A Traveller in Two Worlds

A Traveller in Two Worlds

Volume One: The Early Life of Scotland's Wandering Bard

DAVID CAMPBELL and DUNCAN WILLIAMSON
in Conversation

Luath Press Limited

EDINBURGH

www.luath.co.uk

First published 2011

ISBN: 978-1906817-88-6

The publisher acknowledges the support of

towards the publication of this volume

The paper used in this book is sourced from renewable forestry and is FSC credited material.

Printed and bound by
MPG Books Ltd., Cornwall

Typeset in 11 point Sabon
by 3btype.com

Contents

Acknowledgements

I WISH TO THANK the many people whose help, enthusiasm, interviews and written contributions have made this work possible.

For transcribing over 30 audio tapes of Duncan Williamson and others I am grateful to Sally Kawamura, June Tonks and Duncan's widow Linda Williamson. I wish to thank Barbara McLean for her help in the initial stages of the book and subsequent critical help from her readings of the text. I wish especially to thank members of the Williamson families for their kindness and help. I thank Diana Cater, Jennie Renton, Catriona Murray for their insights, Gavin MacDougall for his suggestion for the structure of the work and Cathlin Macaulay for her help in giving me access to the archives of The School of Scottish Studies.

I wish to thank Celine Leuty for her endless patience in accommodating my idiosyncrasies while typing and reading and re-reading the work.

My special thanks go to Linda Williamson for her immeasurable support, promptings and encouragement.

For permission to use the photographs I thank Robin Gillanders, Tim Neat, Catriona Murray and The School of Scottish Studies.

The financial support of the literary department of the Scottish Arts Council made the research, recordings and writing of the work possible.

David Campbell

Duncan and David telling stories in a school together (master and apprentice)

Preface

Duncan Williamson is the Scottish folk tradition in one man.

HAMISH HENDERSON, folklorist

Do I contradict myself?
Very well then I contradict myself,
(I am large, I contain multitudes.)

WALT WHITMAN, 'Song of Myself'

He was quite simply the greatest bearer of stories and songs in the English-speaking world.

HUGH LUPTON, poet, author, storyteller

I often think of David and Duncan's unique and sometimes prickly relationship as a joyful celebration of love between two rare men.

NUALA HAYES, Irish actor & storyteller

THE NUMBER OF people whose lives were touched and transformed by the magnetism, magnanimity and friendship of Duncan Williamson would be sufficient reason to occasion a biography. The fairy story of a barefoot tinker boy born in a tent becoming an acclaimed international storytelling star is another. His living for the day and total lack of regard for possessions make a parable for our acquisitive and hoarding times.

Timothy Neat has described Duncan's qualities in these respects as Christ-like, though at times his behaviour could readily be described as devilish.

The work will be in two volumes. This first one takes us through his early family life in the tent, his Huckleberry Finn boyhood wildnesses and wiles, his springing the nest to meet extraordinary characters, his 'jumping the broomstick' into his first marriage and concludes with the death of his wife Jeannie. The source material of the book comes from our journeys and conversations together, 30 tapes I recorded of Duncan's recollections, along with visits to and taped interviews of his family and companions from both worlds he inhabited.

Meeting

IN THE LATE SUMMER of 1987 in my dusty, somewhat dilapidated, Ford Transit van I drew up in the backyard of Lizziewell's Farm Cottage, by Auchtermuchty, Fife. He stood, John Wayne, at the back door scrutinising my approach with his vivid blue eyes, lacking only a holster and a six shooter.

'Duncan Williamson!' he announced.

'David Campbell.'

'BBC?'

'Yes.'

'You want to broadcast my story 'Mary and the Seal' on the radio?'

'Yes.'

'But you don't like it the way it is!'

'I love the story. I just don't think it will fit into my 20 minute radio programme, but I love it.'

Stepping forward, he seized me in one of the hugs I came to know so well.

'David Campbell, youse and me are going to be great friends. Come in.'

'Wait a minute.'

I returned to the van and fetched a bottle of Glenfiddich.

That was the beginning of my first ceilidh and my see-saw, black and white, delightful and dreadful friendship and journeys with Duncan Williamson, his wife Linda, their children Tommy and Betsy; the Williamson family. Although I could not have guessed it at the time, this meeting was to set a future course and shape a new phase of my working and professional life.

From then until his death aged 79, 'raging against the dying of the light', I was his travelling companion, fellow storyteller, flyting adversary, city home for himself, Linda, Tommy and Betsy. And as my friend Catriona

Murray said at his funeral, 'Not everyone knew of Duncan's third marriage, to David Campbell.' And like a marriage it often seemed: protestations of undying affection, jealousies, dramatic estrangements and reconciliations, ultimately a bond and underlying mutual affection. To be with Duncan always had an intensity. He was hungry to devour every moment, living with a *carpe diem* and *carpe noctem* insistence, his joys transparent and fiery, his glooms dense and dampening as bleakest November. His appetite for company was insatiable and without it he was soon bored. I had never known anyone to be bored with such demonstrative and demanding conviction. I used to feed him people, elixirs. He sprang to life and charmed each one. Equally, his anger could simmer and erupt like Hekla, into clouds that lingered long and darkly over months.

After this meeting Duncan and I were to travel thousands of miles together, to every corner of Scotland, the length and breadth of the British Isles, through Europe, Iceland, Canada, Israel. In these travels we entered one another's world and in our 'odd couple' relationship the seed for this book was sown.

Appropriately, its genesis was on the shores of Loch Fyne and beside the same tree under which he was born: 'I was born here before my granny,' he joked (his granny, the midwife). 'This is where my life began. This is where it all started and here I am standing with the BBC Manager (he frequently inaccurately elevated my position) making a programme for the radio. I've come a long, long way, David.'

'You should tell the story of your life,' I said.

'You're the scholar, you write it and make a book of it.'

So the rocky journey started and a shape began to evolve. We would set the time aside to record his memories, visit places of his travels. Over ten years or more Duncan and I would sit in my flat in Dundas Street, my caravan in Glenuig or almost anywhere in Scotland in my campervan talking and recording his memories; I also gathered tales, impressions and recollections from his friends, family and wayfaring companions as far as was possible. As these pages will unfold, the fear of Duncan's displeasure muted some voices.

My reasons for writing these impressions of his life are my love for the man, gratitude for the meeting, a promise made, Duncan's conviction that in our stories we live on, and mine that he was one of the most remarkable men living in Scotland, in his own way one of the 'choice and master spirits of the age', a man born in a tent who was to become the best-known storyteller in the English-speaking world, with a legacy of many disciples. I had no wish to produce a hagiography of my charismatic friend of many weathers. As the book evolved, in parallel with the stories of Duncan's life, it inevitably became a narrative of our close relationship with its sometimes severe hiccups.

Duncan recording in David's home

When Duncan and I discussed the book we conjured many titles, and one evening as we sat in the spacious drawing room in Dundas Street, he smoking his nth cigarette, we sharing a whisky, he looked around.

'What are you thinking, Duncan?' I said.

'It's a different world. Where do I belong? Nowhere!' he said.

'In both worlds,' I said. 'You can take the man out of the tent but you can't take the tent out of the man.'

'You're very clever, sometimes,' he laughed.

Out of that came a working title he liked: *A Traveller in Two Worlds*.

Duncan's passion was collecting stories, his mission offering them as gifts. With him, coming from a totally different education, I shared the belief that stories are a vicarious experiential education, replicating life in the wonderhouse of the imagination, sources of real learning and knowing. He would call my way of expressing this 'classical shit', but our convictions were identical, 'Stories was wir education'. More succinct!

It was not Duncan's storytelling genius, not the huge repertoire of story and song that made him the world's best-known and best-loved storyteller: it was the sheer storm force of his being, a force that expressed itself in tireless generosity and lavish giving, punctuated for those at close quarters, by prima donna tantrums, sulks, rants and behaviour that was sometimes hard to forgive; but mostly he was forgiven because of his own generosity and charm.

Duncan recording the melodeon

An old Celtic saying describes the generosity of the hero Finn McCool:

If the leaves were gold
And the waves of the sea silver
Finn would have given them all away.

In this Duncan was Finn's spiritual descendant. From the Alaskan north to the antipodean south pilgrims trod their paths to the open door of his hospitality.

A page from the visitors' book he briefly kept in 2002 speaks of the impact of his warmth and vividness, his unparalleled gift of putting people at immediate ease and fastening friendship like his own sturdy hugs.

> I've know Duncan for six years and I have always believed that he is the greatest storyteller in Great Britain. His command of pitch, rhythm and colour, his sense of detail and structure, his power to inhabit a story – these are unrivalled qualities that are unique in my experience. I have visited him, listened to him, laughed with him and been beguiled by him.
>
> Duncan's power to connect with an audience is both an artistic power and a moral power that marks him out as a truly great performer – who leaves his audience not only aesthetically satisfied but also with the conviction that it is possible to be a better person.
>
> RICHARD NEVILLE 19/02/02 – writer, poet, storyteller

I have quoted this in full as, like all stories, it is the shortest way to the truth, expressing the artistry of Duncan's craft and above all the contagious warmth of his heart.

So, to our first morning's recording. Duncan was staying with me for a few days on one of his frequent visits, sleeping in his preferred place on the sofa bed in the living room under a big wool Campbell tartan plaid he'd christened his 'Broonie' blanket; no sheets, no pillows, just the thick wool blanket, a philamore. Over a nightcap of whiskies we'd agreed to start the next day. We had both prepared. As ever he was early afoot, washed, shaved, and when I came into the kitchen he looked spruce, ready to record, carrying already a sense of occasion and expectancy. He declined my invitation to join me for porridge.

'No, David, I've had my three course breakfast, a cough, a fag and a cup of tinker's tea!'

The lingering smell of bacon gave lie to this assertion but Duncan 'never let the truth stand in the way of a good story' (one of his own adages).

I had my usual porridge and herbal tea, sacrilege to Duncan. I had tidied my bedroom, which is large and quiet, at the back of the flat, away from the traffic. I had set up two seats, microphone and Sony pro recorder (used in my BBC days).

Duncan had been thinking over what he would say, revisiting the people and haunts of his early days. I could see that he had donned a fresh shirt – always a sharp sense of dress – and had even trimmed his eyebrows! This was to be a performance even for an audience of one: me.

He would have said 'classical shit' but he shared with Shakespeare the sentiment:

> 'So long as men can breathe, or eyes can see
> So long lives this, and this gives life to thee'

for he was already speaking through the unwritten pages to the invisible audience of posterity and struck his stage mode as soon as I turned on the microphone.

'Well, David, we're sitting here in your beautiful house in Edinburgh, a great privilege, and I'm going to tell you the story of a Traveller boy born in a tent on the shores of Loch Fyne a long, long time ago.'

Kindling

LIFE TO ME AS a boy way back in the '30s was hard, being born into a large Travelling community of pipers, ballad singers and storytellers. Very hard being brought up in the middle of an oak forest. Of course it was the prejudice, not the lifestyle we lived that was the problem. In Furnace, the prejudice was the heart of the aggravation. Even attending our primary school you weren't allowed to be a little cleverer than the children in the village. Other than this was the problem that if one little thing went missing in the village from someone's garden, whether it be a carrot or a cabbage, it was the tinkers up in the wood; they called us 'tinkers' in these days, us Travelling folk. So I'm going to tell you what it was like as a little Traveller boy, to grow up in a community and then to leave the community of Travelling people, to go out into a wide world among people who are prejudiced against the tinkers.

Now my father, a soldier in the War in 1915, 17 years old, was a piper. Here was my mother living in a tent at home on the west coast of Argyll, just a young beautiful Traveller woman, small and blonde, fair, short, curly hair, and she had her first baby when she was 14. She went on to have 16 kids. My mother made herself older when she was going to have her first baby because father was in the War. She said she was 17 so they could get married, so she would get the 25 shillings, old soldiers' pay. But while my father was in the army she stayed with her mother and father and when he came back, he wanted privacy for his own little wife with him.

* * *

Embarrased to be unable to read or write, Duncan's father Jock, like many others serving in France in that dire war of the trenches, had to find a friend to write a letter to his young wife and she in turn had to ask the local minister to read it and frame her reply. The shame of this determined Jock Williamson to make sure that, if he survived, his children would learn to read and write.

Duncan Campbell, eighth Duke of Argyll, was a Captain in the Argylls and Duncan's father a piper in the same regiment. The Duke owned the forest land round Loch Fyne and gave Jock and his family grace-and-favour tenure to camp there for life. He was a faithful friend to the family. 'Keep the woods clean, Jock,' he said, 'burn all the rubbish and dead wood.'

* * *

> He used to come down from Inveraray with an old Bentley car way back afore the war, and even after the war. He wore the kilt, it was full of moth holes. And his stockings was full of moth holes. And the eyes of his shoes was full of verdigris. And he wore his Balmoral. Old Duncan Campbell, related to the Royal family. Pulled up, and walked from the village where he left his car, up to the woods where Father had his big tent.
>
> In these days in the shops in Inveraray, you could get a big lollipop, oh, as big as a potato, and when you sucked, it changed colours. I remember it just like yesterday!
>
> 'Daddy, here's the Duke coming.'
>
> My father would wait for old Duncan Campbell, he would sit outside. Wait till you hear this strange story.
>
> 'How are you, Mr Williamson, how are the children? I brought them a sweetie.' Big bunch of lollipops. 'I'll pay the doctor's bill the next time if they get ill!' It was half a crown for the doctor's visit.
>
> Then my father would say, 'Just a minute, Duncan.' And father would go in and get the open razor. He stropped the open razor, then he would take old Duncan's shoe off. The old man would take off his big old socks with red ribbons

around the leg. He put his foot on my father's knee and my father would pare the bunions, and the wee bits of skin would fall off his feet on the ground, you see!

After the Duke departed my little sister, Jeannie, a wee girl about three or four, would make a wee wooden cross and she buried the wee bits of skin, covered them with sand and put up the wee wooden cross and nobody was allowed to touch that. She went crazy, she went mental, she said, 'That's his wee bare skin and that's his wee cross,' because he'd brought the lollipops. Old Duncan Campbell, he never married.

But anyway, life in the tent as a child with my parents: it was a comfortable way of life. I mean, it was always warm inside the tent and we always had a good fire on the floor. Inside the tent the ground was polished, hard swept by my mother with her birch besom. We'd all sit around the fire after we had a little evening meal; mother would share it. We just got a plate in wir hands. Father used to make them himself, tin plates. And then the evening came in, he'd light the cruisie. He'd made this lamp himself, it was like a teapot. He took a piece of rag, cotton rag, screwed it in as a wick, in through this little spout and pulled it right down inside the little teapot, and we'd fill it full of paraffin oil. We used to go off to the shop, wir bare feet: a bottle of paraffin was thruppence and that would do a week.

The love of the evening in the tent, by the flickering of the fire, was when father would light that little cruisie, hang it on the cleek. I remember wee bubbles of soot would gather at the point of the wick and he'd poke it with his finger and the flame would fly up again, make it brighter. The smoke would reek out because there was a hole in the roof. There was no smoke inside the tent. The way that tent was constructed with a peak in the middle, it was like a kind of a chimney, would draw the smoke up. You just sat on the ground. We never had any chairs or anything: we had boxes for holding clothes. You were lucky if you had a seat on the box. You moved, and somebody else took it over, you had to just do without.

I mean, the only thing that we really suffered from was a shortage of food because there was so many of us, so many little mouths to feed. As you grew a little older, when you were ten and twelve, you were allowed to try and find enough food for yourself. And, I mean, finding food, not what you would get today in the shops. We had to hunt for rabbits, we had to poach the odd salmon, we had to collect shellfish, we had to guddle trout in the river, we had to hunt hares in the hills, but there were restrictions against this. If you were caught with a hare by the gamekeeper, you were in trouble. If you were caught with a salmon, you were in trouble.

I remember one day I caught a salmon in the river. I was about ten. Mother had no food, the kids were hungry. Because, you see, the river ran into the sea. When it was in spate the salmon used to come up, but when the rain stopped and the river fell, the salmon would make for the biggest pool that was in the river, but the biggest pool would only take you up to the knee.

There's a salmon lying in the stream, and he's going back and forward like that, he's an old fish, you know. So, you had yourself a long stick and you got a rabbit snare. You put it into the stream and you put it right down and you moved it gradually: he's lying in the stream, and you put it over his head and you waited till the snare was behind his gills, and then you pulled. The rabbit snare tightened behind his gills and there's no way in the world he would get away from that.

I poached the salmon; put a snare over his head and pulled him up. But then, I saw him in the distance, a gamekeeper. Whiskers we called him, because he had a beard. He had two dogs with him and a gun under his arm. Deer stalker's hat. I knew there was no escape.

Then I took the salmon and I bit two big bites from the back of his neck! I chewed it and swallowed it: it was like cucumber, fresh salmon. I put my finger in his gill and I walked up onto the road by the riverside. He saw me immediately.

'Here you, come over here, what's that you've got?'

I said, 'It's a salmon.'

'Where did you get that?'

I said, 'I got it in the river.'

'You'd better give it to me,' he said, 'you're in big trouble.'

'No, I'm not,' I said.

I held it up, I says, 'The law states in Argyll, any salmon lying in the river killed by the otter, the owner is the first person who finds it.'

He says, 'Show me!'

And I showed him, turned him round and there was my teeth marks on the back of his neck. This is true. There were my teeth marks on the back of his neck.

'Now,' he says, 'get going and don't come back.'

And until the day he died he never knew it wasn't the otter that bit the salmon in the neck. These were the clever little tricks you had to learn. So we had to be very, very careful how we poached and hunted for food. This is why it was so hard.

Now let me tell you about the tent itself. It was a large structure about the size of this room. Round, made of big saplings – hazel, birch, rowan saplings ten, 15 feet long – bowed over to each other in a great big semi-circle. Round the tent was all these small departments: there was one for the girls, one for the boys, one for my parents. There would always be an extra one for storing stuff in. So the girls could go into their own department, pull down a cover in front and they could have their privacy. The boys had the same thing, parents had the same thing. Now that tent took a long construction, it would take my father, maybe, say, three days to build that. You can build a little bender tent that you move, to use daily or weekly, in 20 minutes.

First, he had to go to the forest and cut the sticks. He had to choose the saplings, the ones he needed, then had to carry them back. We would go with him if we were old enough. And then he had to find the spot that was high enough so that it wouldn't be flooded with water. You couldn't put it too high because it would catch too much wind. Now naturally

Family of Townsley Travellers

while we were doing that with our father we were also learning. This is what it was to be born in a Travelling community. Life could be hard. My mother was born in a cave.

My mother was born in a cave because grandfather and granny went walking one night to visit some friends, about a five mile walk, and it came, a storm. My grandmother was pregnant, ready to have her baby, and he wouldn't leave her behind when he went off to visit for a crack or a ceilidh. Five or six miles was nothing to the old Travelling folk to walk to some other encampments of other Travellers. Maybe have a wee dram and they would walk back. They would always take their wife with them. They'd leave the oldest one of the family to take care of the children while they were gone.

That night my grandfather and my granny went off to visit some friends and about five miles from home they were caught in a storm, near the little village of Muasdale on the

Traveller's tent

way to Kintyre, to Campbeltown. Just couldn't go on, the storm was too strong, but there was an old cave there at Muasdale the beggars and the tramps used to use. If people stayed in it overnight they would leave sticks in it for the next person that came along, and there was dry bracken and a stone floor. Many people had spent the night there. So grandfather and grandmother thought that it would be a nice place to have shelter till the storm went off. But that storm raged all night and during the night my mother was born. Granny gave birth in the cave! And she maybe took her undershirt off, or her blouse, whatever she had she just wrapped the baby in it, because all Traveller women always used to carry a shawl over their shoulders instead of a coat. That shawl was always with them, in case of emergencies.

Life in the old tent in the forest where we lived was wonderful because we had the whole forest to run round in, play wirsels by a little stream running through the forest, trout in the little stream and sometimes sea trout came up from the sea. Father working in the quarry, mother hawking the doors, us attending the local village school. The oldest ones had probably left the school, the girls, just before the war started, some 13, some 14. They stayed at home. They

> would take care of the younger children, wash their faces, fold and mend their clothes and do things around the tent while my mother was off hawking.

* * *

That life in the tent sounded to me like a youngster's paradise. In my old Ford Transit van, when Duncan and I one day fell into reminiscent and nostalgic mode, I told him of the quarry in which, aged 12, I had my own little gang. That place too was a miniature haven; with trees, little hills, a small pond, sand pit, where we 'ran our heedless ways', built huts, cooked rhubarb, played hidey amongst the corn stooks, wrote and performed plays, held our own Olympic games, had a radio system made by a precocious whizz kid. I broadcasted stories to the gang gathered round a campfire on winter nights. I had the first pangs of love and wrote my first love poem. Only hunger called us home at meal times.

Duncan was quiet, somewhere in his own memories. Tears in his eyes, he burst into an angry lament for how the Travellers' way of life had been broken by prejudice, law and 'school education'.

His sorrow and anger recall an incident Ben Haggarty, the English storyteller, later described when Duncan famously hurled a copy of his Silkie book into the fire and sobbed, 'I wish I'd never made any of these books, it's changed my life forever.' It reminded me too of what his first son Jimmy said of his father. 'He just fell out of the Traveller world completely. He's in a kinda void. He's between two worlds. He's in neither one nor the other.'

Already in Duncan's boyhood the 20th century's tentacles were beginning to suck the life blood from that whole Traveller culture, but the real dismantling was in the future and 'Time let *him* climb golden in the heydays of his eyes.' Duncan's bright blue boy's eyes were drinking the richness of the Traveller world.

* * *

> In my father's spare time, at night-time when he came back from the quarry, he would have plenty of material for making baskets and scrubbers and besoms that my mother could hawk during the day. She would probably trade these things for food and clothes for the kids, you know. A lot of

them were very good to my mother, Betsy, and to my granny. Oh, they loved my granny. Oh, granny was their favourite, she was never turned away from their door in a million years.

She was a good hawker and she was a fortune-teller. She could read palms, teacups. The most amazing thing was, when we used to wander the countryside with her, granny was always took into their houses. Bella, they called her. 'Come in, Bella, and sit doon!' They would give her a cup of tea. We had to stand at the door. We were never invited in. Granny would go in, she would be a good wee while in the house with the people, and, 'Oh wait and I'll boil you an egg, Bella.' When the woman's back was turned, she slipped the egg in her pocket. She knew her little hungry grandson or granddaughter, would be standing in the cold, waiting on her. They would give her some tea and sugar, maybe give her a sixpence. My wee granny.

And they would get their fortune read, they would get their palm read, they would get their cup read. 'Did you see what old Bella told me yesterday? As sure as the God is fair, every word she said was true,' they would tell each other. And then the word spread: 'Oh, you read Mrs MacLean's hand yesterday, Bella, how about mine today?'

* * *

We fell to discussing grannies at this point. My own granny, I told him, used to read tea leaves, tim the tea out and tell you what she saw, illnesses, deaths, journeys, and people loved it. 'And could your granny really tell fortunes?' I asked.

'Just as good as me,' Duncan said. 'I barely ever tell Traveller tales, but I'll tell you this one, a tinker story. Put on your recorder.'

* * *

There was a laird and his wife. They had a big house. And the Travelling people used to come and camp on his land but he didnae worry about them. 'Oh,' the laird said, 'they never do any harm.'

But one of the old women, old Maggie, was like my granny and she used to go and hawk with her little basket and she would go to the back door of the big house, and the lady of the house, she loved the old woman because she was crazy about her fortune telling. The laird didn't mind, but he was worried about his wife.

'That's only nonsense,' he said. 'Nonsense! She's just telling ye lies. These old people can't foretell the future.'

But she said, 'She's an old Traveller woman, she's told me many wonderful things, ye ken, in the past.'

'Look,' he said, 'it's nonsense. I don't mind ye give them a penny or two, or give them something from the kitchen, but I dinnae want you to believe all the nonsense!'

'But,' she said, 'I love it!'

'Well,' he said, 'I'll tell ye, I'll make a deal with ye. If they can prove to me that they can foretell things,' he said. 'I want you to invite her up tomorrow, to the house on her own, and I'll ask her a question and if she can foretell that question correctly for me, she can come here till the end of time. She can tell you the stories till you're a grandmother, and I won't interfere.'

She said, 'Thank you.'

He goes to the gamekeeper, right! To Donald, the gamekeeper. He says, 'Donald, I want you to catch me a fox.' They were catching a lot of foxes in these days, you know. 'I want you to catch me a fox and I want you to keep it alive and I want you to put it in a box and bring it back to the big house.'

Donald says, 'Of course, I'll bring it to the house.' But anyway Donald catcht the fox, put it in a wooden box. The laird brought it in. The old woman came.

'Oh, come in, come in, Granny,' he said, 'come in, sit down!' Glass of wine, maybe whisky, whatever it was. Right, laird's wife sitting there, in the big house. This is true, a true story, actually happened.

He says, 'They tell me you've been telling my wife her fortunes, reading palms on her.'

'Aye,' she said, 'I've been doing that all my life.'

'Well,' he says, 'look, I don't believe one single word of all the rubbish you've been telling my wife. But to prove it, I want you to tell me what's in that box, and if you can tell me what's inside that box, I'll never interfere again with you or my wife. And you can come here to your heart's content.'

The old woman hadn't a clue.

There were an old saying among the Travelling folk: that if you do things that are not natural, some day you're going to get caught. And they say, 'Long run the fox but he's caught at last!' So she knew she had a long run, she didn't have a clue what was in the box and she walks over, and she puts her hand on the box. She says out loud, 'Long run the fox but he's caught at last,' meaning herself. An old expression used among the Travelling folk. And the laird was completely flabbergasted!

He stood up and he shaked the hand with the old woman, and he gave her a full glass of whisky and he said, 'You can come here as long as you like and I'll never interfere with you and my wife again.' And neither he did.

Granny used to tell us that story in the tent, you know!

Life with granny was the best thing that ever happened to me. She smoked a pipe and she wore these old fashioned boots, you know, buttony boots, we used to lace them for her. And she wore a long black dress coming to her ankles and a little shawl over her shoulder. She was only five foot two, and her feet were so small, she could never get a shoe to fit her because she had feet like a wee fairy woman. She'd only wear children's sandals and I felt sorry for her sometimes, especially in the snow with the bad weather; you know, wearing sandals in the snow!

When we were kids with granny – I'm talking about when I was six or seven years old, we loved our granny dearly – she had some of these droll sayings: talking about a person if he was thin she'd say, 'His porridge must have been thin'; a lazy person, a sleepy headed person, she would say, 'The cock will never crow in his morning'; and see a person with a ruddy complexion, 'His face would light matches.'

> I expect you know what that means, David, she couldnae read, she couldnae write, she couldnae tell the time. The only time granny could tell was when the two hands was on 12 o'clock. 'It's 12 o'clock,' she would say, '12 o'clock.' But it was magical.
>
> Time to feed the dragon, David.

* * *

Duncan began to smoke at the age of seven or eight. The habit of nearly seven decades had to be obeyed so we took a break.

Ken Shapley, a young storytelling friend of mine recalls that he'd sit on a chaise longue at my house and roll fags for Duncan. He told me, 'One time I said to Duncan, "I sank so low I'd pick up butts from the street to smoke." Duncan understood perfectly. "Och, it'll do you no harm," said he as he reached for his bag full of more bottles of pills than anyone should ever have to keep them going. We'd smoke our roll-ups and bemoan rainy days when all the fag butts were sodden. Duncan advised looking in bus shelters!'

These nicotine fixes demanded and determined the breaks in our recording sessions, during which he often transformed into one of his favourite roles as 'James': cook, butler and dishwasher. This was Duncan, the thespian, entering his part with absorbed enthusiasm and disappearing into the kitchen, from whence issued in his melodious tenor, snatches of his current favourite song or ballad. He was always singing when he wasn't in a gloom! A knock at the lounge door.

'Dinner is served, my Lord,' in a grandly deferential pose.

He was a good cook and on the menu might be oxtail he'd bought and brought; a flavoursome dish, red flannel hash; a mash of beetroot, tatties and corned beef; his own sturdy flapjack, a solid pancake-like creation; or 'incinerated' meat, bacon, beans and potatoes, not green vegetables and never mushrooms. Dessert was strong tea, another fag and we were ready to go on.

* * *

> Now back to granny. She had wandered far and wide because my grandfather was a wandering piper. They had a big family – he lost three sons in the First World War. As

they got older they used to wander together. Grandfather went on the booze and died in the mental hospital. He was buried near Lochgilphead. Then granny had no place to go so she came to stay with us. This is back just before the Second World War. Life with granny was wonderful, because granny always seemed to have a thrup'ny piece in her pocket. Getting a penny then in these days was magical, a penny.

Now, in the little shop where we lived, the tobacco used to come in rolls, called bogie roll, two little white dogs or a black dog and a white dog. At each side of the dog was a roll of tobacco – like a piece of rope. On the side of the little dog was a little blade, and the old store-owner would pull a little bit of tobacco out. He had a little brass scale and when people came in and asked for an ounce – I can remember it just like yesterday – he would take a piece of tobacco and put it on the little brass scale; the little ounce weight looked like a pound coin. He'd put a bit tobacco on and if it was too heavy he would cut a little bit off to give it the right weight. These small pieces, he would throw in a little drawer, and this is what granny used to get. He had a little brass scoop, and he'd make a little twist of paper with his finger, put a scoop of tea in, press it with his finger and put it on the counter. And he'd make a twist of paper – sugar. We gave him the thruppenny piece. Granny's tea, granny's sugar, granny's tobacco, thruppence.

Then we ran home through the village in our bare feet, up to the wood. Granny would be sitting in the tent with her wee drum, like a little billycan with wire over it. She'd have a stick, and she'd hold this little drum over the fire and let it boil. She would put a handful of tea in it and a wee bit sugar. Then she would sit down. Our father had made her a little tin cup. Then she lit her clay pipe. 'Granny, would you tell us a story?'

'Wait a minute noo, weans, and I'll see what kind of story I have for you now,' and she opened up that little pocket and she brought out a story. Some of them's Jack tales, some of those tales that's in *Fireside Tales*, you can read for yourself, granny's stories. Wonderful stories. She would never tell you the same story twice in a night, oh, it was always a different story. We loved the stories from granny. Then, we'd go and collect firewood for her, for her wee fire, for a story. And there was me, little sister, little brother Jimmy, Willie, Dodie, all sitting round.

Now, the thing we did in the summertime. Before we moved in the summer we burned the big tent, the winter's tent, we burned it to the ground. We built little bow tents, one for granny, one for my father and mother, one for the girls, one for the boys, four of them and we put them all facing each other. Everybody had their own piece of canvas, cover enough to sleep four or five boys, three or four girls. In summer granny always had her own little tent. Little door flap came down at night-time, granny had her little bed in one corner and her little possessions that she had; her basket with the stuff that she sold, hawking basket, and all the wee bits and pieces that she needed, wee bits extra clothes and things.

Now the reason why I've got to bring this up to you is because in bygone times these old ladies, they didnae have a purse or a handbag. They had round their waist a large pocket homemade by themselves, and they put it round their waist, like you would wear a sporran on your kilt, and it hung to the side, and all their worldly possessions was in this pocket, the little money they owned, and everything they had was in this pocket.

* * *

Many, many times I heard Duncan tell that story of his granny's purse. Sometimes, he averred from that moment he determined to be as good a storyteller as his wee granny. At other times, he gave different origins for his story collecting and telling vocation. It depended on the occasion and the company but in every mention of his wee granny she was 'magical'.

* * *

My story takes you to the summer month just before we left. Granny called me and my sister together and she said, 'I want you to go down to the village for a penny's worth o' tobacco for my pipe!'

'Right, granny! We'll get a story.' So she gave us a thruppenny piece, with a big three on it, silver thruppenny piece, and we ran down to the village. Penny's worth o' tobacco, penny to Jean and a penny to me. We got a cake of McCowan's toffee for a penny each, it's lovely. We came back up, granny was sound asleep. She'd tooken off her pocket, this pocket that we had got many wonderful stories from and it was lying by her side. She was sound asleep.

She was just like a wee Indian maiden, you know, she was only five foot high with long dark plaits as she lay there sound asleep. So we took the little poke with the tobacco and we placed it by her side. And Jeannie says to me, 'Look, how many stories d'ye think granny's got in her pocket?'

'Oh,' I said, 'she must have hundreds.'

'Well, let's take it and see!'

We took the little pocket away from granny's side, went behind a tree in the forest and we opened it up for the first time. And it was like Aladdin's Cave in there! There were pieces of jewellery, there were rings, things that she collected from people when she was reading fortunes, beads, brooches, there were ha'pennies and farthings full of verdigris, so old they'd been in there for so long; buttons, needles, all the things that an old woman would need – but not a single story could we find. So we took the pocket, closed it, put it back by her side. She was still asleep. We left it where we found it and we went off to play.

In an hour's time we came back. She had her little fire kindled in front of her tent. She was making some tea for herself. Granny was sitting by the fire with a billycan on the open fire outside because it was a sunny day. Her tea was so strong you could never drink it. She never took sugar or milk, just black tea in this little billycan.

She says, 'You wantin some tea?'

'Aye, Granny, we'll take a sup o' your tea.' She gien us a wee sup o' her tea, she always gave us a sup of her tea.

'Did yese get my tobacco?'

I says, 'We left it beside you, Granny.'

She took out her little clay pipe (now I have the pipe and the purse here today) and she lighted her pipe up. You could see the marks on the clay pipe where the stem was broken, four or five times, little square pipe. What granny used to do, if she sat on it and it broke, she would wrap a piece of string round her finger and she'd take her needle and she'd jab her finger till the blood came out, and she'd take the blood and put it round the broken bit of the stem and hold it together till the blood dried, like Super Glue. When the blood dried it would join the clay. You could see the marks where it had been joined two, three times. Once that join was joined with that blood from her thumb it wouldn't come separate. Granny lit her pipe.

'Granny, you promised us a story for going for your tobacco!'

'Well,' she says, 'of course I did.' So, she picked up her pocket and she put it round her waist, and she buckled it on and she says, 'Wait a moment and I'll see what I have for you tonight!' Now I had many, many stories from granny's pocket, some of them are in my books today. She opened the pocket up and I swear on my mother's grave, it's the truth. She looked at my sister and she looked at me for a long time.

She said, 'You know I cannae tell you any stories.'

I says, 'Why, granny, why can't you tell us a story?'

She said, 'Someone opened my pocket when I was asleep and all my stories are gone.'

And from that day on granny never told us another story. I swear to you, she never knew that we had opened her pocket because we were so careful. I remember the look she gave us. I was 17 when granny died, a young man, after doing a lot of travelling, meeting hundreds of Travellers on my travels, but never again did granny ever tell us a story.

I seen me standing in school, hungry, and I would see

granny with her wee sandals and her shawl over her shoulder, and the basket on her arm making her way down past the school. I would sneak out, jump the dyke and follow granny. Granny wouldnae take you with her if you were in school. She wouldnae take you away frae the village, but if you followed her, keeping behind her for a while, till you were about a mile away from the school and you come up, she wouldnae let you turn back on your own. She'd say, 'It's too far for you to go back now. You better come,' and this was a day out with granny. It was fun.

I saw me waiting a half hour for her, sitting on the step waiting till she read palms. Or she'd go to a big house and she used to take the maids, read their palms and they'd give her a silver sixpence. Granny would always give you a penny at night when she came back.

She used to send ten shilling notes away to Glasgow and it was COD, cash on delivery. And the postman would say, 'Here's a parcel for your Granny.' We'd take it home. And it'd be a brown paper parcel, and she would open it, ten shillings worth, wee stuffs of tape, leather laces for men's boots, wee combs and razor blades and all the little things that was hard to get in the local village. She would hawk them with her little basket. She'd put the basket down at the door and the woman would help herself.

'How much is that, Bella?'

'Oh, that's thruppence.'

She used to buy a book of stamps, two and six for a book of stamps. She would charge the woman three shillings for it, a sixpence o' profit.

Oh, yes! Father would make heather scrubbers for scrubbing the porridge pots because in these days they made big pots of porridge. There were a lot of big families among the local community as well as the Travelling people. It was all these iron pots. You could be boiling a pot of herring and tatties – you couldna put your hands in the hot water, but if you had a heather scrubber, then you scrubbed the pot with the heather scrubber. These things were very perfectly made,

> you know. And they were very, very popular at that time when we were young just before the war. Thruppenny each. My father used to sit there and make two dozen. My father made baskets and carpet-beaters made of wands, made of willow, and clothes pegs at night-time with his pocket knife, big blanket pegs and small pegs. Very popular.
>
> My mother used to hawk them at the doors. Granny used to hawk them. Life with granny was magic. She collected clothes and food and potatoes from the people. They'd say, 'I'll give you a boil of potatoes, Bella.' We'd go with her and help granny carry anything she got. My mother would cook it and divide it and granny always was first to get shared; if it was making tea, granny got her tea first. If we were making soup, granny got her soup first. It was the custom. Granny and father, then we came up next.
>
> The more we grew older the more love and respect we had for wir grandmother. Granny stayed with us till her daughter, my mother's older sister, Bella, thought she would take granny off with her for a wee visit to Paisley round Glasgow. They lived round there. We were sad to see granny go, and I never saw granny again. Granny took pneumonia and died.

* * *

Among the many visitors to my Dundas Street flat was a small, round, genial storyteller who lives in Inverness, Davie Muir. What I didn't know was that he had known the Williamsons when the family lived in their tent in the forest outside Furnace.

He called in on a visit to the Guid Crack, Edinburgh's storytelling club, while Duncan was staying with me and was hailed, hugged and insulted by Duncan in his frequently outrageous way.

'Ah, Davie, great to see you. When did you last catch sight of your tadger?'

This robust greeting Davie accepted as it was intended, a token of sturdy friendship. People Duncan liked best, he insulted most, and this could turn into a playful game of fierce flyting. He often asked our mutual friend and frequent visitor Lindsay Porteous, also not a lean man, 'And when is it due Lindsay, do you think it will be a boy or a girl?'

Anyhow, while Duncan went off in search of an oxtail to cook for the evening meal I was able to record Davie uninhibited and uninterrupted.

* * *

> 'I was a young boy growing up in Argyll in the '50s, in a wee fishing town on the shores of Loch Fyne. I met Duncan's parents first of all because his mother, Betsy Townsley, used to come round to our house hawking goods. They were mostly brushes and combs; things any woman would find handy for the home, all wrapped up nicely and presented in a kind of straw basket she would carry. And things Duncan's father had made, wooden flowers, beautiful things, hand-made wooden clothes pegs. Jock, Duncan's father would have pots and pans. If you wanted something made he could make it for you. Betsy would come round pretty often and my mother was the kind of woman if somebody came to her for help she would give all the help she knew of. We didn't have much money ourselves; we were a poor family, but we were rich in hospitality. My mother, every time Betsy came round would buy something from her, at least one thing and put them in one top drawer, storing them for a rainy day. We had plenty rainy days in our family. So these goods kept piling up and the drawer gradually got full.
>
> My father would say, 'When are you going to empty that bloody drawer? I can't even open it now.' He had to take out the bottom drawer to get the top one out!
>
> So we hit upon a plan. I was eight or nine at the time and crazy about Duncan's sister Rachel, my age, but that's another story.
>
> 'You love going with Rachel, don't you?' Dad said. 'Well, you could take some things back to Betsy and she could sell them to somebody else, you see?'
>
> 'Aye. Aye, Dad.'
>
> So that's what we did. Always left the drawer about 80 per cent full, and I'd go down to see Rachel and download a bag, and Betsy'd sell them back to mother again. I often

wonder how often we bought the same things. I don't think my mother ever knew. But maybe she suspected.'

When I was talking to, or recording Davie or Duncan I could see that their memories had the force of reliving, of being there and then, and, depending upon what they were recalling, the times could be wretched and hard or bathed in a summer glow of warmth, the townsfolk pleasant and helpful, or prejudiced and malign. From talking to Furnace people who remembered the Williamson encampment in the forest, I found most seemed tolerant, if not actually appreciative of the Travellers.

In October 2003, I recorded Alastair McKeller. He knew Duncan's eldest brother Sandy and told me, 'They were always well received here.' He added that one of the Williamson girls, when asked why she thought she was a native to Furnace, replied, 'I was born at the brig and washed in the burn.'

'You can't get more native than that,' he concluded.

Whatever memory Duncan visited he told with passionate immediacy.

* * *

The tinkers had this terrible name: they were thieves, they were stealers, they were child stealers, you couldn't trust them. All this prejudice down through the years, and you had to cope with this kind of thing. The Travelling men were classed as lazy, but they were only lazy to the people who did not know their lifestyle, because in reality they worked really hard. They done many wonderful things to help bring up their family. They would collect old boots from the dumps and the old skips and places where they were throwing out, and they would cut out pieces of leather.

Now daddies done the work at home and looked after the children while their wives were out hawking. Of course men were good cooks, some were wonderful cooks. The boys helped and my sisters could do anything I could do. The girls were really clever. Night-time was especially for the girls – stories – and the Traveller women were good storytellers.

They told stories mostly about princesses, how the princess kept herself tidy, how the princess kept herself clean and all these beautiful things of these stories, as an educational thing for the children so that the girls would comb their hair and look after theirself and someday they would meet their prince, which would just be somebody they fell in love with. Sometimes the boys sat in and listened to the storytellers too.

Now, to the boys and the wee laddies, father would say, 'Come on laddie and I'll show you how to carve a wooden flower. Show you how to make a leather lace.' He would take a wee strip of round leather cut off an old boot and he had a wooden block, and he'd stick that knife in the block. Sharp as a razor! A little piece of stick with a little chip on it, about the breadth of a leather lace. And he'd place it against the face of the knife and he'd bring that piece of leather right up against it and he'd make a wee strip of the leather, and he'd pull that little strip. The most amazing thing was, when he pulled that strip that piece of leather started to run round, round and round, and as it ran round it came out in a long thin strip because it couldn't get any wider than the little stick with the nick on it. It couldn't get twisted and it would come out in a long strip, maybe say, six foot long, and he'd cut that in four and make four leather laces, rub them on a piece of carbolic soap, tie them in a roll. And he would say, if he got his pipe, he'd say, 'Ye want a wee shot, laddie?'

Now if the laddie made a mistake, and the same with basket making, father never controlled the boy for making a mistake. 'Oh well, you tried, and that's okay, but you'll get better as you go along.'

Take a woman hawking for eight miles, calling on the farms away on the hill, carrying a bundle on her back with potatoes and oatmeal which she traded goods for. They didn't beg. They bartered. They gave the laces for the farmers' boots and the shepherds' boots; they received potatoes, maybe a bit o' cheese, maybe homemade butter, maybe some milk in their can. But if the people didnae have any kind of foodstuff to give them, they would give them a little money, not very much, maybe a shilling or a sixpence. And woe be to the woman who came back with the stuff that her husband had made! She wasnae a good wife.

I'm not saying the men were all good. There were some pure bad ones among them too; beat up their wives, wouldnae do nothing, wouldnae even look after their children, chased their children after their wife saying, 'I'm no watchin' your weans, take them away with ye.'

But say 90 per cent of the men from the Travelling community were very good to their wives and very, very fond of their children. I remember my father standing around the campfire, one of the wee boys running in front of my uncle, and my uncle took his boot and kicked that little boy. My father swung his hand and hit that uncle on the side of the jaw, knocked him scattering about ten feet away. And he says, 'Never again, ever you lay your hand on a child in front of me. I don't touch my boys and I don't allow the like of you to hit a child before me.'

Now, today some people would turn their back even in the street if an old woman gets mugged. But you see, if a man beat his wife some of the men would step in, and say, 'Right, that's enough. Don't touch her. You can argue with her, scold her, but don't lay your hand to her in front of me.' And some of these men were very, very hardy.

Roots and Lore

Duncan already as a youngster clamoured to know the family genealogy, delighted in the near mythic anecdotes of the past stored in the mind of his paternal grandfather.

ALAN BRUFORD

* * *

NOT LONG AFTER I met Duncan he invited me to join him visiting a care home where he was to tell stories. He breezed in as if he lived there, greeting staff and residents like long lost friends, shook several by the hand and fished out his Jew's harp asking an old man if he had ever seen such a thing. A couple of folk remembered them and at once he put the harp to his lips and played 'The Hills of Perth', one of his favourites. Out came the mouth organ and, something I was to hear many times in the coming years, a robust vamping of 'The Bonnie Banks of Loch Lomond'.

'Come on now, join in.' And those who could did and earned a great applause from Duncan.

'And now for a story.'

He told the fairy story of 'Archie and the Little People' and when a couple of folk dozed off, one snoring vociferously he seemed not to notice and continued walking around the circle telling the tale.

'Now, I have a special treat for you. My good friend David Campbell, manager of the BBC, is going to tell you a story. Give him a good welcome.'

I recovered from my surprise and told Duncan's story of

'Mary and the Seal', the story that had occasioned our meeting. At the end, he clapped enthusiastically.

'Wonderful, David. Wasn't that wonderful?' said he to the audience.

'David Campbell, you told my story better than me, that's your story now.'

Duncan was always a convincing liar!

Soon after that he said to me, 'David, come to schools with me,' and so began our travels.

Usually the night before our visits I would drive to Lizziewells farm cottage near Auchtermuchty, spend the evening in the company of Duncan, Linda, John Barleycorn, the kids Betsy and Tommy and the dog dodging around the place. Early next morning I would drive us off in my campervan. He would often say that if our day didn't start off with a disagreement it was going to be a bad day and we would pass the journey teasing, flyting, exchanging jokes and stories of our very different lives, our two worlds.

'Now, David, why would you, a university educated man, a scholar, manager of the BBC, be wasting your time with an ignorant tinker, an old uneducated Traveller man?' (Fishing!)

'That's what I ask myself, Duncan. I think it is sheer good nature, kindheartedness, and the faint hope that one day I might just learn something.'

'David, I've taught you everything I know and still you know nothing.'

'You are right! Absolutely right!'

Duncan was curious to know about my family, my childhood. What was my father like?

'A bit like yours,' I told him.

My father had little instructive sayings that I still remember: 'A place for everything and everything in its place.' 'If a job's worth doing, it's worth doing well.' 'Never grumble when you lose but laugh like blazes when you win.'

He also in a mild but firm way insisted on our respect for older folk; we couldn't refer to mum or granny as '*she*'.

'Who?' he would enquire.

'Granny.'

'Yes, Granny.'

The skills he taught us were very different from those Duncan learned, but with endless patience he taught us to play golf, family card games, chess, how to kick a ball, how to make soup, custard, stew, and every Sunday morning he brought the whole family breakfast in bed. The price my brother and I who shared a bedroom had to pay, was a little bit of guilt, as he surveyed the disarray around us.

'It would be a great help to your mother if you boys would tidy up the room.'

We did.

Duncan was much impressed and wanted to meet my mother who at that time was in her 80s. She lived in a small, neatly kept flat in Morningside, in Edinburgh. Duncan professed to love her ever after because she greeted him, sat him in a comfortable armchair, offered him a cigarette, a cup of real tea, made from loose tea leaves. She never used a tea bag. Real tea.

As often as not on our journeys, Duncan asked about my family life. Compared to his knowledge of family antecedents my knowledge was lean. He set great store by where he came from.

* * *

Not many people know about their background and their ancestry, but it was the custom among the Travelling people, especially boys sitting round the campfire, to ask questions. They always listened to the old folk. You had to call them 'Uncle or 'Auntie' or Grandad' or 'Granny'. You could not call an older person by their first name. So, the question we used to ask wir grandad or wir granny was: 'Tell us about your Grandad, tell us about your Granny.'

So, we'll go back to the beginning. Back to 1812, which is a long time ago. There's a man in Orkney by the name of Mosey Williamson. They called him Moses because he had a long white beard. He had a wee run-down kind of farm, grandfather would say. Now Mosey had three sons; there were Billy, Jimmy and Sandy the youngest. Mosey died and was buried in Kirkwall old cemetery in Orkney.

Whatever he had, he left to the three boys to share between them.

There was an argument over the farm. They probably had a drink, then there was an awful fight. The youngest brother Sandy was killed and this is where it started; the whole Williamson migration to the mainland. No one was charged but the two brothers fled to the mainland.

Billy's son John went to Islay. That was my grandfather's father, my great-grandfather, John Williamson. He settled down and he had married an Islay woman. They never moved from Islay. They had a son Willie, my father's father, my grandfather. He later got the name 'doll', Willie the doll, because he was just a small man, only five foot two, but he was very beautiful; blue eyes, fair curly hair, little fair moustache, white teeth, a great Gaelic speaker and never went to school in his life.

Now, it happened a Traveller family came to Islay as many did, and among them a young woman Betty McColl; big woman, tall, over six feet. Her father was Irish; she was part Traveller, part Irish. A lovely singer. And grandfather, 'the doll', took an interest.

'I think Granny would be 20 when I met her,' he said, 'she was a bonnie lassie, a bonnie lassie. I think,' he said to me, 'her hair was what attracted men most of all. It was hanging down, near touchin' the ground.' And to the day my granny died she never cut her hair.

I remember my granny away back when she was, maybe, in her 50s. I would see her sitting here with an old bone comb and combing the hair over her knee, Bett McColl, grandfather's wife, the folk singer.

They left Islay and they moved to Tarbert in Argyll. They stayed in Tarbert, Loch Fyne, for the rest of their life. My father was called John after his great-grandfather, the old man that went to Islay for the first time, John.

Sometimes, Grandfather, 'the doll' and Granny Bett would visit us in the tent at night, they would have maybe a few bottles of beer, maybe a wee half bottle. It was a great pleasure to hear granny sing. Even as an old middle-aged woman she was a lovely singer.

Granny and grandfather... grandfather died when he was 86, and granny died when she was 82, both buried in Tarbert, Loch Fyne. But I dinnae mind my big grandfather, my mother's father, because he died the day I was born, in 1928. I was told that he was a piper, great piper. He took the blues through the drink and they put him to the mental hospital up in Lochgilphead and he died there. So I don't mind o' him, but I'll be remembering his wife, my little granny.

When old grandfather died, my wee Granny Betty came and stayed with us in Furnace as I told you because my mother was her daughter, Betsy. My mother was the daughter of Bella MacDonald (her maiden name), and old John Townsley.

Bella and my big grandfather never married. They just lived together all these years but they had a big family; they had three sons killed in the First World War. They never settled down because grandfather was a wandering piper. Sometimes they visited, but I don't remember because I wasna even born when grandfather was a piper and come visiting. Granny lived many, many years after grandfather died.

But my mother's side of the family; not much about them at all, because granny didn't know much about the Townsleys. No, all granny knew was that her father's people were foreigners, French she said. That's as much as I got from her. But I got the whole story of my father's side and grandfather, yeah. Right from Norway to Orkney, from Orkney to the mainland, from Elgin right down to Moray, right down to Islay, to Tarbert, Loch Fyne, where my grandfather finally died. That was the whole story, the Williamsons, where they actually come from.

Now, I would like to tell you more about them, my grandfather and my grandmother on my father's side. Well, the most interesting thing in my life was my grandmother, big Bett McColl they called her. Many people ask me in many places where I get the old traditional songs I've collected down through the years, 'cause I don't read songs from books or anything like that, as you know well. All the songs and stories that I've collected were told to me orally by people. Especially when it comes to old ballads and old traditional songs, I go back to the days of my grandmother. A little Traveller boy, tinker they called us in these days, little tinker boy with my bare feet, six, seven years old with grandmother, big Bett McColl, tidy big woman, blonde hair, big bun on the top of her head, big bone comb stuck into it, big shawl over her shoulders and a big brooch on her breast there, you know, like a big old lady warrior, and she would sing the streets in Tarbert.

Grandfather as I told you was just a wee mannie, 'the doll', five foot two, and grandmother, big Bett about six foot two. 'Wee Willie' she would call him. She was a wonderful folk singer and her father being Irish, she had between the Irish accent and the Scottish accent, the Highland accent of the West Coast.

Tarbert was mostly Gaelic speaking there at that time when I was a boy. Granny was fluent in Gaelic herself and so was grandfather. He would teach us swear words in Gaelic, which was to get me into trouble many years later. But oh, he was a wizard on the little chanter, the old practice chanter. He could play anything – jigs, reels, strathspeys, anything – and he would take it with him in his pocket when he went to the bar. He would go into the little bar in Tarbert and get a pint of beer and granny would be on the street with a shawl over her shoulders walking up and singing in the street. A lot of fishing boats coming in, tourists forbyes. Tarbert was a busy little place back before the War. And granny could make a good living singing in the streets in Tarbert.

One of the songs she loved, and I used to love granny singing was 'The Corncrake'. I think it was wrote by Robert Burns and this is the song before I tell you the rest of the story.

O the lass that I looe'd first of all was handsome, young and fair,
And many's a happy day we spent alang the banks o Ayr,
And many's a happy day we spent where thon wee burnie rows,
That echo mocks the corncrake amongst the whinny knowe.

O we loved each other dearly disputes we seldom had,
We were happy as the pendulum, our thoughts were always glad,
We fought for joy and found it where thon wee burnie rows,
That echo mocks the corncrake amongst the whinny knowe.

Now the corncrake is gane awa, the burnie's tae the broom,
The whinny knowes are happed with snaw, tae top the highest whin,
We fought for joy and found it where thon wee burnie rows,
That echo mocks the corncrake amongst the whinny knowe.

And I remember big Bett MacColl, granny, standing in the street singing away. I'd be singing, standing a wee bit away from her with my bare feet listening to the song, taking in every word, liking it as much as the people standing around the circle listening. Then you would see a couple of old drunk men come a-wandering up the street with each other's arm, few drinks on them, old fishermen talking to each other.

'Hi, Bett, give us a song, Bett, come on, give us a song!'

'All right,' she'd say, 'I'll give ye a song. Stand there and I'll give ye a song.' This is the one she used to sing to the men, they loved it.

O Johnny you're a rover, I may meet you drunk or sober,
But Johnny you're a young man forbye,
But if I had it in my power with you I would spend my hour,
O beneath thon shady bower my Johnny first I met.

O there be millers, brewers and bakers
And journeymen and shoemakers
And ever kind of countrymen forbye,
O beneath thon shady bower my Johnny first I met.

And they'd, 'Well done, Bett, well done, that was very nice. Hey, here you are, my lass,' hand in their pocket and took whatever they had in their pocket, whatever change they had, they never even looked at it. And they would wander on till the next couple came up, maybe a man and his wife. 'Come on, Bett, give us a song!' And that was the way she made a living. Then when she came home her and grandfather would get a couple of these pale ale bottles of beer, a little stone cork with a rubber band on it, red rubber band. This cost a sixpence each, and granny would buy one for herself and two for old Willie. Then we would come in and say, 'Granny, give us a song.'

'Oh aye, I'll sing you a song, wait till I get my wee drop beer, laddie, I'll sing ye a song.' But she didn't smoke, it was my wee granny old Bella that smoked a pipe. Not big Bett McColl, wouldn't smoke because it would affect her voice, and old Willie didna smoke. She wouldna allow him to smoke! He would pick up his little practice chanter and they'd have reels and jigs and strathspeys, went on for ever and ever. Fantastic old couple!

His job was mending umbrellas. He was a 'cheeny feeker', they call it, and he would collect all the umbrellas. He took care of the local tip. The Tarbert tip. In these days it was all done by horses and carts, carting the rubbish from the village to the tip. He collected the bottles, he done everything. He never got paid for it, but he collected all the old broken umbrellas, the handles, the silver bands and the ribs and the stays of the umbrella, took them all home with him, and he'd make enough with the old broken umbrellas to pay for his work on the dump. He could take an umbrella to pieces, and within minutes it was back again. And all the people came with their umbrellas, and that was the cause of the separation of little Willie 'the doll' and Big Bett McColl: an umbrella.

There was a woman with a house up some steps as you're going to Tarbert, Loch Fyne, and he had got this umbrella to mend for this Mrs

Campbell. That old couple were together for maybe nearly 35 years, the Travelling folk got each other when they were young, childhood sweethearts.

Willie had an umbrella from Mrs Campbell. It was a cold morning, and Bett said, 'I'll walk in wi' ye to Tarbert,' because it wasnae far to walk, maybe about a mile fae where they lived. They lived out in a place called Cuparcraigane. They had a lovely little place out among the rhododendron. The laird had given them permission to live there all their life. So, this particular morning, Bett and Willie walked into Tarbert, granny and granddad, and he said, 'Just you stand there, Bett, and I'll go up, and gie the woman back her umbrella.' Sixpence to get it mended. But it was a cold day and Mrs Campbell came out and she said, 'Willie, you must be frosted. Just wait a minute and I'll bring you a cup of tea.' She went in, she wouldnae be but five minutes in and she came out with a sixpence and a cup of tea. Willie tried to sup the whole cup of tea, thinking about Bett standing.

Big woman standing watch, 'Where in the hell is he, what's keeping him?' By the time he had the tea supped she was furious. And when he came down she said, 'You were in the house with her, weren't you? You were in the house with her! Well, you'll never, never stay with me again till the day you die.'

Oh, she moved out, built her own little place beside him and they lived separated for 30 years. She had tea with him, she talked with him but she never again ever slept with him. Five minutes, Mrs Campbell handing in the umbrella and she gave him a cup of tea. That was granny. Never again did she ever sleep with him. No, she told the story many times, 'Me standing in the road,' she said, 'and him up there in the house with a woman.' Grandfather told it: 'I was five minutes. I would never hae gaen in a house!'

No Traveller man would go in the house with a woman. Never would, that was the custom, you never walked in. Old Willie never was in the house, he would never, never break an old code. Five minutes overlong, because maybe the tea was hot. Poor old soul, eh?

They went to the town together. He played in the pub, she done her singing, they bought their messages, came home, had their tea together, but they never lived with each other again for the rest of their life. But the two of them's buried together in Tarbert.

Here was another one of granny's songs, 'Lonely I Wander'.

O lonely I wander through scenes of my childhood
That bring back sweet mem'ries of happy days of yore;
O where are they now all those scenes of my childhood?
The young ones are scattered, the old ones are gone.

There's no fire in the hearth, there's no light in the window
No light in the window, no welcome for me
So why stand I here like a ghost in the shadow
It's time to be moving, it's time to pass on.

* * *

So, we make strong tea for Duncan, tea bag left in the cup, milk and sugar, black coffee for me and we adjourn for our 'break' to the lounge.

'I like that song,' I say.

'Well,' says he, 'sing along.' And in the Traveller mode he sings it *into* me, 'eye to eye, mind to mind, heart to heart'. Again and again he sings it, and afterwards on our journeys to schools until I have it more or less to his satisfaction, not having an ear as quick and adept as Duncan's. About this he is endlessly patient.

At ceilidhs in my house, I have seen him from his own inner divining select someone in the company and sing the song he has chosen to that person directly, intently, and fasten that person to his unwavering blue eyes as one newly in love. Often as not, ancient mariner-like, holding them with his hand. Caught and held in this way it was impossible to escape and the recipient's initial astonishment or embarrassment invariably became a transfixed delight to be the Princess or Prince of this royal tinker's song.

But as his close pal and multi-instrumentalist and obsessive collector of tunes and instruments, Lindsay Porteous said, 'Duncan never knew when to give up and when someone came in with a bottle of whisky he'd drink the lot.' So, early on in the ceilidhs in my house or wherever, Duncan was the self-appointed *Fear an Tigh* and everyone in the circle would be called forth, but as the evening

> progressed and the bottle emptied Duncan took over until there was only one performer, Duncan.

* * *

They never lived together again in the same tent but oh, they were both jealous. Oh, wheesht! You've no idea, he was worse than what she was, that's why she took me with her, with my bare feet, sometimes my brother George, sometimes one of the lassies, Rachel or Nellie or Susan, always took one of us when she went singing. Ye couldnae take children in a bar in these days so she couldnae speak to a man because she had a kid with her. This was the kind of deterrent, safeguard, because these men were very, very jealous. Oh, she was worse than him. The two of them was the same. She knew as long as she had one of her grandchildren with her, grandfather wouldnae be jealous; he would say, 'Oh right, ye're back, Bett, come in and have your tea and sit down,' and everything was well, 'did you bring me a wee bottle of beer?'

'Yah, I got you a bottle of beer.'

'Okay,' that was a good night. And he would take out his chanter and play, he was happy, and she would sing a song. But she was never allowed to go off on her own.

Oh, I remember my wee grandfather and my big granny. They would come for a visit, bring a few bottles of beer or maybe a bottle of whisky! Bottle of whisky was only 12 and sixpence! Of course, they would have a sing-song. My father always kept a practice chanter in case the boys wanted to learn to play. My little grandfather, he was a wizard on the little practice chanter, but he never learned how to play the pipes. My father would play the bagpipes, he was a great piper.

My father bought a set of pipes in 1918. It cost 14 pounds and he paid for them with rabbit skins. Would you believe that? After the War, he came back in 1918 and he bought the pipes. They were made in 1914. They were four years old, silver and ivory bagpipes from Lowry in Glasgow. Rabbit skins were in great demand. A rabbit skin was worth a sixpence. When we caught a rabbit he would skin that rabbit, he would stuff that skin with paper and stretch it and hang it out in the trees to dry. I remember the little blue tits coming peck, peck, picking the wee bits of fat off the skin. We would chase them but Daddy used to say, 'Oh leave them alone, they're just picking the fat, they'll no break the skin.'

Father would dry these skins and he would parcel them in a two dozen brown paper parcels and a bit of string. He would post it to a man called Sax in Glasgow, a fur collector, and they would send him a postal order. My father sold rabbit skins up to near the end of the War. He paid them up, then the bagpipes came with a set of reeds to Furnace Post Office.

My little brother Charlie died with pneumonia when he was only a year old and I remember him sitting on my father's knee and he loved the pipes. My father used to put the blow stick in his little mouth. My father would squeeze the bag and little Charlie would laugh, a year old, and he took pneumonia and he died.

After that day my father never played again. He took the pipes up to Inveraray and he sold them to a sailor from Lewis, a fisherman. Never again did he play after Charlie died.

We grew up in the middle of the forest. We knew everything, everything about the plants, the trees and nature. We were nature's children. But this didn't stop the people of the little village of Furnace where we lived from having all this prejudice against us. If a little child came up and called us 'tinker' we couldn't say one single word to that child, otherwise, my parents would have been told that we were bullying the wee local children. The parents would tell my mother when she was hawking the doors, my mother would tell my father and then we'd be in big trouble.

Now, the actual village of Furnace itself was a nice little village. What kept the village alive was the quarries. Granite stone quarries. Boats would come into the pier and collect the stones, great ten-ton boulders for Holland, to build a kind of sea wall. They exported stones and chips and gravel around the world. It was a great novelty for us when the little puffers would come in, the little puffing boats, and the stones would go into the boats. But back to the village itself. The village was small; it would take it tight, I would say, 200 people. The whole community, when I look back now, was just like one big family that agreed with each other on some things and fell out with each other on other things.

The wee village itself was close, and we were the tinkers up in the wood. We were a different class; we were the tinkers, because we got on with everybody. 'Ach, they're just the tinkers, they dinnae know any better.'

Springtime

THE SCHOLAR AND SINGER/SONGWRITER, Adam McNaughton, has the well-known song 'Yellow on the Broom' describing how the Travellers would take to the road after a fraught wintering in town. Duncan has a song of the same name and he assured me that he wrote his song long before Adam's. Duncan's was for a fellow Traveller to sing to comfort his wife who was depressed in the bleak winter of Aberdeen and longing for the open road again. He sang it to me as he recalled his own feelings of excitement when his family moved from the winter tent at Furnace in the springtime to be on the road again.

> Come sit beside me Peggy dear
> I hate to see you gloom
> And I will take you from this place
> When the yellow is on the broom.
>
> When the Angus hills are free of snow
> And the swallow is on the zoom

[He interrupts the song to make sure I understand this line and then fluently continues]

> Oh, I will take you from this place
> When the yellow is on the broom
>
> So put a smile upon your face
> I hate to see you gloom
> And I will take you from this place
> When the yellow is on the broom.

* * *

We always looked forward to one particular time, and this time was April. Because my father worked piece-work he could give up the job in the quarry any time he felt fit. So in April month when we had our 220 attendances in school, the police couldn't bother us; father would set fire to the big tent in the forest, clean up, take everything we needed, and put fire to the rest, burn it all, make a big fire. The first step would be the Furnace beach, down to the shore near the tree under which I was born. We'd camp there for about three or four weeks in the summer, and we'd have the enjoyment of playing on the shore and collecting the whelks and shellfish and fishing. We kids loved the shore. Go swimming, you know, we never had a shoe on our feet, bare feet all summer long.

And then he would say, 'Well, weans, we'll move tomorrow.'

So then he'd move, just a little handcart for carrying our possessions, blankets and tent stuff, sticks for the tent, and the cooking utensils, children's clothes and all the bits and pieces we needed to keep us through the summer. We gradually went down the west coast of Argyll. We'd be all little children at this time, all steps and stairs, maybe mother had one at her bosom, carrying one, maybe one in her belly, you know! We were all entitled to do something, carry something to help, down to Lochgilphead and into Tarbert, and Daddy would get jobs with the local farmers cutting hay. He was a great scythe man. Daddy was well known in the West Coast, he would get a few jobs on the little farms, casual work, like gathering stones off the farmers' fields, digging drains, things that the local community didn't want to do themselves. 'Jock Williamson and his family, they'll do it for you.' Then during October month, he would come back to Furnace and he'd put us back to school, nine of us.

Anyway, every day was a source of learning when you lived with your parents in the forest. Parents would make sure their children had the best teaching and the best learning to see them through the life that they were supposed to lead as Travelling people; they knew fine their children were not going to do a nine-to-five job, they were going to try and survive in the world to the best of their ability. They had to learn how to put up a tent, they had to learn how to collect shellfish, and where in the world would you learn it? Right with your parents and your grandparents! But also, there was the dos and the do nots.

The dos and do nots were: when you went to the shore to collect shellfish you only took as much that you could use that night. When you went to fish, you only took as much that would do that night. When you went to the hill to hunt for rabbits, you only took as many as would do that night. My father used to snare rabbits, taking two rabbits and letting the rest of them go. It was the same if we took some shellfish, he would make you walk back, nearly a mile, and say, 'That's enough for the night. You go back and put that back on the beach where you got it. Somebody else may need a wee drop shellfish. And if you keep destroying all the shellfish, what do you think's going to happen to the future?' These are the things you had to learn down through time, the dos and the do nots.

I remember one strange story when I was a little boy with my little sister. The little river that we camped beside went dry, and he gave us a pail and he said, 'Go to the well!' There were an old well about a mile away, it never went dry. It was covered in green moss but the water was crystal clear, and all these little boatmen, ye call water spiders, running along collecting little pieces of straw to make their nests and things on the top of the well. But me and my little sister, we just ducked in the pail, and carried it back. My father was sitting in the tent. We gave him the pail of water. He looked at that pail, and there was a little boatman or water spider.

He says, 'Look what you've done to that little water spider.' Now he says, 'You'll go back to the well and you'll carry that pail of water back all the way, and don't empty it out before you get there. You'll put the little fellow back in the well where you got him. Who do you think's going to keep your well clean? These are well washers, these are little boatmen, these little fellows collect all the pieces of grass and stuff that keep your well clean for you. Now, if you take two or three off every time that you go for water to the well when the little river is dry, these things will die out and there'll be none to keep your water clean for the next time.'

You see, he was teaching us many wonderful things. Then you had to go to school. Now school life. Ye're five years old and you go to school. So, when you went into the classroom, the teacher didnae put you in among the class with the other children. Teacher was an old teacher called Miss McFarlane. She lived in a little schoolhouse in Furnace with her mother; she never married. She was our teacher, but she was prejudiced against the Traveller children because the Traveller children were very, very clever, especially about the nature things.

I remember one time, I won the little award for poetry called the dux medal, a little aluminium medal. We had to up and recite a poem. I was

Duncan's schooldays at Furnace, 1937
(back row, third boy on left)

about eight and I won the medal and beat the rest of the children, the local children. It was not presented by the teacher; it was presented by the manager of the local quarry where all the people went to work. And you know, by me winning that medal in school, my mother had to suffer because of me when she went and hawked, 'Oh no, we don't want nothing fae you today,' because here was me a little tinker boy, I'd won the dux medal in my classroom for reciting a poem. I was a tinker.

They were even prejudiced against the quarry manager. Why should the quarry manager give it to a little tinker boy? The quarry manager gave it to the best, as he told many of them, but that didn't satisfy the local people. They were very, very prejudiced against us in school. The teacher would keep us by ourselves, as if we had lice or beasties or something on us. Life in the school was really, really hard. The only consolation was we knew when we got this attendance quota Daddy would burn the big tent, and then we'd move on down the West Coast, we'd be off for the summer, but then we'd move back.

When the winters came life began to get hard once again. Hunger began to catch. We had plenty firewood, that's one thing we did have. Hunger was the problem. We waited for the snow. The snow was the most important thing for us. You see in the hills in the West Coast where I lived the heather grows about four or five feet long, and under this heather is the tunnels with the white mountain hare, the blue hare. Now he never runs in the snow. When it's really deep, he runs in the tunnels under the snow and he can't run very fast under his tunnels among the heather, so we used to follow his footprints in the snow till it came to the tunnel. We searched round about the snow. He never came out! He's under one of these tunnels under the snow and then we'd creep up, we would see him and dive on top of him in the snow and we'd pull his neck. It was a pot! It would feed the whole lot of us for one night. Only one! No, two hares wouldn't do, daddy wouldn't allow you to bring back two. It was the same with rabbits. We learned to hunt, we learned to guddle, we learned to poach salmon, we learned all the things that stood us in good stead down through the years to come.

When we were small boys and my father had a wee job, he would say, 'Come along, laddies, if you cannae dae nothing, ye'll maybe learn something.' He was a great scythe man. Say he got a contract to cut a field of hay for the farmer, no machines for cutting the hay. Naturally, he would sit down and take a smoke, 'Try it,' he would say, 'laddie, try a wee shot of it!' Then we learned to cut and there were no machines for tying corn. You learned how to tie the corn into little bundles, little sheafs, and stook it. It was the same building a dyke. He would say, 'You put the stone, you do that wee bit!' It was the same when you were digging a drain, it was the same when you went to cut timber. 'Get the other end of the saw,' big, six foot cross-cut saw. You pulled one end, he just pulled it back, he pulled it, you just pulled it back. Zoom, zoom, zoom, zoom. The same with the axe, the big, seven pound axe he had for snedding his trees, and we laddies could barely lift it, but we could manage. When you become 12 you were qualified. You learned so much.

You see that's what happened to me when I left home at 13, what it's all coming to. I had an education above my quarter, being a Traveller. I could work a horse. Father carted with horses in the barn, carting out dung, cleaning out the dung reeds, carting in the harvest. He'd take the big Clydesdale horse out of the stable and say to one of the boys, 'See how quick you can put a harness on!' And he'd put it on. He was yoked up on the cart. On with the braces, on with the chain. Then he would take the harness back off and he would say, 'It's your turn!'

I seen me, hardly able to reach up, so young I could hardly get the collar on the horse's head. But gradually it came to you and you got so good at it. I could yoke a horse in three minutes. On with bits, on with the collar, on with the bridle, back him into the cart, pull down the shaft, put the rope under the belly, cleek up – three minutes time! I was only 12 years old.

If there was a wee bit job, 'Oh, you're Jock Williamson's boy,' and I would get a wee job on the farm. I was a qualified farm worker at the age of 13: I could handle a horse, I could dig drains, I could dig ditches, I could build drystone dykes, I could handle a 14 pound axe, I could handle a scythe, I could use a cross-cut, the old fashioned cross, long days before power saws. I could build a fence, I could set fence posts and I could build a little haystack. I had the same ability and the understanding my father had: he had taught us all the things that he had learned as a farm worker. You got an education past the common. And I think that if I hadnae been taught the ways of my father, I wouldnae have managed to cope when I left home at the age of 13. And you were supposed to be able to sing a song when you were three years old, you were supposed to be able to tell a story by the age of five. In the whole close knit community, the family, the old Travelling people enjoyed the children to participate, to tell stories, sing songs, they were encouraged to do this. And that's the way I grew up.

We had no books unless we had them in school, and of course we never got any Christmas presents or toys or nothing like that. The only thing we lived on was stories and songs at night-time round the fire because we needed some source of entertainment. You can imagine! Well, we wouldnae have all been there, 17 kids, at one time. Mother would maybe have nine in the tent at the same time. Funny thing, she had boy-girl-boy-girl-boy-girl all down her lifetime. Sitting in the tent, girls would be doing things, maybe sewing. Boys would be annoying each other, father would say, 'Be quiet and I'll tell you a story.'

I remember it was Christmas morning. He took one orange, one single orange. He always carried a pocket knife. He took his pocket knife and he cut that little orange in strips; he gave each of us a wee bit out of it. Christmas morning in the tent in the wood. All the children in the village enjoying their Christmas presents. See with us, one orange! And this is the words he said, 'Do you know weans, I wish I could afford to buy you something special for your Christmas but I dinnae have nothing to give you for your Christmas.' He knew that he was going to give us something far more important than the most expensive toy he could have bought for us. He said, 'I'm going to tell you a story for your Christmas.' And so he did. He said to me and the rest of the children, 'You know some day, when I am gone and you're grown up and have your own family, you will remember that story. I hope you do. But you wouldna remember a present if I could give it to you. Because presents doesn't last, but stories last forever.'

He'd been brought up with stories. So that's where we learned most of our trades, from father, it was passed down to all the children.

Now, I'll give you a riddle, a present:

It will never break
It will never wear out
You can keep it forever
You will never lose it
You can give it away and still have it
Every time you give it away it gets better.
If you don't give it away it is of no use.

You don't get all you need in school even today but it was worse in my day. Even in school I knew every herb, every plant, every tree and every bush. I knew about animals. They didn't have a clue! Look at it this way Miss McFarlane was not very good to us kids. She had this big leather strap, a big belt. I got the belt many times, cross-hands. The worst belting I ever got from Miss McFarlane was for drowning a bumblebee. Drowning a bumblebee! That horse trough is still there where I drowned the bumblebee. It was only fun, you see.

There was a group of girls standing around and there was a bumblebee crawling up the side of the trough and I caught the bumblebee by the wings. I knew how to catch them, right. I pulled a piece of thread off my jersey and I tied the piece of thread round the bumblebee and I got a wee stone and sank the bumblebee into the thing and drowned him.

The three girls ran across and told the teacher, 'Duncan Williamson drowned the bumblebee, Miss, in the horse trough.'

'How did he drown it?'

'He tied a piece of thread to it. He tied it round the bumblebee and he tied a stone to it and he sank the bumblebee in the horse trough.'

'Duncan Williamson, did you do this?'

'Yes, Miss. I just wanted to see how long a bumblebee could survive in the water.'

'Hold out your hands!' Cross-hands that time, the big belt. 'Now, go over there and sit down.'

Anyhow, we went to school in our bare feet, no boots all summer long. We had in school a wooden floor, bare wooden floor. No carpets. No linoleum.

I told my brother, told my sister, told some of the wee kids I could get on with in the village, 'Let's walk in the puddles. When you get in the puddles close your toes. Close them tight before you go into school. When you get into Miss McFarlane's class, open your feet up!'

And we made these big wet slobbery duck marks on the floor with our feet. She gave us the belt for bringing in mud with our bare feet. We went back out, we brought in more mud with our feet till we finally made her stop giving us the belt for bringing in mud with our feet. When she stopped giving us the belt, we went into the wash room and washed our feet before we went into class. We washed our feet and dried them with a big old roll of bath towel and came in and sat down. There was never another word. No more belt for bringing mud into the school with our bare feet.

So we teached her a lesson. Quite simple. We never argued, we never fought, we never cried. We just done something to annoy her that she didn't like. This was a way of paying her back for giving us the strap for bringing in mud with our feet!

On a Wednesday the teacher, when I was seven years old, used to do her books with her big pen. She would take some of the older kids, then she would take the little ones, pull a glass partition and get the little ones, one girl at a time, make a wee shop with them, do things, learn them to draw, to paint, kindergartens, five- and four-year-olds who had come from the village. Not many, about eight or nine.

But one day, I don't know for some reason, she said to me, 'Duncan, would you like to take the wee ones over?'

I'm seven years old. And of course, she pulled the partition. They were all sitting in little chairs.

And I said, 'I'm no going to play a shop with you. Today, we're going to have a wee story.'

'A story?'

I said, 'I'm going to tell you a story.'

And I told my first story in public when I was seven, to a group of kindergartens. The old traditional fable was 'The Fox and the Crow,' how the fox was hungry when he had come so long a way, and he smelled a beautiful smell. 'And then, children, he looked up and sitting on top, upon a branch, was a big crow. And in the crow's beak was a lump of cheese. And this is where the smell was coming from. Now,' I said, 'that fox was hungry. And he wanted to get that piece of cheese for himself. But a fox can't climb a tree, can he?'

'No!' Little one.

'Now, he's got to get that piece of cheese. How's he going to get it?'

So I told them the old fable.

'Once upon a time there was a fox. Och, he had wandered here and wandered there looking for something to eat, but he could not get a thing. He was as hungry as could be! Chased by the hounds, chased by the hunters, he was tired and wearied and could not get a bite.

So he says to himself, "This will never do. I'll have to eat or I'm going to die. There's only one cure for it; I'll have to go to the village and see if I can get something."

On this path leading down to the village there was a tree. And sitting on the branch of the tree was a crow. This crow had managed to get hold of a big lump of cheese. Oh, a beautiful lump of cheese! And he had flown up on the branch with it, and he's sitting there with his foot on it, you see! When down comes Mister Fox, trotting wearied and hungry. He looks up. He sees the crow sitting up in the tree, oh, well out of reach with this lump of cheese.

He says to himself, "That is a lovely lump of cheese. I wish I had that! That black bird has got it, and I'll never get it. But I'll have to rack my brains to see what I can do, if I can get that bit o' cheese."

Now, when the crow saw the fox, the crow took the cheese and put it in his beak, so's it would not fall! Mister Fox came down under the branch and looked up.

He says to himself, "I'm going to have that bit o' cheese! I must get that bit o' cheese." He thinks and he thinks and he looks up again.

He said to the crow, "I heard my father saying a long, long time ago that there were bonny, black birds flying about. They called them crows, and they were the bonniest birds he'd ever seen in his life. But I'd never seen one before. And I think to myself, that this one I see up there now

– man, that is a lovely bird! Look at the way the sun is shining on it! Look at its feathers. Look how black and glossy they are. And look at its lovely beak and its lovely feet. I wish I had a bird like that for a pet!"

And the crow sat listening. But no, it never let the cheese go.

So the fox says, "I heard my father telling me a long time ago that these black birds, them crows, they were the greatest singers in the world! They could sing, and their singing could put you to sleep. I've never really heard them, but I'd give anything if I could hear one of these birds singing!"

The crow could not stand this any longer. He opened his beak, "Caw, caw," and the big lump of cheese fell!

The fox picked it up and ate it. He looks up at the crow.

He says, "See you! You black, dirty bird – you silly black crow! I thought you were fly. You're not – it's me who's fly – I'm the fly fox! I've got your cheese and you've got nothing. I'm on my way and I feel better now."'

And this was the story I told the kindergartens.

And they're sitting there, the children, so quiet listening to me. So, here was all the little ones and me a seven-year-old. And I'm telling them a story. Then they're so quiet the partition opened, the teacher looked in. She was wondering what was going on, she stood there with her head in through the door listening to the end of the story. And from that day, our teacher Miss McFarlane completely changed. I don't know whether it was the story that changed her, when she heard the end of the story, or was it the quietness of the children or the way I sat there with the children – she knew I was a little tinker boy, right! After that, when it came to Wednesday afternoon they didna want anybody else, they wanted me to tell them stories, the stories my father and mother and granny tellt me. I took an interest in stories ever after that. That inspired me that I was going to become a storyteller; I was going to be as good as my grandmother.

In 1976, I got a letter from the head teacher in Furnace School. Would I come back and tell some stories to the school children? I wrote and told her I would be privileged to come back. Miss McFarlane was living in an old people's home but she came to the school to listen. I sat there for an hour, told stories and told about my travels and my wanderings, and during the break Miss McFarlane came up.

'Duncan, I would like to buy one of your books.'

I said, 'No, Miss McFarlane, you can't buy one of my books.'

She says, 'Why? What's wrong? Why won't you let me have one of your books?'

I says, 'Miss McFarlane, you're not buying a book. I'm going to give you a book! A present from me.'

She says, 'That's very kind of you. Will you autograph it for me?'

I says, 'Yes, I'll autograph it for you, but,' I says, 'look, if the writing's bad you can only blame yourself. You taught me!'

I think it might have been the first greatest smile I had seen on Miss McFarlane's face, and she says, 'You know, Duncan, after all these years you haven't really changed very much!'

That was the last time I ever saw her. The local press – I've still the clipping at home – wrote, 'Local Boy Makes Good.' Headlines in the paper, my picture, picture of the kids in the school. *'Traveller comes back to Furnace and tells stories at school where he was first as a child.'* And I remember it as if it was yesterday.

* * *

> My visits to schools with Duncan became mutual places of learning. Duncan was nothing short of magical with his capacity to connect with children of all ages. He would pull out his little Jew's harp, get the kids to guess what it was, tell them it taught him his ABCs and 123s and then get it to sing these sounds, waking wonder in their eyes; they were under his enchantment.
>
> 'David, when you make friends with people you can tell them any story.'
>
> In his company, I learned much and as time went by I was delighted to see him incorporate some of my storytelling ways. In his mellow moods he would fulsomely acknowledge this. I was always amazed by his memory.

* * *

Let me tell you a strange story.

When I was a boy, when I was really young, my father used to take us up to Kilmartin and work on the farms there, cut hay with his scythe and gather stones in the farmer's field. And at Kilmichael Glassary are the Pictish tombs, the tombs of the Picts. I played there as a boy. All round the Pictish tombs there are cairns and under the cairns are the little Pictish graves, always dry. Oak leaves blow with the wind and gather under the tombs. We used to camp not far from them.

When I was about five we camped around there. While my father was cutting hay for the farmer, I climbed one of the big standing stones, right up to the top. Climbed it up, five-year-old boy. Father laid his scythe down, because it was next to the field where he was cutting his hay, and he says, 'Come down off of there, boy! Come down. You know you're not supposed to climb a standing stone.' He said, 'Bad luck will follow you, I'm warning ye! Something bad'll happen to you. You're supposed to look at them, worship them, enjoy them, but not to touch them, or climb them. Now remember that. Now,' he says, 'I'll get you when you come down, suppose it's for a week!'

I was feart, afraid. But he went off to work anyhow. And I saw him away at the other end of the field, swinging away with his scythe. Shirt sleeves rolled up, good strong man. I came down the stone. Next to the stone was a little field of corn, about six inches high, just before they came to their heads, before the corn sprouted. It was a warm day, middle of May! I goes out into the middle of the field among the corn and I lay down, I put my head down and I must have fallen asleep. The sun rose high in the sky, passed over. I'm still lying. They searched for me. The big River Add runs by. They searched the river, they cried for me everywhere. I was gone. No one could find me. So for some strange reason, some of the girls walked out in the evening and they found me in the middle of the field. Unconscious! Sunstroke! Mother said put me in a little barrie, little pram, and they hurled me through Lochgilphead to the doctor. Those days it took two and sixpence for the doctor's visit. They paid the doctor, the doctor said it was sunstroke. He said, 'The're nothing for it, just water.' I was allowed water.

And I can't remember nothing from that time on. Nothing. Not a single thing could I remember from that time on. They hurled me for two months in the little pram whenever they moved. I couldn't walk, I couldn't move, I was fairly paralysed.

Then later in the year, my father goes back to the same farm. This time the hay was all cut, made into little stacks: he had to go back to cut the corn. Put his tent in the field among the daisies, not far from the Pictish stones, same place he'd camped before. My two brothers, George and Willie, were out catching gulls. Now, when I mean catching gulls, they catcht gulls just for fun, for amusement. They done them no harm, they petted them, they loved them and then they let them go.

How did they catch the gulls? They threw pieces of bread which is just scraps and the gulls came flying around. They made a little hook, made from a pin, no barb on it and on it they put wee bit of bread. They watched the gull till he put that wee bit bread in his mouth, then they ran at it, chased him, and he flew off and the little hook stuck in his beak. Never got in his throat or he never swallowed it, it stuck in the side of his beak and give them as much time to catch the little gull, little black headed gull, maybe a big grey gull. And they sat, would pet him and they would look at him, admire the gull and then they would let him go! They wouldn't lay a finger or take one feather out of the gull.

And here was me three months later, and mother had sent me out with them in the pram to look after me while she was busy. And the first thing I watched – I opened my eyes – and here was a gull. And he was caught. I sat up, and I looked at them. I says, 'What are you doing?'

That was the first word I ever uttered for three months. They said, 'We're catching gulls.' They came over, and they gave it to me, a little black headed gull. I petted it and I let it go, and I climbed out of that pram, for the first time in three months. I was completely sane, but I could not remember one thing, what happened. I remember my father warning me, 'Come down from the standing stone!' I remember coming down. I remember lying in the field. And from that it was three months blank. Completely blank. Nothing. But I can remember just like today, of the two boys giving me that wee gull that was caught with the pin. That three months is gone, but I can remember many things that happened before that.

I can even remember my mother taking me to old Duncan Maclean the minister, into the little church, the little office, I smelled the cigars. I was nine months old. She sat there with a shawl over her shoulders and me on her knee. The minister came with a little wooden bowl. He had gold rimmed glasses and a wee black string over the back of his ear. Nose was red. I didn't know then what made his nose red. But you probably know! He put his fingers into a little bowl and he spread water on my head, 'I baptise you Duncan James MacCallum Williamson.'

In 1928, there was an old woman called Katie MacCallum. Some of her relations are still alive. I hope they read this in your book. Katie MacCallum was good to my mother. My mother was pregnant. Katie's young son Duncan was in bed with TB, 22 years old. My mother was hawking the doors. 'Aye, Betsy, you're going to have another baby?'

'Yes,' she said, 'I'm having another baby.'

'Betsy,' she says, 'I was going to ask you something.'

'Yes,' my mother says, 'Kate, what is it?'

She says, 'See, Betsy,' she said, 'if you have a wee boy, would you call him after my son, Duncan?' My mother knew her son Duncan was in bed, tuberculosis, nothing but a thread, a hair lying in bed day out and day in. She said, 'Furnace is playing today against Newtonmore on the village green. I wish Duncan could be at the game. But he'll no get to the game.' 1928 Furnace beat Newtonmore, sixteen nothing. That's true. Sixteen goals. Not many people will remember that. That's the day I was born.

When mother went up to Adie MacCallum, the registrar, to register me, she never forgot. Duncan James MacCallum Williamson. Mother used to take the babies through the village and everybody would give maybe a sixpence, you know, handsel the wee baby, they called it. So, mother goes to Katie MacCallum, she says, 'A little boy, Betsy, yah? What did you call him?'

She says, 'I called him Duncan, after your son.'

She says, 'Is that true? Ye really did it?'

She said, 'I did.'

Then she said, 'Well, would you show me the registration paper?' They give you a wee registration paper.

'Ach,' my mother said, 'I have it up in the tent.'

'Well,' she says, 'you bring it to me, Betsy, and show it to me and I'll never forget ye.'

Mother had a box, a wee box for keeping things in, birth certificates of the kids. She took it out and went down to Kate MacCallum, and she showed it to her. Old Kate started to cry. Three days later Duncan died. From that day on, mother had one of the greatest friends she ever had in her life.

I remember her myself. When I was going to school she was still alive. And I could go anytime, and get a piece. She used to make good blackcurrant jam from the garden, and I would get a piece with blackcurrant jam. I would go and knock on the door and she would come out, old Kate. 'Well, Duncan, what is it?'

I said, 'Could I have a little piece?'

'Oh, just a minute, I'll get you a piece.' A big piece and jam then I would go and play with the kids. What a wonderful refuge she was.

Being sunstruck did something wonderful to my memory. Because I was telling you a minute ago, there was nothing that ever happened in my life now from the early days I couldn't recall. I can remember today my sister taking me out for the first time when I was only about a year, and showing me how to have a pee. That is in my mind just like yesterday. There's nothing in the world, every movement, I can't forget names and I can't forget stories. It's not a photographic memory. I think that sunstroke did something to my mind. It didn't destroy anything, whatever it did, it increased the value of my mind. Whether I been struck in some particular place in the head with the sun, I don't know. Any of my brothers alive today or any of my sisters will tell you how much I suffered, though I didn't suffer any pain but something had transformed inside my head with that being sunstruck on the forehead. And it gave me I would say, one of the greatest memories in the world because I can remember every single detail from the day that I saw my two brothers catching the gulls, and that was back in 1933. I was five years old. All the people, all the stories, all the things, all the travels that I had done from 1933, in my memory just like yesterday.

Every single detail I can remember, leaving home, the clipping, the dipping, the sheeping, the farmers' names, the tragedies, the melodies, and the things that happened, the good times, the bad times, the ceilidhs in the Western Isles, and the Hebrides, wandering the glens, climbing aboard the ferry boats, hiding out sometimes and missing the purser when he came around and hiding behind him. All these wonderful things down through the ages are trapped away in my memory, every single detail.

When we camped at the Pictish tombs as I was telling you, in the little village of Kilmartin there lived an old roadman, MacVicar, and his wife. My mother used to hawk the doors and I used to wander with her in my bare feet, a little boy. The old roadman; he had a white beard, and his old woman was identical to him. You couldna tell one from the other. They were like twins, and she'd a long white grey beard. But I didn't know this. They called her Beardy, the local villagers called her Beardy. Anyway, my mother smoked a pipe and she says, 'Duncan, would you run back to Beardy and see if you can get me a match to light my pipe?'

'Sure Mummy.' So I run back and knock. The old woman came out, I says, 'Sir, could you give my mummy a match?'

And the moment I said 'sir' she went completely berserk. 'I'll sue you,' she said, 'you little brat. You'll get no matches here, get out of here.'

I run back, I says, 'No, Mummy, the old man wouldnae give me a match. He chased me.'

She said, 'That's no a man, that's a woman!'

I said, 'Mummy, I never seen a beardy woman in my life.'

But anyway, next day me and my mother was going to Kilmichael. She had a basket on her arm full of stuff; selling stuff and I'm in my bare feet behind her. It was raining. Halfway down the road there was an old rusty bike and here he was sitting, old MacVicar, the roadman. Now beside it is a little birch wood, thick birch wood and a few little spruce trees. In these days the roadmen when they cycled away from home, they took a little billycan with them. If it wasn't a good day, they would kindle a wee fire and boil their wee drum of tea. So here was old Beardy sitting there on the roadside. We came up.

'Terrible day, Mrs Williamson,' he said, 'terrible day, too wet, canna get the fire kindled.'

She says to me, 'Laddie, we're no in that big a hurry,' smirr o' rain coming down. She said, 'Kindle the wee fire for him.'

I just sprang into the wood with my bare feet, and within a minute collected a handful of dry grass, knew where to find the good dry stuff away from the rain, twigs, wee bit, a handful of bushes, a handful of little dry sticks. I just lighted the wee grass, gied a wee blow, put on a wee bit more thin twigs, more twigs, within a minute wee flames gathered and then I put on more sticks. Within five minutes I had a beautiful wee fire going. He held a wee can on the fire, like the size o' a double bean-can burnt black, and within minutes it's boiling.

He had a wee box, maybe they're antiques now: one end of the wee box held tea, and the other end of the box had sugar. Kept the tea and sugar separated. He took this tin out of his wee bag and he shook a wee taste of tea in it, put it a-boil. I watched him, and he opened the other end. It was oval shaped like a wee mustard can, and he shaked a wee bit

sugar in it. He broke a wee twig and he stirred it up. 'Now I can have a wee cup of tea,' and he says, 'Thank you both.' And you know the light in that old man's eyes was something I'll never forget.

Someway, me and my mother just appeared like guardian angels. She put the basket on her shoulder and to pass the time away, she'd sing all beautiful songs, 'O Johnnie you're a rover, I'll meet you drunk and sober', to break up the journey till she came to the door.

It was kind o' strange to me then, but now when I look back at it and see what kind o' life was in the village then in Furnace, it was just one big bloody family. But for us in the forest it was, oh God, I'll tell you, it was a hard life when I thought about it, especially in the winter time, the cold winter nights and the gales in the forest and the flapping of the canvas and the old fire burning, the old paraffin lamp. But, when I look back at it today, comparing with life today, if I had my chance to live again, I would like to live that life once more.

For the village folk, Sunday was their day. I think someways when I look back I see that Sunday was a very special day to them, not that they were religious people, but they seemed to celebrate a Sunday as something special, something to go out, see your neighbour you never saw all week and show them your new coat, show them your new hat and take your children with you and show them how your children were looking, how healthy they were and how well they were shod. It was a kind of a show-off thing. You know, Sunday. 'Did you see Mrs Maclean today? Wasn't that a wonderful hat she was wearing? Where would she get that? I bet you her husband had to go to Glasgow for that. He wouldn't get that in Inveraray.'

I heard them many's a time.

* * *

During one of Davie Muir's visits Duncan, Davie and myself compared our Sundays as children. In wartime my family lived in Fraserburgh in the North East of Scotland and Sunday was the day of the crows. Dressed in black the families, mum, dad and the catechism-chastened chicks paraded obediently to church and Sunday school.

From these observances my brother and I were mercifully

free. My father at a young age discovered the name of a young woman in the family Bible scored through: she had had a child out of holy wedlock. He determined never to enter a Christian Church and so we were never in one either.

In Fraserburgh no children could be heard or seen playing on the Sabbath. Everything was closed, the swings in the park chained up, the shute and roundabout disabled. My brother and I were confined to the back garden for our games, or most frequently dad took us for a walk on the long and beautiful beach. He also took us to a farm where the irreligious farmer gave him blackmarket eggs. This was wartime.

Davie told us his Sunday tale:

'Rachel and I had met up in the usual space beside the drying wall and she said, "Do you fancy going fishing at the Corn Burn?" The Corn Burn was the local burn for fishing and it was really good. When the tide came in you could get salmon in there, but what made me hesitate a bit was it was Saturday when we met and she mentioned it for Sunday.

Sunday, if you understand, in the Highlands was a defunct day for doing anything. I mean, you would stand a good chance of meeting the Devil himself if you were doing anything untoward like. So there I was challenged, you see. I was challenged and I don't think Rachel ever realised how much I was challenged but I said to her, you know, it was Sunday, it was the Sabbath and she said, "What do you mean, the Sabbath?"

For Rachel, you see, the Sabbath had no meaning. Every day was the same as the next. It was a struggle to survive whatever it was and if you could get a few trout in the meantime, what harm? Poached or otherwise! I said, "Alright, I'll go for it."

So, anyway, there I was, down the potato garden, not digging for potatoes but digging for worms, a wee jeely jar

and my rod beside me. I realised that I would have to be careful how I did this and see that I didn't get caught, 'cause I didn't know what would happen if I got caught. I knew my father would be mad with me, but I didn't know what would happen, so I had to plan it in advance and I realised that if I ran across the green, there was a gap in the hedge at a certain place, and then there was a gap in the other hedge, and after that I thought, I'll be pretty safe, you see?

I got round the main part of the town by the sea wall and I ran across the green, jeely jar in one hand, rod in the other hand, and held them back like this, you see, then I poked my head out the hedge this way and before I could poke my head that way, a great big ham of a hand descended on me, grabbed the back of my shirt and my kilt and hauled me off the ground; hauled me through the hedge and lifted me and there's me perched on nothing with my jeely jar in my left hand, and my rod in the other and carried unceremoniously to church for about half a mile through the entire village, with all the people in black of course. For some reason, people in the Highlands wear black when they are going to church so they look as if they're going to a funeral rather than going to enjoy themselves.

The minister was in place, all the congregation were in place, and he patched me down next, or very near next, to my mother and father who were sitting there. The glares they gave me were inexpressible and there wasn't a word to describe what all hell was waiting for me.

In these days, in the church, the congregation would be sitting on one level and there was a penitent seat slightly higher so that the sinner would be on show to the righteous above them but below the minister. The minister would be ten feet above the congregation and he glared down at me. For an eight year-old it was absolutely terrifying, absolutely. I have never been so horrified in my life and of course, as a believer, I was positive that the Devil was stoking the fire up especially for me, you know, I would be a regular guest from now on.

At every mention of Hell and Damnation or the Devil, the minister pointed to me.'

We laid aside the tape recorder. On that afternoon of Davie's visit, Duncan had decided to crack open a Super Lager or two. Davie and I had Glenfiddich whisky and the talk ran free. It started to rain and Davie's tale took the topic to sin and guilt. I told of how my brother and I had never been in church as children, and then aged 17, I met a baptist Evangelist in school called Tommy Mayo, attended chapel with him in Rose Street in Edinburgh and my conversion was complete when I fell wildly in love with the head girl of Jean Brodie's old school. This girl, amongst her other attractions, was a dedicated Christian.

I became a road to Damascus disciple. Simultaneously by snail-slow but steady progress from holding hands our sexual explorations were advancing until we each deliciously but guiltily lost our virginity. In the end, glands were winning the battle over powerful Presbyterian preachings and ultimately I abandoned my resolve to become a minister.

In fact, deeply drunk of an evening, I knocked on the manse door to inform the minister Rev James White that I was drinking, gambling and fornicating and had given up the trinity. He was a wise man and casually remarked that I could, to go deeper down the path, add the sin of spiritual pride to my repertoire.

Despite his ironic lightness of touch, I gave up the church, and in the meantime, God.

'You should put that story in a book, David,' said Duncan. 'But there isn't a God.'

'And what do you believe in then?' said I.

'Put on your recorder and I'll tell you.'

So we had a sample of Duncan's metaphysical reflections.

* * *

Now, some people believe in God and the Devil and some believe in ghosts but they don't have any proof.

To me the Broonie is real. Not a real person that you can talk to or of flesh and blood like you and me but a living spirit that never dies and has the power to do many things. To the Traveller People, or people of the road or tinker folk, whatever you like to call them, the Broonie has always been there.

Let me tell you a legend about the Broonie. When man first came on earth, as the legend says, he had a choice between God and the Devil, between good and evil. Some chose the Devil, some chose God, but one person stood alone and when he was called upon to be good or evil he would be neither. So, he was left in the middle, a spirit that would not take sides, the Broonie. Down through the ages he became a spirit alone, never good or bad who wanders forever with no place and no end. And he will help people if they are good or if they are bad. The Broonie will always stay in between helping them, good or bad. As the old folk say, 'You can be as good and as bad as the Broonie.'

* * *

Often Duncan would tell people that he was the Broonie and as such he 'married' several 'couples'. Alison Millen, Duncan's friend and apprentice told me of just such an occasion when Duncan used his Broonie powers during the 1988 Edinburgh Storytelling Festival.

'Early November 1988, I was assigned the task of being Duncan's minder. This involved sitting in the pub for hours at a time. Over a period of about three days we sat there on and off more often on then off. At once completely at ease he was soon like a life-long crony of the Royal Mile locals and regulars.

"See these two," he said, pointing out a man and woman sitting together, "they're neighbours. They fancy each other and are too shy to tae dae anything about it."

After the last festival concert we were all in a euphoric ceilidh mood. Friday night, the pub was packed. It was time to go back to David Campbell's to carry on till whenever.

"Away out and order a taxi," Duncan said, "I'll no be a minute."

In the taxi Duncan laughed. "I tellt that couple I was a priest – well I am a Broonie priest – got them to join hands and married them in the pub." We were both greetin' with laughter. I knew it was true.'

Village Tales

Memorys

If only I could see again those things that haunt my mind
As through the ages and the years they seem so far behind
So far away that distant land to me it is so real
As though those childhood memorys this longing that I feel
Some fleeing thought or picture that brings them from the past
As in a dream those memorys not from my mind be cast
That longing that is in my heart yet so distant in my mind
If I could somehow bring to life those things so far behind
To see again those places then some peace I'd find.

DUNCAN WILLIAMSON

COMPARED WITH THINGS THEN, you've got everything today, but really today you have nothing. You havenae got the human spirit that you used to have. If we were short a wee puckle tea we'd go to Mrs MacVicar and we'd say, 'Ach, Mrs MacVicar, can I have a wee drop sugar frae you? I'll gie ye some later on.'

Doors would lay open, nobody ever locked their door. They hung their washing just scrubbed on the washing board outside to dry. Nae washing machine, nae dishwasher, nae freezer, you know what I mean! It was a kind of primitive life but it was a good life. They never had nane of these cash cards or anything like that. They went to the shop, they got their messages all week, never paid money; it was marked down in the book. On Saturday when the men got their pay, the wife would go in and pay her bill, the week's messages, maybe four pound, that was a lot of money then.

At Christmas time who'd be the lucky one? Everybody wanted to go with Mummy on Christmas Day, 'Good morning, Betsy.' 'Have a Merry

Christmas, ma'am.' 'Merry Christmas, Betsy.' They would all give her a wee ammas [a token or blessing or wee gift in return for hawking or begging]: some would give her a couple of oranges and some would give her an apple. She would fill her basket, they would help her out, they werenae mean. It was the local public that kept us alive, mostly, in the village. Some were hard-hearted, but not them all. No, no, there were good and bad among them all. There were some nice people among them. They're all gone now, they're just a memory.

* * *

Memory was Duncan's Fort Knox. Parodoxically, he vividly inhabited the moment and yet the past lived in him with the force of the present. He loved to hear and often invited tales from my past. We shared the conviction that 'By their stories shall you know them.' Their stories told you who the people were. Davie Muir, Duncan and I were talking one day about our memories and I broke into a pop song I recalled.

Memories are made of this
Sweet, sweet the mem'ries you gave me
Take one sweet and tender kiss
Sweet, sweet the mem'ries you gave me.

'When was your first kiss, David?' Duncan asked.

'I fell totally in love when I was 12,' I told him.

We'd come from Fraserburgh to live in Edinburgh. We kids had the run of a disused quarry near Fairmilehead. It was more like a paradisal, disused, private playground for me and my gang. I fell in love with Izzy, Isobel, a slim, blue eyed, blonde pig-tailed self-confident mystery of my own age. To the clear and vociferously expressed disapproval of my small gang, she occupied much of my time and attention and showed minimal interest in our usual athletic pursuits.

One day, early on a summer's evening we were alone in the quarry and I suggested I build a fire and we cook some rhubarb.

'I'll make the fire,' she announced. 'I know the proper way to light fires.'

I had the confidence of experience and said it would be better for me to make the fire.

'We'll both make a fire,' said she, 'and see whose is the best.'

And so we did. We agreed to have a ration of three matches each and in no time my fire was ablaze. Hers smouldered for a moment and died.

'So my way is best,' said I.

'No,' she said, 'my way is the proper way. It is how we learned in the Brownies and it is the best!'

'But mine is lit and yours is out,' I protested.

'That doesn't matter, this is the best way to make a fire.'

She stood, slim, upright, unchallengeable in her certainty. Beautiful! Completely confused and bewildered by this logic from the alien female world, I clasped her and planted a baffled and brief and inexpert kiss upon her lips. Then we cooked the rhubarb, each a little startled.

Duncan loved this story and subsequently asked me to tell it at festivals and celidhs. Now it was time to hear the story of Davie Muir's love of Duncan's sister Rachael.

'Rachel was Duncan's wee sister. How I met Rachel was I was stravaiging one day down by the shore. I had a wee pot my father had given me for my birthday. I loved it because it had a lovely Celtic kind of design on the bottom, homemade. My father bought it for me. He said it was tinker-made for me especially and I was really proud of this wee pot. So I would stravaig along the sea wall picking up whelks and mussels – I would make my own wee fire and cook up my whelks and mussels.

I was busy stuffing myself and was sitting on the bank and this wee lassie, same age as myself, six or seven, dunked herself down beside me and said, "That's my father's pot you have!"

I looked at her aghast. "What!" I said. "You're lying. My father gave me that specially."

She said, "You're Davie Muir, aren't you?"

"Yes," I said, "I'm Davie Muir."

"Well," she said, "your father may have given you it but it was my father gave it to your father to give it to you! It's a tinker pot isn't it?"

And I said, "Yes, it's a tinker pot, aye."

And she said, "My father got an order from your father to make a tinker pot for you, for your birthday."

I was totally amazed and said, "So, are you a tinker lassie then?"

"Oh aye," she said, "that's what you call us, you townies, but we don't call ourselves that. We're just Traveller folk, you know?" And she said, "Come and meet my parents anyway, they'll be here shortly."

"Alright," I said, "I will." And I went with her.

So they camped me down beside the fire; they had a big fire and they had an iron thing that you could swing out from the fire to cook on.

Duncan's father said to me, "Would you like some tea?"

I said, "I'd love some tea." So they gave me a mug.

They poured in some sugar from a bag. The tea was absolutely solid black, no milk or anything. I was used to tinker tea. My father used to say, "Are you going off to have a slice of tea?" I've never seen them change anything in the pot: they just pour in more tea and more sugar and it would just continue on the boil and that was how I met them and they were great folk; they were the finest folk ever.

I fell in love with Rachel, aye, she was gorgeous.

I had some friends, you know, a little gang of us that used to go around, but as soon as they heard about my involvement with Rachel, that was me cut dead. They used to call me a 'Tinker Lover' and try and beat me up. I didn't mind that so much, but I hated Rachel being called anything. I was a terrible fighter. When I was knocked down I would stagger up and say, "You're not going to say that about my Rachel," then down I would go again and so it went on every day, never stopped.

Rachel was hard in some ways, I mean you had to be hard to be a Traveller because the winters were hard, but

> names would just get to her. I never knew how to comfort her really, I didn't know the words to say; all I knew was that I loved her and that, as far as I was concerned, she was the best but I never ever found the words to say so.'

* * *

> Never to be outdone we had to hear Duncan's first sexual encounter.

* * *

Now I'll tell you when I had my first sex experience.

Sometimes we had other Travellers passing by. They didn't come and camp in the forest because they weren't allowed but there was a camping place nearby, and sometimes the parents would walk up and visit my father and mother, have tea with them and sit in the tent and discuss old times.

I remember a certain woman and her husband coming up and they had two girls with them. I was 13 years old. I was going to fish on the rocks over in the sea and I says to one of them, 'You want to come along and see if we can get some fish?' She says, 'I'd love to come along with you.' A little Traveller girl, she would be about 14, beautiful girl. I'm not going to mention her name.

We made love on the way back in the woods. Oh, it was real fun. It was something new. Something I'd known about, how children were made and kids were born, but I'd never actually experienced it myself. After we caught some fish she coaxed me, she cuddled and kissed me when we came through the wood.

She threw her arms round me and we sat down and I felt this strange experience. She kind of brought it out of me. That was my first sexual experience. Believe me, I enjoyed it. Anyhow, by the time we got back her parents were ready to leave. They knew nothing of this not even until this day and the next day they moved on. And after that I felt different. I could sit down with my father and talk to him and talk about life and the things that were going to happen in the future.

Now back to the village, the saddest thing was I just remember it as a dream. And it never was accounted for. There was a hall in the village.

We had a box player, wee Duncan MacMillan; he played the wee melodeon at the dances at night-time. There was no drink of nae kind in the village unless somebody had a bottle of beer with them in their pocket. Wee Duncan played the dances and for some reason that we'll never know the dance came out that night about 12 o'clock and Duncan never came hame. Wee Duncan never came hame.

He would be in his 30s. He worked in the quarry. Wife and two wee kids. I heard my mother and father speaking about it. Duncan would fall out wi' nobody. He never hurt nobody. And nobody ever hurt him, and nobody would argue with him.

The're a big tree by the bridge in Furnace and lovers used to kiss and cuddle under it. They got wee Duncan sitting there the next morning. He was sitting in below the tree and his throat cut from ear to ear with an open razor and a wee melodeon by his side.

Oh, there was a big hullabaloo in the village, a police enquiry, but to this day nobody knows who killed wee Duncan MacMillan. Whoever killed him never was gotten and they lived with it all those years. You'd think the secret would have slipped out somehow. Whether some man was jealous of him, whether he'd spoken to some man's wife or something, I don't know. We'll never know now.

The local people, they all ended up in the graveyard, all in Minard, every one of them. My mother's mother, my brothers and sisters, my father's and mother's in Minard. All our families buried in Minard.

Aye, oh, the're a big stone, and the stone's for my brother and father. It says JESUS WAS A FISHER OF MEN on the stone.

Now I discovered a great secret one time. I had a Klondike on my hands, like Fort Knox! You're no going to believe this. There's an old man called Dan MacDonald, and he had a wee small shop in the village where I lived, shop is still there today but it's not under his name anymore. He had a little wee Ford van, and he used to wander with his wee van selling groceries. He collected jam jars and an old lorry used to come from Glasgow with boxes, like the lemonade lorries today, collecting the jam jars.

Ye got four wee half pound jars, a penny; a pound jar, a ha'penny; and a big two pound jar was a penny. Now you had Keiller from Dundee produced clay jars, they're antiques, clay jars, made of white clay. This was the love of his heart. He loved collecting jars. He paid us for the jars over the counter. He'd take the jars and he'd take them round behind and put them in a wee shed, and locked that shed with padlock and chain, and bolt! He kept many things in the shed forbyes, a tank of paraffin and everything, but he had a special place for his jam jars.

The shed was close up against a wall that led up the brae to the post office. You could walk in between the wall and the back of the shed and I was bursting for a pee one day. I walked in between the shed where nobody would see me to have a pee, and I perched a plank on the shed, and the plank moved. I pulled it aside and I looked in, and there was a Klondike. They were piled upon the dozen, jam jars! Within arms' reach. And that sleeper was never mended till I left home. It was just slices of trees split and turned back to back, made the little shed, and I pulled one aside, and when he slid back into place you'd think he was nailed up. I don't know how it came slack, but it just left enough space to get your arm in to get a jar. Oh, this was a secret I was going to tell nobody. I says, 'Tonight I'm coming down with a bag, and you'll keep till tomorrow.'

So, that night, late at night when it got dark, I sneak down canny to the back of the shed, pull the bar. Shop was closed. He was in the house with his old wife, prob'ly sitting in to a good evening meal. Young Traveller boy, I didn't feel I was doing anything wrong. And I reached in, two-three-four-five-six-seven-eight... two dozen, big ones, Keiller clay jars! Into the bag. Carried them gently. Didn't take them home to the camp. Hid them behind a tree. Next morning, took them to the river and I washed them all clean.

Took them down, I said, 'Dan, I've got some jars.'

'Oh, how many have you got?'

'Two dozen.' 24 jars was then two shillings, two silver shillings. Having two shillings then was like having two thousand pound in Furnace. I mean, I was only nine year old. Back in the '30s, late '30s, just the year before the war, I had a Klondike. Nobody knew. He put them in, I took them back out. He didn't know. He put them in, I took them back out.

I made a lot of money, not a big amount of money, I didn't want him to miss them, but one day, sad to say, all good things must come to an end.

In come the lorry from Glasgow and crate by crate, crate by crate, all my jars was gone. And the lemonade bottles. These lemonade bottles were worth a penny. They had a naked man on them, completely naked. They were antiques. If you had one today you would get a fortune for it.

Tuppence for a naked man. Lawson's lemonade. It was great to have a naked man, a naked man was worth five fags, tuppence.

I went down and I pulled the plank. Shed was empty. Not a thing was left, they were gone. My Klondike was gone.

I think myself, if we hadna been clever and intelligent enough to survive, we'd never have made it. Never in the world would hae made it. We never hurt anybody, we never did anybody any harm. We werena vandals of any kind, we never bullied the local children in the village, we kept ourselves to ourselves. Most of the best parts of our life we spent in the wood with our parents or on the hills hunting rabbits or hunting hares or going fishing or going collecting shellfish. We were too interested in survival. We didn't want to go to the village and hang around doing nothing. We went for an odd time to play with the kids.

One thing my father wouldn't have, he wouldn't let us touch mushrooms. But all the herbs and plants and the wee things, all the things about trees and bushes we knew and names of the wild flowers. It was quite simple, that was the easiest bit.

Travellers had many, many good cures. I remember my granny had many rings she'd collected as an old fortune-teller. She had rheumatics in her hands, rheumatism. Some days her fingers were curled up so she could barely hold her wee teacup. She would get us to go out and pick nettles for her and we'd pull the nettles for granny. She'd fill her wee skillet full of nettles. She'd put a wee drop salt in them and she would bring them aboil. Then she would take a big silk handkerchief and she would pleat it across and she'd strain the green nettle juice, like pea juice, strain it into another wee skillet and she would drink that. Within two days she could take off all the rings. That's the only way she could take the rings off her fingers, after she had – we used to call it 'Granny's Poison'. Nettle juice, the green brew off the nettles and a wee bit salt. Then she could run to catch old Linkley's bus. Granny could run like a weasel in her 80s, I'm telling you, and her feet were only tiny. Oh, she loved her nettles, granny's nettle brew, 'Granny's Poison'. That was only one thing. She used to heat a stone, get a big flat stone at night-time before she went to her bed, heat it and wrap it in a bit of cloth and she'd sleep with that hard stone in her bosom all night long, not too hot. It kept her warm all night long.

Magical stuff! You learned these things as a kid. Survival. You can make soup with earth nuts, pig nuts we called them. And you can make hazelnut soup. We used to collect the wild hazelnuts to mother, sit and pop them on a stone and break them and give her a bowl of broken hazelnuts to make soup.

But to live off the land without rabbits and hares or without fish you couldn't do it. You couldn't keep yourself alive on two, three herbs, even if you did eat mushrooms. We used to catch the birds no problem at all, pheasants when father worked on a farm. He used to put his hand in below the horse before he left the stable at night, pull the horse's tail. Horse hairs. He'd thread a horse hair through a raisin, tie a knot on it and throw it down and scatter a few other raisins on the ground. Pheasant gobbled up the raisin, and the one with the hair on it, with the hair sticking out the side of his beak he just started to run in circles trying to get rid of this. You could walk up and pet him and catch him.

Set snares. I could set snares like nobody on this earth. Catching rabbits, twisting a stick in the burrow. Art of survival.

Actually being a Travelling person, when it came to the art of survival, I think if there were another war, it would be only Travellers that could survive. Say for instance nuclear war, Travellers know how to build a shelter for themselves.

You see, it was the same with kindling fires. When I build a fire the smoke goes straight up. This is the art of kindling a fire.

* * *

Duncan didn't exaggerate his fire building skills. When he took me, on a day of drizzly scotch mist, to see that tree under which he was born on the shores of Loch Fyne, he conjured a fire on the beach, knocked some limpets from the rocks, cooked them in their shells and presented them for me to eat. Until then, I didn't know you could eat limpets and they did have a rubbery consistency that I would not readily add to my cuisine but it was '*survival*, David.'

Helen East, a storyteller to whom Duncan was mentor, second father and adored friend recalls another of the fire wizard's miraculous combustions.

* * *

'I think my best memories of all are of camping with Duncan, along the seashore, in the woods, up in the hills, a whole new world opening up for me. What you can eat: limpets boiled in their own water, soup flavoured with wild sorrel. What wood to burn and why (and why the wood I collected was always wrong). What this bird says, how that animal lives. Stories and knowledge of the natural world blending seamlessly together – through magic.

The open fire is an essential part – but occasionally, in this modern world of fire regulations and police presence it causes some anxiety.

In Norway, in June, it's forbidden to light a fire in the woods. We were stopped just outside Bergen and I was nervous about being caught with a fire but Duncan refused to stop without one. Our little primus stove was an insult to him and he refused to drink tea with water boiled that way.

Finally, in desperation, I pointed to a river running through the woods, deep on either side, but in the middle shallower with a few stones almost showing in the water.

"If you can build a fire in the middle of the river," I said, "then we can have one. Otherwise, not!"

Duncan is nothing if not obstinate. He built that fire, hot enough to last us all night, and I had to stand in the running water to cook the evening meal.

Never ask Duncan an impossible task – by hook or by crook he will do it.'

* * *

Now, this shows you what the people in the village were like. I was about 11 at this time, and I felt great because I was 11 years old, you know, qualified to sit in at night and listen to the bawdy tales and sing bawdy songs in the tent and things like that while the wee kids was off to sleep.

Then, 1938, diphtheria broke out in the village and the whole school was closed. Now there were nine of us in school, two at home that wasna school age, 11 kids in the forest in the wood. Of course, we had to go to the village. Two of my mates I used to play with took the diphtheria and was took away to Glasgow.

Their mother forbade her boys to play with the tinker boys: would learn them bad habits, would teach them bad language, they'd maybe get lice off us; we were full of lice! She wouldnae even say hello to you in the street if she met you, wouldnae even look at you. If you went in the shop and she was in she'd move away. That's the kind of person she was.

Meanwhile, Betsy Williamson's boys and girls were having a ball. We'd run through the village, had fun swapping sweets bare feet, little urchins. Fair, blonde, everyone was blonde.

I was walking down the street by her cottage one morning, and she stopped. She said, 'Hello!' to me for the first time in her life. She says, 'You're Duncan?'

I says, 'Yes, I'm Duncan.'

She says, 'Are ye hungry?'

I says, 'I'm always hungry!'

So she says, 'Come on with me!'

And that was the first time in my life I was ever inside a house, first time in my life I was inside a house! She took me into her boys' bedroom and on a table there was a bowl with some apples. And she gave me the apples, three of them. She says, 'Take the three with you and give one to your brother and sister.'

I didn't know that diphtheria was contagious. I had no idea. I think she tried to give me diphtheria. She was so jealous to see all these blonde kids running through the village like wild urchins. Both her boys died with diphtheria. She tried to commit suicide after that and her husband moved away to get her out of the district, went away up north.

That school was closed for six weeks and not one of Betsy Williamson's children took diphtheria of any kind. We guddled the burn for trout, we hunted the shores for shellfish, and while the school was closed we were still getting our attendance.

War

BRITAIN DECLARED WAR on Germany on my fourth birthday, 3 September 1939. Duncan was 11. Both of us had lived in Fraserburgh, so after we had told stories in the Central School where I had been a pupil, we explored and reminisced, walked along the glorious beach, surveyed the hugely changed harbour. No longer was it thronged with little fishing boats in shining prime colours bearing mysterious women's names and smelling of rope and fish. The herring girls were gone.

I showed Duncan the house we'd lived in. Fraserburgh for my younger brother and me was a wonderful place to grow up during the war. Because of the importance of the fishing fleet the crews had extra rations and so we had plenty of meat and, of course, endless supplies of sea-fresh fish. We were never short of food. At the top of our road was an anti-aircraft gunsite that we kids visited and the soldiers gave us chocolate!

My big brother was a flight engineer in the RAF, stationed somewhere in England; my sister was working in the office of the munition factory, target of frequent night bombing attacks. My father, too old for call-up, was in the ARP (Air Raid Precautions), and one time he told us of a wall blown off a house and marvelously a bed was hanging by its two bottom legs. An old woman was held aloft perched on the headboard. She refused to be rescued without the mattress. Sewn into the mattress were her savings.

My parents kept an open house for the young British and

Commonwealth aircrew stationed for training at nearby Cairnbulg airbase, so it was always abuzz with what seemed to us kids giant laughing men, who were actually almost all in, or barely out of, their teens.

On 20 July 1943 our family was devastated by the death of my brother in a Stirling bomber that crashed on his 20th birthday. The grief and shock aborted the child my mother was carrying. He would have been our younger brother. In a way my mother never recovered and every year on 20 July until she died aged 94, I could feel the undertow of grief when I visited her.

'The war changed everything,' Duncan said.

* * *

Now life in the tent in the forest had its good times and its bad times, but actually it took the war to change our life in that forest. In 1939, when war was declared, my three brothers were called up for service and three sisters left for the Land Army. My mother, at the age of 47, gave birth to her last child, Mary. I was still in school.

Then the evacuees came from Clydebank and from Glasgow when the Germans started to bomb the big cities. The local council and the education authority gave people money to foster these children. There were about 15 of them in Furnace School alone. Our school had swollen to over 70 children. These little boys and girls came from the back streets in Glasgow, from the Gorbals, from Possilpark. They were a little like Traveller folk, ken what I mean, the way they were brought up in the walled closes and the slums in Glasgow. They seemed to mingle with us a lot better than the local villagers.

They had to be put up in foster homes with the local minister, the doctor, the bell ringer, beadle of the church. Each people took two children because the State was paying seven pound each for them per week. That was a lot of money in the '40s. Argyll was a very religious place at that time. They still observed the Sunday and they were holy. There were Catholics and Protestants and they had Mass and they had church, Sunday school for kids, though we never went to it.

We seemed to get on really well with the little evacuee children. When grandfather used to come and stay with us – my father's father – a fluent

Gaelic speaker, as I told you, we used to say, 'Grandfather, teach us some Gaelic.' A lot of the people in the village spoke Gaelic, local old men and the old fishermen and the old quarry workers. We could understand some of it but we wanted to learn the dirty words, you know, because you learn the dirty words easier when you're learning Gaelic!

Some of the children in school had Gaelic, their parents and grandparents were Gaelic speakers. When the evacuees heard us discussing this language between ourselves, 'What were youse talking?' they would say, 'What are you saying, mister?'

We would say, 'We're talking Gaelic.'

'Oh, we'd like to learn some Gaelic,' in a nice Glasgow accent, you know?

Of course, we said, 'We'll teach you some Gaelic.'

They got a few pennies from the foster parents they were staying with and they would always buy these big penny caramels, great big chocolate caramels. We'd say, 'Give us one of your sweeties and we'll teach you some Gaelic.' We'd sit on the dyke around the school and we'd make them repeat over and over again till they got it fluently and they would say it back to us. My sister Rachel, my sister Jeannie, my brother George, brother Jimmie, brother Willie – we knew what was going to happen: they were going to go back to where they lived and say, 'We learned some Gaelic today!'

'Och, they're not teaching Gaelic in schools, now are they?'

'No, no, we never learned Gaelic in school, we learned from some of the children.'

'Well, let's see what you were learning.'

And they would repeat what we had told them.

'You've been playing with the Williamsons again, weren't you? These wicked children!'

I was a good shinty player – me and my three brothers used to play in a little clearing in the wood among wirsels. We made wir own shinties, because a good shinty then would cost about one pound fifty, like a million pound at that time. We could cut wir own natural bends in our spare time: break an old lemonade bottle, get a piece of sharp glass and shave it and polish it and then scrape it, and just make it a right natural bend, a camlach. We used to dribble in the woods in among the trees with the ball. The three of us, we three brothers played wir little game.

Anyway, in 1940, I was asked to play for Loch Fyneside. And oh, I was delighted! Sometimes, Newtonmore would come to Furnace, sometimes Kingussie, sometimes Glendaruel across the loch. We'd be off at playing games away in Carnoch, playing games in Kingussie, Newtonmore, Kyles, Inverness. Sometimes we played at home. And the whole village turned up! There were not a soul in a house while the shinty team was playing in Furnace in the 1940s.

Shinty was then like what football is today. Everybody was shinty crazy. If you were going to shinty you were respected. Brothers going off to war, sisters going to the Land Army, me beginning to play for Loch Fyneside, things changed.

People would stop to talk to you on the road and ask you how you were getting on, and, when do you play next. Would you come and dig my garden? Because of old Churchill *Dig for Victory*, everybody grew their own vegetables. They'd say when you went to dig their garden, 'If you find any old vegetables, take them home with you.' Good old cabbages that sat through the winter and big carrots down in the ground that the old folk had missed; we took all this home to my mother. Maybe got paid two shillings, half a crown.

So it took the war, it took the war. The young Travelling people who went to the army, they were used to living in tents all their life, sleeping on the cold ground, sleeping in some stall: now they got clean clothes, they got hot baths, they got a lovely place to stay. The Travelling people didn't take the discipline so hard because they were disciplined with their parents when they were wee: children got away with nothing. They had to do what they were told. So going into the army was a complete change but it wasn't really hard for them.

This is from talking with my own brother, Willie. They were out in Burma somewhere, their captain was leading them through a kind of forest or jungle, or what it was there, a place I've never been. One of the officers took his rifle and shot a little monkey. He told the group he thought it was a Japanese up the tree. My brother walked up and hit the captain on the face with the butt of his rifle and broke his jaw in three places. He said, 'If you cannae shoot anything better than a little monkey – that's only a little creature,' he said, 'not a Japanese or an enemy.' Willie got a court martial and was whipped back and he done 18 month in Colchester. After he came out of there, it said on his

Discharge, '*Failing to fulfill Army physical requirements*'. I remember the words well. Brother Willie, William, died of cancer about five years ago.

In these war days the coal came in by boats. Father and another few men would get a chance to empty this coal boat, maybe 60 ton of coal. I used to go up and bring him a bottle, a wee screw-top of beer my mother would send down for his lunch. He was as black as that tape recorder, stripped to the waist.

He would come out of that coal boat completely covered in coal, nothing but his two eyes shining. Then, he would have to go to the burn and wash himself when he got home. He was accepted too because he was an old soldier in the First World War – he had old friends who were soldiers in the First World War, his three sons were off in the army, his three daughters in the Land Army, I was playing shinty for Loch Fyneside.

He still stayed in the wood. My father never moved during the war. He couldn't afford to because you see it was the Blackout. There was no way you kindle a fire in the Blackout. My mother couldnae cook, couldna make any food for the children. They had the air raid wardens going about the village warning 'Out with the lights!' We had to keep our fire and tents secure. We could have a fire and the cruisie inside the tent burning, and you could walk in the black dark and not even see a beak of a light; that tent had to be so covered that there weren't even a little hole in the canvas that a wee bit light would shine out. Otherwise they would come up and chap on the tent with their sticks: 'Get that light out!'

Now, what father used to do the summers before the war, take us off down through the west coast of Argyll and away to Campbeltown, away round by Kilberry and up into Oban, where he used to get all these little jobs – that had to stop. That had to stop for five years. We had to go to school just like the local children in the village. We only got holidays at Christmas. No more long holidays for us anymore. Daddy had to find a job. He got a job in the stone quarry, him being a big, strong, powerful man.

There was a big stone-crusher in the quarry and every man had a ten ton wagon, like a big steel skip, that you would see today. You started at seven in the morning, winter and summer. You had to have that ten ton wagon loaded by ten o'clock. Three hours to load ten tons on your own. A little steam engine – a puggie engine, they called it – came into the quarry, and went right round, and if that wagon wasn't full, it left. And you lost your eight shillings. Eight shillings a day, two pounds a week, paid every fortnight.

You can imagine... six of us in school, mother with a little baby, two pounds a week. But with that two pound things began to improve a hundredfold. The only thing we didn't have like the rest of the people in the village was a house. See, if we had hae lived in an old house in the village, I'd never have been the person I am today. I would have prob'ly grew up like the local lads in the village.

One particular thing I'll remember will stick in my mind till the end of my life was this little evacuee girl. And I loved her. I was 11 years old, and I loved her dearly. She was so down to earth. But she was so ugly. She had everything that a little girl should not have. The kids didn't hate her or bully her, there were no bullies in the school, but they teased her. They made fun of her and called her names. And this upset me very much.

Well, she had rickets in her legs, God forgive the mark. Rickets was very common things in these days, and she wore bifocal glasses, she was so short sighted. She had a pug nose, freckles, short cut hair. To be quite honest, looking back at her, she was sheer ugly! The local kids called her Pansy Potter, off the old comic. But I loved her. I taught her how to guddle trout in the river. We used to collect shellfish together on the beach, had the little can for boiling my whelks. She used to sit, and I used to sharpen a little stick like a needle and show her how to pick whelks with a crook. We roasted limpets on the fire. She was an adorable little companion, I loved her like nothing on this earth. I wouldn't hurt a hair on her head. But this caused a terrible animosity.

You see, there were other little girls – I mean I was a beautiful little boy. I was 11. Barefeet. Just a little urchin, you know. Blonde, blue eyed. And these other little girls maybe fancied me in the school because there were a lot of them there forbyes. This caused a wee bit trouble.

One day this boy, he was a year older than me – Patrick Carr was his name, his father was Irish. I got him in against the bridge, I beat the life out of him, threw him over into the river, because he was calling Nancy some names and teasing her. They used to call me Scrapper for a nickname in school. Everybody had a nickname in school. Scrapper was mine because I was very hardy. I could fight like big guns, you know! Everybody my own age would leave me alone, some of the older ones would neither think to attack me. Somebody rescued Patrick Carr from the river. They phoned the police.

I remember the young policeman; he would only be in his 20s, red hair, he came down on his bicycle, up to my mother's and father's tent, pitched his bicycle against a tree, and he ordered me out. 'You, I want to talk to you,' he says. 'Look, young man, if you want any more fighting, you go to the army when you grow up and you'll get plenty more fighting. Now, I never want to see you laying a hand on anyone else again as long as you live!'

Policeman never bothered us in any way in my day.

Father said, 'You know, boys will be boys.'

'Aye, boys will be boys, but,' he said, 'it was intentional. He threw the little fellow over the bridge. He could have killed him.'

From that day on I never touched another soul in the village, never touched another soul.

I've smoked a long, long time. I'll tell you about that. Time to feed the dragon again.

* * *

So we adjourned to the kitchen. Duncan rolled a cigarette and slaked his tannin withdrawal symptoms with strong black sweet tea.

'Did you ever smoke?' he asked.

I told him aged eight I had pinched a packet of ten Players from my mother, sneaked off to a nearby field, smoked several and was dizzily retchingly and wretchedly sick: cured. Apart from later, out of bravado in the local gang, smoking cinnamon sticks, sweet and also nauseating. After that, I didn't smoke again until fashion and a love affair seduced me into it when I was a student at university in Edinburgh.

'I wish I'd never started smoking,' Duncan said. None of Duncan's children smoked or drank.

His daughter Edith told me, 'When my brother John was nine he smoked some fag ends. Father caught him and says, "Ye want to smoke?" And gave him a whole cigarette. "Smoke that!" John was so sick he never smoked since.'

Duncan was a great teacher. 'His way of teaching was by demonstration,' said his son Jimmy.

'When I was about five or six maybe,' Edith said, 'Daddy taught me there was a kelpie in the river. We were staying beside the river and Daddy wanted us to keep out of the water. "You go in there and the water kelpie will take you away." He put a frog in the water and told me the water kelpie was a frog. "It will change into a horse and gobble you up." To me the frog was this horrible looking thing that was going to eat me. So we didn't go near the water. We didn't realise that we were being told just to teach us of the danger. It was a deterrent.'

* * *

I'll tell you how it was with me. My mother smoked a pipe. She smoked a pipe all her life. My granny smoked a pipe, my father smoked. In the front of the store was a little cigarette machine and you put two pennies in and it went click, and you pulled the little drawer and you got five Woodbine in a single packet for tuppence. Five Woodbine. We used to split, I remember four of the boys and myself. We couldn't put ha'pennies in the machine so we'd go into the local post office and get the woman to give us two pennies for wir four ha'pennies, and we'd pop the two pennies into the little machine and pull out the little drawer. Five Woodbine would fall down, but we'd keep the door open because about an inch above that there was the arse of another packet of Woodbine ready to drop for the next two pennies. So my idea was, we got a long pin, a big safety pin, and we straightened it and made a little hook we could reach up and stick it into the end of the arse of the little packet and pull it out and it would fall doon. Another one would take its place. We could rob that machine for two pence. Five to you, five to you, five to you and then we'd close it again. Wouldn't take them all. If there were five of us we got five fags each. Then we went under the bridge and we smoked cigarettes. That was my first smoke, that was, cigarettes.

I was now 13 years old and the local lads in the village; we'd become friends. I grew up with them; I went to school with them. I fished with them, I played shinty with them. I was accepted. They were 13 years old. They'd no need to listen to their parents anymore. 'Don't play with the tinkers; they've got lice and beasts.' They didn't give a damn what their parents thought about us. I was the boss, I was the leader. We could smoke together, we could fight together, wrestle, go fishing together, see who could climb and jump the highest from a tree. I could do anything with them. They'd do as they were told. We could go and hunt snakes on the hill. They loved hunting snakes. I used to take them.

In the village there were dogs we hated. I hated the dogs. An old man called Neil ran the butcher shop and round the back he used to have a bin. What he couldna use, I mean there were no freezers in these days, he used to put in the bin with a lid: bits of fat, wee bits of bone, wee bits of mutton, maybe sheep's tail, things ye couldna eat. We used to sneak round behind the back of the shop, open the lid, take out a piece of fat, maybe a wee bit of meat on it, maybe a sheep's tail, wee sheep's tail. 'Come on boys, we'll go snake huntin'.'

There were a few dogs in the village. They would bite you, and they would race at you. The owner didn't keep them under control. We'd go snake hunting in the hills. We'd come up through the heather, find the place where the adders were, big adders lying curled in the sun, baking in the sun. Snakes like to bask in the sun. And we'd aggravate them! We had this piece of meat on the stick and we'd aggravate them. When we got them real angry, we'd hold their tails, and they'd *pfut, pfut pfut*! He would sting it and you could see the poison, like a rainbow going round the meat. We'd keep that on the stick. We'd plunk it to the dog we didn't like. Next day he was lying, legs swelled up, dead. Nobody knows about that but yourself till this day. How dogs was dying in the village. Vets would come and take them away. They couldna discover what was killing them. They were dying with snake poison in the stomach with the wee bits of fat we gave them. This was our secret.

All this time the war was going on and everybody had an Identity Card. I always left mine in case it would get lost or get wet, left it with my parents.

I was walking home to see my parents and a police car pulled up, and the policeman said, 'Your name!'

'Duncan Williamson.'

'Do you have an Identity Card?'

I said, 'It's at my Mother's. It's at my home, my Mother's.'

'Get in the car.' He put me in the back. They drove me to Inveraray and put me in jail in the police station.

I says, 'Look, I'm only 15 years old.'

'We'll soon find out,' he said. 'You should be in the army.'

I said, 'I cannae go in the army. They'll no take me 15 years old in the army.'

Brought me a wee mug of tea, and I laid in that cell all night and the pigeons went coo-coo coo-coo. They phoned Donnie, my friend, who went into the Metropolitan police and he became a policeman in Argyll. And Donnie tried to tell them.

'I know him. He was born the day my uncle died,' Donny says. 'Look, he's no age for the army. I've known him since he was a wee boy.' He told the sergeant straight. He said, 'I'll tell ye something; in school the Williamson children were the most intelligent children there. There's only one thing we had that they didn't have, that was a bloody slate roof over our heads. They had canvas, we had slates, that was all the bloody difference.'

He tellt the policeman. Do you think he would listen? No, he wouldn't listen, and they kept me overnight and then phoned Adie MacCallum that was the brother of the stonemason that taught me how to build dykes. Adie was the Registrar at the office in Auchindrain at that time. Sergeant Weir was the policeman.

'We have a boy here,' he says, 'says he's 15.'

'What's his name?'

'Duncan. One of the Williamsons. Jock Williamson, Betsy's boy.'

'Ach,' he says, 'aye, wait a minute.' Looked in the book. 'Aye,' he said, 'born on 11 April 1928.' Then they let me go.

So you see life was, I would say, strange. It was nice when you were a wee boy in the tent with the fire burning and the lamp lighted, cruisie above your head. You felt safe and secure. But then when you left home and went out on your own, there's a new world out there. There's people to meet, people to talk to, there were things to learn.

I remember me and my mother walking into Inveraray one morning and just before you get to Inveraray the road comes right to the shore. There's a deep drop to the sea below and when the tide comes in, it's pretty deep. The tide goes out, it's just bare shingle. Just as we came into Inveraray, here was the police car. A lot of people standing looking over the dyke. I wondered what it was.

My mother said, 'Stall, look at the wee gadgie, deek, deek,' she spoke in Cant to me, Travellers' language, meaning 'Look!' And there he was lying. The tide had went out and left a man, his two feet in the water, wee soldier. He had fallen over during the night. A British soldier. They were there to pick him up, the ambulance and the police from Inveraray and a few people. Maybe he had fallen over when the tide was in and drowned and the tide went, left him. Somebody saw him and reported him.

We had over 50,000 soldiers in Inveraray at the time of the war. We had trainee soldiers from all around the world, commandos training in the hills. Over a thousand merchant seamen. From Lochgilphead to Inveraray was chock-a-block with boats, all lying in there because it was in the middle of the hills away from the bombing. This is where they brought them in for repairs and things.

Sometimes, I would go up to Donald MacIntyre in Inveraray and I would work in Argyll Farm with Donald. Donald was the undertaker but he had the farm forbyes. He had the milk-run in Inveraray and he supplied the milk to the hospital ship with the big Red Cross that lay out in the loch. A speed boat would come in from the hospital ship and Donald would give him four or six big cans of milk. They would leave the empties and they'd take the full ones away. The next day they'd bring back empties.

Donald MacIntyre had over a hundred milk cows. Now these cows had to be cleaned, they had to be mucked, they had to be fed. They had to be milked! Didn't have a milking machine. I would help wash the cans. He had a wee van, a wee Austin van for taking the milk to the pier for the boat coming in. You could always get a job from Donald.

He paid you every week, end of the week, two pound ten shillings a week. It was good money. And you got all your meat in the house, because Chrissy the housekeeper (who later went to Achnagoul), she was the woman who did all the cooking. You got plenty milk to drink at the milk house when you were cleaning up.

And we had the Polish camp, Castle Camp. Now and again Donald and me would go and get the ashes when they cleaned out the fires. We used these ashes to put on the farm roads, mucky old roads that went into the fields. He had an old horse and lorry and we'd load it with ashes. Sometimes we'd go to the kitchen. But the best people to us was the Poles.

That was the first time in my lifetime I ever saw – I thought it was rosydendron leaves these big leaves – the Poles used to put them in their soup. They invited me and Donald in for a plate of soup at dinnertime. We came in and they gave us a big bowl of soup for dinner. I looked and there was a big green leaf and I took it out. Didn't I think it was a blinking rosydendron leaf, same shape.

I said, 'Donald, I'm putting out the rosydendron.'

'Nah, Duncan,' he said, 'that's no rosydendron leaves, that's a herb. It's quite good.'

So they gave us a bowl of soup and we got a cup of tea with them. And we loaded the ashes: we'd go and put them on the farm roads.

The Poles wasnae prisoners. When Germany overrun Poland in 1943 all the young able-bodied soldiers were whipped over to Britain. They were going to fight with Britain: they were going to be British soldiers but they were Polish.

When the war finished a lot of them went back, but a lot of the Polish lads, I ken five in Fife, never went back. One became a postman, all his life the postman. One kept a wee farm up near Peat Inn where we used to stay. Another one married the daughter of a nursery gardener, and when the old folk died they got the nursery to theirself. Another one married old Dick Brunton's daughter, an electrician. He was clever. He ended up with a big electric shop in Cupar. Poles were great people. They werenae prisoners. They were great folk.

But we had about three or four thousand Italian prisoners in Inveraray, in the prison camp in Inveraray. They had all these patches, crosses on their body, green coded patches on. They were not allowed out unless they went for an out march. When they took them out, maybe say 50 for a march, the Italian prisoners, they took them through Inveraray. They weren't allowed to go into the shops. They weren't allowed to do nothing. You had five armed soldiers in front, five armed soldiers in back and five armed soldiers on each side. They were Mussolini's men. They were captured. Prisoners.

We had some German prisoners forbyes. They had patches on their back so's you would ken the German prisoner if he ran away, because they only gave him one set of clothes. A few escaped and tried to make their way back, but they were always captured and brought back again.

Things was good for us at that time, for these five war years. No summer travelling but we had enough. Daddy had a job and we were accepted.

* * *

Alastair McKeller and Alex Campbell were pupils at Furnace School at the same time as Duncan in the 1930s. Neither of them could recollect the school closing for a diphtheria outbreak nor that Duncan played shinty for Lochfyneside. They acknowledged that he would play shinty at school with the other pupils.

My researches with Brian Wilkinson, a local shinty official, suggest that Lochfyneside didn't exist as a shinty team until after the war. I could not find records to confirm whether or not there was a diphtheria outbreak in Argyll at that time.

However, the details Duncan provides in describing these events either endorses his stunning memory or his genius as a storyteller. Readers are invited to make their own conclusions.

Aunt Rachel

WITH ALL THE KNOWLEDGE and understanding I had, I took a notion it was time to leave home. Not for good, but to go out into the world because I had qualifications beyond my powers. I could do anything to keep myself alive, all the things my father had taught me down through the years and I thought it was time for me to move out of home and leave whatever food was behind so's that the little ones could have more. Another one less to feed.

I was qualified, I was 13, I was five foot nine, I was 12 stone, I was able to fight, I could hold my candle with any man. I was ready to gain a new experience. I had all the stories I ever needed from the Traveller society. I had songs I could sing, stories to tell and out there would be a new culture. I wanted to meet other people, I wanted to meet other Travellers like myself.

So one morning, I had saved up a couple of shillings from my jar pinching, closed the door and said goodbye to my little Klondike. I told my mother, 'Think I'll go and visit my Aunt Rachel in Tarbert.'

'Ah well,' she said, 'I'm sure Aunt Rachel'll be glad to see you. But come back when you get fed up.'

I said, 'I'll come back when I get fed up, Mother.'

It was two shillings on the bus from Furnace to Tarbert. I took the bus to Tarbert, come off in Tarbert and walked up to Aunt Rachel's.

Now let me explain, Aunt Rachel also lived in a tent, a place where her father and mother had lived. By that time, granny and grandfather were gone, dead and buried in Tarbert.

Aunt Rachel didn't stay in a forest, Aunt Rachel stayed in the most beautiful place of all, in a place covered in rhododendron. There was a drive and she had permission from the local laird, because her father before her and her mother before her had stayed there all their time. They had never moved except for a wee while in the summer. Aunt Rachel stayed in a big tent, same kind of tent but maybe not as big as the one my father owned, because she only lived by herself.

Not far from her, about a hundred yards away, was her sister Nellie. This was my Aunt Nellie, the other older sister. She lived alone. They barely ever came in contact with each other unless they walked together to the village, Tarbert, which was half a mile away.

My father's sister Rachel had never married, but one thing about Rachel was she had attended school. Rachel could read and write, very clever in school she was. She was a big tall woman. Five feet ten, not stout, beautiful pale features, blue eyes, long golden hair like a Viking lady. I remember her sitting there in the tent long ago combing her hair across her knee, long yellow hair going down the side of her, could reach to the floor where she was sitting on her chair. Then, she would plait it in these two big plaits and she would take them and tie them up. She would put them in a big bun on top of her head; she would stick a comb in the top, like a bone comb. My father's youngest sister was a beautiful woman. She never had a boyfriend, and she stayed with her parents until they died.

Now I walked out to Aunt Rachel's. She was pleased to see me.

'Duncan!'

I was one of her favourites.

She had tea and she said, 'I'm going to Tarbert.'

I said, 'I'm walking with you to Tarbert, Aunt Rachel.' Walked with her to Tarbert, talked about many things, asked about my father, asked me about the boys and any word from your brothers in the war? Not very much about them. Nothing from my sisters. I stayed with Aunt Rachel for a week.

I said, 'Aunt Rachel, any jobs around?'

She says, 'What kind o' job are you looking for?'

I said, 'Any kind of job, I cannae depend on you, to live off you. I need to get something to do for myself. I've got qualifications.'

'I know, I know,' she said, 'your father taught you well,' she says to me. 'Have you ever done any tiger hunting?'

'Tiger hunting, Aunt Rachel?' I says. 'What's tiger hunting? I thought tiger hunting was things that people do away in Africa, and away in foreign countries.'

'No,' she said, 'it's just a nickname.'

I said, 'What is it then?'

She says, 'Mat mending. You know, the doormats.' Aunt Rachel was to teach me a new trade that stood me in stead for years, and I done it for years after I got married to my first wife. You know these doormats made from Sparta rope that people wipe their feet on, and sometimes the outside gets worn? Aunt Rachel was an artist. She could make them. She went to the farmer and she got all that big Sparta rope – you know they're made with Sparta grass. They were very popular in these days, and she was an expert!

Duncan weaving baskets.

She said, 'Laddie, all you have to do is take a bundle of sparky rope under your arm and a big bag needle and some string, and go from door to door and ask if people's needing any mats mended. Tell ye what I'll do with ye, come with me tomorrow!'

She was an expert. She was the real tiger hunter. I'd never seen this before. Father never mentioned it. This is what she made a living with. She also was a good basket-maker from the word go!

She said, 'I do jobbing.'

I said, 'Jobbing?'

She says to me, 'You never done any jobbing?'

I said, 'No, Aunt Rachel, I never done any jobbing. What is jobbing?'

She says, 'Baskets.'

I said, 'Ah, I can make a basket.'

'Oh,' but she said, 'I dinnae make baskets. I wander the town, I mend baskets. I go round the doors and ask the folk if they got any baskets to mend, broken lips and broken bits, piece of basket needing a new handle. I carry a bunch of willows under my arm and I mend them. I sit on the step and I mend them.'

I said, 'Aunt Rachel, I never knew that could be done.'

She says, 'You come with me tomorrow.'

Me and her walked to Whitehouse, little town not far from Tarbert. She said, 'I havnae been in Whitehouse for a while.' We must have mended eight mats that day. Two shillings at that time. Sixteen bob. She gied me eight bob for me: she kept eight for herself, halved it with me. I was delighted. This was something brand new to me. Mat mending!

She learned me how to plait a border, put a border around the mat. She learned me how to sew the border in, and how to mend an old mat that was really worn, the people was about to fling out. She could make that look like brand new. For two shillings or half a crown. Saved the people buying a new one. That's where I learned to make my mats, and I became very good at it. She said, 'We'll go jobbing.'

She got a bundle of willows, white willows, she cut the willows. She peeled them, me and her sat and peeled them that night, and the next day we went to Tarbert. We went away up round the houses of the back street of Tarbert. She went door to door, and I carried the willows. She got up a basket, the handle was burst, took the handle off, and I knew how to stick a new stick in, put a new handle on it, handed it back to the woman. Money. We done that for a few days. I really enjoyed it.

I walked into Tarbert myself and I walked down to the pier. I walked out to a bunch of fishermen at the fishing, because one thing I didn't have much knowledge was for fishing. All the knowledge I had was of the shore, where I collected shellfish. I lived by the shore. I was born by the shore, but I never had any knowledge about how the fish came in and how the people sold. I used to delight to go down early to the market and see the auctioneer bidding on the boxes of fish. I wanted to learn what they were saying. I really loved to hear them bidding on the fish. Local people came and bade on the boxes of fish. I stayed with Aunt Rachel for a month.

During the night-time, this was the real pleasure. Aunt Rachel hadna far to go to the sea. She was only about, I would say, maybe three or four hundred yards from the seashore. It was all rocks, cliffs, along where she lived. Never any trees. Rhododendron. When these bushes were in full bloom it was a beautiful place. She would walk there.

She had one great love apart from anything else; that was the seals. She was completely tooken over with the seals. She loved the seals. She would walk on the beach, sit on the rocks and for some strange reason they didna seem to bother about her very much.

'Come, we'll go a walk to the shore Dunkie,' she says.

I says, 'Right, Auntie.'

She'd sit with the seals, and at night-time she would tell me all these beautiful stories. You can find some in *Tales of the Seal People*, in that book Linda and I produced. These are mostly my Aunt Rachel's stories of the seal people.

I said, 'Aunt Rachel, do you really believe that there's such a thing?'

'Aye,' she said, 'Dunkie, there is such a thing. I hope some day I'll be going to join them.'

'Ah,' I said, 'Aunt Rachel, how could you?'

'You never know,' she said, 'maybe I'll join them some day.'

I says, 'Auntie, you'll never join, you'll no become a seal person.'

She says, 'Ye never know.'

I could never forget Aunt Rachel's idea about the seal folk, and I thought to myself, was this really happening, because in the tent with my father, my granny, my grandfather and all the stories and things I'd heard, I never heard a silkie mentioned.

Aunt Rachel took out a purse and she says to me, 'This belongs to your granny, my mother's purse. And I'll show ye something.' She opened up old granny's purse and in granny's purse she brought out a piece of skin, a piece of real, genuine sealskin.

'I don't know where,' she says, 'my mother got it, but my mother used to keep it for telling the weather, forecasting the weather. My mother, old Bett MacColl, could tell us if it was going to be a good day, sunny day or a dry or a wet day or a cold day. And all she did was check her sealskin in the morning, and put it back.'

I said, 'Did you ever discover, Auntie, what she could read off the skin?'

'Well,' she said, 'I managed to get it out of her when she had a wee drink on her,' she says. 'When the seal hair lies soft and flat on the piece of skin it's going to be a good day or a good weather coming in. But when the hair stands up, we're in for bad weather. And this is what my mother used to check.'

'Aunt Rachel, how could the hair rise on the skin when the animal's dead?' You know, very clever I was.

'Well,' she says, 'I don't know. That's what I tried to find too, but she believed in it, and she was never wrong. I seen her and my father were going to walk to Kilberry, which is a long way away, 12 miles away. And she would check the skin and she would say, "I dinnae think we're going to gang the day because the weather's no too good looking", and check her skin and put it back in her purse.'

The funny thing was, three years later we were collecting something in the post office and we got a little postcard from Aunt Rachel – Aunt Rachel had never wrote to us in her lifetime – to her brother Jock. She called my father Jock, she says, 'I think you should go down and see me soon because I think I'm getting married.'

'What in the world,' my father said, 'is Aunt Rachel getting married for? She never had a man? How in the world unless she met some fisherman she's fell in love with.'

She says, 'Ye come down next week, you and any of the family, when I'm getting married and I would like you there.'

And it's true, as I'm sitting here, my father, my mother and me and brother George, sister Rachel, we all went down to Tarbert. We never went to Aunt Rachel's marriage, we went to Aunt Rachel's funeral, for Aunt Rachel had went down to the wharf along the rocks, among the seals and she drowned herself. The last time I saw her lying in her coffin, and the plaits down by the side of her coffin and her teeth as white as that book you're writing on. Beautiful woman. That was the last memory of my Aunt Rachel, apart from the memory of her stories. But her stories will last me forever, the stories of the love of Aunt Rachel's seal folk. She believed that some day that she would join them. For all we know, maybe she did. She drowned herself and they found her body floating in the sea. But where did the spirit go? There yet, still there in Tarbert, in Loch Fyne.

* * *

A seal story occasioned my first meeting with Duncan Williamson. It was one of Aunt Rachel's stories, 'Mary and the Seal'.

I read this story in Duncan's first book, *Fireside Tales of the Traveller Children* and at once fell in love with it. I was producing a schools programme for BBC Radio Scotland, 'Scottish Magazine', for an audience of 12-year-olds and this story was perfect. However, like my entire years of friendship with Duncan Williamson, the journey was not to be simple.

My programme slot was 20 minutes and I reckoned 'Mary and the Seal' would need to be cut. The publisher was Canongate. Stephanie Wolfe Murray phoned me to say, 'Duncan Williamson says you can't use his story.'

'Why not?'

'He says that it can't be changed or cut.'

'I think I'll go and see him.'

'A good idea,' she said, 'good luck!'

Another impulse apart from the story prompted me to make this visit. Before I'd ever read 'Mary and the Seal' or heard of Duncan, I'd been introduced by a friend to Alan Herriot in the Abbotsford, a great haunt in these days for actors, poets, broadcasters and all. Alan was the illustrator for *Fireside Tales* and that night in the pub he said to me with sudden conviction, 'David, there is a person you just have to meet: Duncan Williamson.'

These two promptings took me to Duncan's door at Lizziewell's farmhouse cottage near Auchtermuchty where Duncan's wife Linda plied us, Highland fashion, with tea, sandwiches, scones and joined us, while the Glenfiddich I brought contributed to that first of countless whisky fuelled evenings of story, song, and wild flytings. Duncan promised: 'I'll tell the story for you if you can record it in a school.'

Duncan sang, I sang. Linda sang, tellingly, one of Duncan's own songs: that song essentially described Linda's own journey from American music student, to the wife of a Scottish Traveller, Duncan.

> I'll give away my money and I'll give you my land
> I'll sell my mansions three
> And I will go on the road tonight
> And a tinker I will be.

'Well,' said Duncan, 'Mark Twain said it all when he said, "Don't let reading or writing interfere with your education."'

And that evening was the Genesis of my long, undulating, fiery and fond relationship with Duncan, like a strange marriage of a kind.

Dangerous Corners

DUNCAN AND I TRAVELLED thousands of miles together visiting schools, telling stories. Often these trips lasted a day or two, sometimes a week. Duncan's second wife Linda, a genius in marketing and organisation, planned our itinerary. The Scottish Arts Council subsidised these storytelling sessions, accommodation and travel. Linda had an expert ability to interpret forms and apply for funds.

These journeys were a full exposure to the weathers of Duncan's moods, from glittering sunshine to sultry storms. He was pontifical, dogmatic, contradictory. He would give away his stories saying they belong to everyone, the next moment jealously own them and condemn any tiny change in their telling. Reverently he averred that he told the story as he'd been told it, yet I never heard him tell a story in the same way. If he wasn't paid at once and in cash he was outraged and frequently ranted at the very Arts Council that was feeding him. He fell in with people as if he'd known them for ever and if he thought he was slighted he fell out with black finality. Arm around shoulder I was the greatest friend he'd ever had, he loved me more than a brother and when we fell out there was no name black enough for that David Campbell. Travel was not dull and there were always stories and songs to shorten the road as well as robust genial arguments, mischief, teasings and flytings. We were off to visit schools in Skye. I planned to visit Sorley Maclean and his wife Renee in Braes and in the van put on a cassette of Sorley reading 'Hallaig' and other poems. I loved Sorley's reading.

Duncan fell into a broody silence, suffocating me with

endless cigarettes and eventually said, 'I can't stand this rubbish. For God's sake turn it off, David.' To establish peace for our journey, I did.

After telling stories in a primary school we visited the Macleans, were welcomed with tea and sandwiches by Renee and we'd brought a dram to share. So Duncan and Sorley met, two different parts of my world but both of them men who could and would meet anyone with deep intent interest in the person who was before them. They were like old pals chatting before the fire, Sorley knowledgeable about Skye tinkers, and curious as ever about the genealogy of the Williamsons. Of course Duncan could tell him and Sorley could unravel connections.

Sorley at some stage said to Duncan, 'Did you know that David Campbell is a streaker?'

Fuelled by a good few malts I had this propensity and one new year in Skye, visiting Sorley and Renee at their house in Braes when I was going out with their daughter Ishbel, I walked out divested and ran naked and happy through the snow and then back into and around the house. I recall that Sorley and Renee and the company surveyed this with only curious equilibrium.

This incident Sorley related to Duncan, concluding in his marvelously octave-leaping voice, 'I wonder what makes David Campbell a streaker?'

This trait of mine was incomprehensible to Duncan. In the years of his marriage to his first wife he had never seen her naked. Thus intrigued he was inspired to write about my snowy Hogmanay jaunt.

Come lissen to my story and I'll tell you by and by
About an Edinburgh streaker on the Isle of Skye
The people will remember all their lasting days
When they saw the streaker running through the Braes.

The people gazed in wonder as he ran down the street
As naked as he was born from his head down to his feet
'Ha, Ha,' old Sorley cried, 'in all my living days
I have never seen a streaker a running through the Braes.

Old Angus Mckay was drunk that night as he staggered on his feet
When he saw that shameless streaker coming down the street
For he gazed in wonder and gave a drunken sigh
That's the biggest snow flake I ever saw on the Isle of Skye.

Then old Kate McLean she ran out from her wee bit but and ben
Saying, 'I'll never get a chance to see a thing like that again'
For she gazed in wonder the way that he would go
And she fell in love with that streaker in the snow.

Old Jean McNeil she gave a cry as he went running by
Said, 'I'd rather have him in my bed than all the gold in Skye'
But on and on the streaker went as fast as he could go
Even though his willie was frozen with the snow.

But it still remains a mystery only Sorley knows
The man who went a streaking in his birthday clothes
But people will remember as years and years go by
The day the Edinburgh streaker came to the Isle of Skye.

In our companionship we had huge fun but travelling with Duncan was fraught with dangerous corners; corners which brought our recording for the book to a sharp halt.

While the Scottish Storytelling Centre was evolving it had an office in my house and a secretary employed by the Netherbow theatre on the High Street. Duncan was booked to tell stories at a school in Dundee.

At that time he was staying at my house. I was lying peacefully asleep in the morning when there was a loud knocking at my bedroom door and an incandescently irate Duncan arrived at the foot of my bed. 'I'm not happy about this,' he began and embarked on a vociferous complaint about the inadequate payment he had received for his work.

'Duncan,' I said, 'stop this machine gun of words. We'll talk about it when I'm awake after a shower.' He left the room. By the time I had showered he had gone. Off to get the train home.

I followed him to Waverley Station and found him, a bull with head down, on the platform. I approached. 'Duncan, let's talk about this.'

'I'm going for my train,' and he set off across the platform.

'Well, that's the wrong train,' said I and pointed to one on the adjacent platform. 'That's yours. Duncan, look at me, look me in the eye and we'll try to sort this out.'

He raised his fist below my chin, 'Fuck off, or I'll hit you.'

I said nothing and left. After that we did not see or speak to one another for 18 months. Inevitably the reconciliation was as dramatic as the parting.

Duncan's wife Linda, both of their children Betsy and Tommy, were saying to me that Duncan was regretting this breach and eventually I decided to visit him in his Fife fastness. When I called at the cottage he was not at home and so I left a brief note, *David Campbell called.*

Duncan's reply in his usual scrawl came more as an explanation than an apology. 'Things was difficult for me at the time, and I was not very happy,' and so our journey and the process of the book recommenced once more and he came to stay.

I remember the day well. We sat together at the kitchen table. 'David, you've always wanted to know my story, 'The Flying Horse of Earthdom'. I'm going to give this as a present for you. Get your tape recorder!' We adjourned to my room where I set up the microphone and he began.

'David, this was a story brought back from the First World War. Where it came from we don't know but this is a present to you from me and it is to say we will never fight again. We will never agrue, we will never fall out. And you can tell this story long after I'm gone.'

I have told that story many times since then. It expresses to me that beautiful part of Duncan's character, his compassion and particularly his inclusion of, and affection for, the outsider and the spurned. For that reason, I include it here as an articulation of this endearing feature of my friend Duncan's character.

'The story begins a long time ago. Back into history, there once lived a great King, where his kingdom was the story never said, but he was loved by some, hated by some, worshipped by some, in fact.

And of course, he lived with his Queen in a great old stone palace, somewhere, we don't know where it was. Now, the love of his heart were his two little twin sons. He loved the boys dearly; he couldn't get enough time for them. Sometimes he'd give up hunting, he would give up battle; he loved these sons dearly. The Queen was loved and respected by everyone and her dearest friend apart from the King was the old hen-woman who lived not far from the palace in a little cottage and kept hens by the seaside. They had spent many happy times together and the longing of the Queen's life, she would tell her friend, was a little baby girl.

She knew how much the King loved their sons. She, of course, too, loved their sons but she wanted a little girl and she kept telling the King of this. And the King would say, "Girls, girls, girls, all we hear about is girls, girls, girls. You should be happy with what you've got."

But after a few visits to her friend the hen-wife, and what passed between her and the hen-wife, the Queen became pregnant. And when she told the King, he was delighted. He said, "Maybe another son." The King loved his sons.

But the months flew by very quickly and lo and behold the Queen gave birth to another son. The King was overjoyed; he was called to the Queen's bedside a couple of hours later and she passed the little, wrinkly, new born baby to the King and she said to him.

"You've got what you've wished for."

And the King took one look and thrust the baby into the Queen's bosom. It was a bonnie little boy, but he had a hump on his back and his spine was bent. The King was so upset he said, "I didn't father that. That doesn't belong to me!"

She said, "Of course, my King it is your son."

"I can't have that," he said, "to grow up and disgrace me."

"But," the Queen said, "it's your son, my King, it's your son."

"That's no son of mine," he said. "My son will grow up strong and tall like me. That has to go out of our sight."

The Queen began to cry. The King said, "There is no option. It has to go."

"But," the Queen said, "what are you going to do with him?"

He said, "Leave it to me. Tomorrow we will have a mock burial. It has died." And he ordered the servant to take the baby away.

The Queen's heart was nearly broke with sorrow but anyhow the next day there was a mock funeral and many people gathered. The little coffin was buried in the graveyard in the cemetery behind the palace.

But secretly the King had the baby in another room with an old woman who respected the King. He called on one of his huntsmen late in the evening and told the huntsman, "Huntsman, I want you to take this baby of mine. Take it out to the forest as far as you can. Destroy it and bring me back evidence."

The huntsman didn't know what to do because he was a father himself and had children of his own, but he could not go against the King's orders. So late that night the King bundled up the little baby and passed it to the huntsman who rode off into the forest, but before going off he called at the house of the old hen-wife. He told the hen-wife the story; he was nearly crying.

"I don't know what to do," he said, "I can't go against my King, and I'm a family man and have children of my own. What can I do with this little baby?"

The hen-wife gave him something to eat and drink and she said, "Don't worry, just a moment." She kept a goat or two and she went away and came back with a big bottle of goat's milk and a little teat and she wrapped it in a little piece of flannel and said, "Take this with you into the forest, till you come to a great oak tree. Sit under the oak tree, then just wait. And if the baby cries, feed him on this." She bid the huntsman goodbye and off he rode into the forest.

He rode for some time with the directions the old hen-wife had given him until he came to the old oak tree, and there he sat and his heart was breaking with sorrow.

"Who could destroy a little baby like this?" He held the baby in his arms and looked at the little creature. Yes, it had a hump on its back but it was somebody's child. He thought of the sadness of the Queen but he could not go against the orders of the King. He sat till dawn was breaking when he heard the clop, clop, clop of feet, like the feet of a horse. He stared down the old pathway and sure enough, coming towards him was an old man, with a long white beard, dressed in skin, goat-skin. He came up. He had a donkey, and the donkey was carrying many little packs, and the old man looked at the huntsman and said: "You look kind of sad, stranger."

And the huntsman said, “Yes, I’m very sad, it’s a terrible thing I have put upon me.”

“What has been put upon you?” asked the old man.

He said, “I’m here to destroy this little one.”

And the old man left the donkey standing to one side and caught the little baby and looked at it and the most amazing thing happened when he pulled back the covering that the old woman had wrapped the baby in. The baby looked up and smiled at the old man and it was only a few days old.

And the old hunchback said, “Never worry my friend, you’ll have no trouble,” and he reached into his pack and brought out a rabbit. He said, “Give me your sword,” and he passed it through the rabbit two or three times. Then he put his hand in a purse he carried by his side and gave the huntsman two gold coins.

“As far as you are concerned,” he said “the baby is gone.”

It was a very relieved huntsman who climbed on his horse with blood on his sword and rode back to the palace and presented himself before the King. The King was overjoyed.

“There’ll be no more of him,” he said.

The old hunchback took the little baby up beside him in the saddle on the donkey and he travelled on through the forest winding his way between the trees and bushes until he came to a great cliff in the hillside. Through a secret passage among the trees the hunchback passed. The sun was just rising and he padded into the most beautiful valley anyone had ever seen.

It was full of little cabins like a market garden and when the people saw them coming they all came running towards them clapping their hands. Some with club foot, some missing a leg, some hunchback, some blind, some deaf, some not able to speak, and there was not a person in the whole crowd, and this must have been 50 or 60, young, old, children too, who was not disabled in some way. They all came laughing and happy around the hunchback and from his pack he gave things to them all and they went on their way.

Through this valley of gardens and flowers went the hunchback. It was the most beautiful place you could find and the hunchback went to one of the largest cabins, gave the donkey to one of them who put it in a little stable by the cabin’s side and there sitting, rocking herself in an old wooden chair was an old woman. He came in with the baby in his arms and she said, "Oh, you've brought me something, another one."

"Yes, my dear," he said, "I've brought you another one but this one is very special."

She said, "They're all very special to me."

In this beautiful green valley the old hunchback and the old woman were as kings and queens, caring for the people of the secret hidden valley of Earthdom. Only the hunchback knew the entrance to this place; no one knew all these people existed. Whenever he found someone the world did not want the hunchback brought them to this secret valley and there they stayed, amongst friends, happy to the end of their days.

In this beautiful hidden secret valley of Earthdom the years flew by and the young humble Prince not knowing who he was grew up with the old hunchback and the old woman. To him they were as a father and a mother. The old hunchback taught him the ways of the moors and the rivers, taught him how to fire an arrow and how to wield a sword. Many happy and wonderful times they had together at fencing and archery, and ranging the secret valley. He took the boy riding. Aside from the old donkey there was only one horse in the whole valley. An old white horse. The creature looked ancient in years but it could be swift enough.

So he lived there content and well till he was 18 years of age. He had grown despite the hunch, tall and muscular and strong, a handsome young man. The old man and the old woman loved him like a son. Everyone in the valley was his friend.

Then one morning the old hunchback called the young man before him.

"My son," he said, "I have a task for you."

"Yes, Father, what do you want me to do for you?"

"Far from here," said the old hunchback, "is the city of the King and the palace of the King. In that place there is to be a great tournament to celebrate the 21st birthday of the King's two twin sons. My son, I wish you to compete in three contests. The archery you are so skilled in; the sword fencing and the best, the horse racing. I want you to do your best for me."

"I would love to do that for you," said the young man, "but I have never been outside this valley. How will I find my way?"

"I will show you the way!" said the old man.

"But, Father," said he, "what shall we do for a horse?"

"We have a horse, the swiftest in the land."

The young hunchback was a little dubious. The old mare had never gone beyond a lazy trot with him.

"Come with me, my son, climb up!"

So the young man swung up, no saddle, barely a bridle and the old hunchback swung up behind him.

"Now, my son," he said, "let's do some speed."

The old hunchback reached over the young boy's shoulders, pressed his two thumbs into the horse's back and said, "Faster, boy, faster!"

Suddenly the wind was in their faces as they sped over the ground.

"Where is all this speed coming from?" said the young man.

"There is yet more," said the old hunchback. And again he reached over, pressed his two thumbs into the horse's shoulders and said: "Up and away."

And all in a moment a pair of beautiful silver wings unfolded and they lifted and soared from the ground, like a bird they floated and circled round the valley. The young man gazed down in amazement and delight and they glided gracefully back to earth. The wings folded and were gone. The old man smiled.

"Tomorrow you shall travel to the palace of the King, my son. If ever you are in trouble or danger, you know what to do; press your thumbs into the horse's shoulders and say '*up and away*'."

So next morning he led him through the cliff passage and the young hunchback went on his way saying farewell to the only one he'd ever known as his father. He travelled for a day and a night and another day and night and on the third day he heard music, saw flags waving from the rampart of the palace. He had never seen anything like this before in his life so he rode into the gate, the entrance to the palace where the great tournament was to be held. He was instantly stopped by two guards who asked, "Where do you think you are going?"

He said, "I have come a long way to compete in the great feats."

They looked at the strange young man and exchanged amused glances.

"Oh, anyone is free to enter. What great feats are you for?"

"The swordsmanship," said he, and they chuckled.

"The archery!" said he, and they laughed out loud.

"And most important, the horse racing." They doubled up.

"On your way, good luck!"

And followed by their howls of laughter he entered the city. He found something to eat, something to drink and somewhere to sleep. Next morning was the great day. He competed in the archery until three competitors remained. Two strong handsome young men, the King's twin sons, and himself. From the royal balcony the King and Queen saw their two sons put to shame by the skill of this stranger.

In the sword fencing it was the same. The stranger out pointed, out manoeuvred, out fought the King's sons and put them to shame. The King was red with fury. And then came the greatest event. The horse race with the finest horses in the land round the wall of the city.

The Queen from the royal balcony dropped a golden ball. They were off, thundering through the city gates. All round the walls the crowd cheered and roared, then fell strangely silent. And then like a whirlwind clear of the field bursting through the gates, past the winning post, the old white mare and its rider, the young stranger. The King's sons followed.

The King roared to the guards. "Bring that man before me!"

At once the guards and soldiers ran towards the young hunchback. Afraid he was being attacked he pressed his thumbs to the horse's shoulders. "Faster boy, faster! *Up and away.*" And the two silver wings unfolded. The horse rose, a graceful wonder, and flew out over the city and disappeared above the distant forest.

The King fell into a fury of obsession. He questioned everyone. No one could tell of this young man. He sent couriers and messengers over the land seeking the flying horse and the young man who rode it but to no avail. One evening as the Queen saw him sitting brooding by the fire she said: "Maybe I could help you."

"You could help me! You could help me? When all my couriers, army and advises riding round the country can't find this man? You could help?"

She said quietly, "Maybe my friend, the hen-wife, could help."

He calmed down. "Do you think so?"

"Ask her."

At once the King set out to where she lived. The old wise hen-wife knew the King, treated him as she would anyone in the world, and she already knew he was coming.

"I know you are obsessed in your mind," said she, "you are looking for the flying horse of Earthdom."

"The flying horse of where?"

"The flying horse of Earthdom."

"I have never heard of such a place," said he.

"In your kingdom there is a secret valley, the hidden valley of Earthdom. And that is what you will need to find."

"Just tell me. I will go myself!"

"Do as I say and you may find it. Take off your coat."

"Take off... " The King removed his coat and inside the shoulder of the coat the old woman sewed a cushion.

"Now, put on your coat!"

When the King put on his coat there was a hump on his back.

"Why this?" said he.

"Without this," said she, "you will never find the way. Without this you will never find the hidden valley of Earthdom. You will wander in the forest, maybe for days, until you come to a great old oak tree. Wait there until someone comes for you, even though you are starving of hunger."

She made him a little bundle of food for the journey.

The King made his way into the forest and wandered for days, lost, but came to a track and at last to the great old oak tree. There he sat all night long till the chirping of the birds ceased and the forest was silent. He woke cold and hungry as the first light of day wakened the birds. Then he heard, the *clop, clop* of hooves. And there leading a donkey was the old hunchback.

"Good day, stranger, you seemed troubled. Are you in pain?" asked the hunchback.

"Just the pains of hunger and thirst," said the King.

"We can cure that – follow me."

So through the forest the King followed the old hunchback and donkey. Through winding ways and secret trails till they came to a great cliff. Concealed among the bushes was the secret passage.

Out they came into the most beautiful valley the King had ever seen. Flowers, fruit trees, beautiful gardens, the air scented and fragrant. And from neat little cabins people came clapping and laughing and surrounded the hunchback; some crippled, some blind, not one without a disability. The King was bewildered and startled.

"Who are these people?" he asked.

"Don't be troubled, they will not harm you. They are my friends, my people."

He led the King to a fine wood cabin and there sitting outside was a young man.

"Son, I have brought someone to meet you."

The young hunchback stood up, greeted the King who at once knew that this was the person he sought. Together they sat and after some food and drink the young man and the King talked long into the night. In the morning they walked round the gardens and everyone greeted the young man with smiles and happiness. The King was amazed. He did not know such a place existed.

At length he asked. "How do you pass your time when you are not tending these beautiful gardens?"

"I practice my archery!"

"Archery," said the King, "ah, that was once the love of my heart but well, with my back."

"Stay awhile," said the young man; and so the King stayed.

Back in the palace the Queen and court wondered what had happened to the King. But when the Queen visited her friend, the old hen-wife, she said. "Don't fret, he is in good hands and will return."

The Queen was content.

Now the King stayed there in that beautiful valley for many days admiring the gardens, talking to the people, getting to know the old hunchback and the young man. He learned once more the skills of archery, of the left-handed swordsmanship and the young hunchback was his teacher. He taught him well. The King became quite expert because, of course, he had practiced these skills all his life.

One day he said to the young hunchback, "You have a wonderful place here young man."

"Well," he said, "this is my home."

"How long have you lived here?"

He said, "I've lived here all my life. I can't remember anything else."

The King said, "I wonder what this place would look like from up amongst the clouds?"

And the young hunchback said, "Would you like to see it from above?"

"Oh," said the King, "it's impossible. I'd need to be a bird to fly up there."

"Come with me then," said the young hunchback, and he led him to the stable beside the little cabin they lived in, and he took out the old white horse, put a bridle on his head and said to the King.

"Climb up on his back!"

The King climbed up. The young hunchback jumped up before him and they rode for a bit, rode for a bit and another bit and then he pressed his thumbs into the horse's neck and the King heard the words plainly, "*Up and away*." And just like that out came the silver wings once more. The King gazed down, they were not too high, just above the valley, and all the people were staring up at them and the King gave them a little wave, and round and round they went and landed once again near the little cabin. There stood the old hunchback. He turned to the King and he said: "You can come down now, your Majesty. You've got what you came for. Take off that coat!"

The King dismounted and took off the coat and there he stood, straight and tall.

"Now," said the old hunchback, "you've found what you want."

The King said, "Yes, I came looking for a young man who put my whole palace to shame and now I have found him."

And the old man turned round to the young hunchback and said, "My son, do you know who this is? This is the King, this is your King... not only your King but also your father."

"My father?" said the young hunchback, "but *you* are my father."

"No, my son, I'm not your father. This is your father, the father who sent you to be killed in the forest with a huntsman because he was ashamed of you because of the hump on your back."

The King was put to shame. He stepped towards the young man and the young man stepped away from him.

"Son," he said, "son? *You are my son*?"

"Of course," said the old hunchback, "he is your son. He is the son you sent to the forest to be killed because you were ashamed of him. And all the people around us here – are you ashamed of them? Are they not your subjects? Not your subjects because they have a hump on their back or a club foot or want an eye or cannot speak or cannot walk or cannot hear? Are you ashamed of them?"

The King's eyes filled with tears.

"I never knew this place existed," he said, "but please, my son, will you come with me? Will you come and see your mother and maybe she will forgive me?"

The young man looked at him.

"I cannot come with you. This is the only father I have ever known and I will not leave this place and these people who are my friends."

The King begged him but his son would not leave Earthdom.

"I ask one thing," said the King.

"You are the King," said the young man.

"That I may bring your mother, the Queen, to meet you here."

"I would love to meet my mother," said the young hunchback.

Next day, the old hunchback led the King through and out of the beautiful hidden, secret valley, back to the old oak tree and from there the King made his own way home to the palace, but said nothing to anyone.

From that time on, mysteriously the King and Queen were gone from the palace for weeks at a time and I'm sure wherever they went they were very happy. For where they went was to the beautiful hidden secret valley of Earthdom.

So there you are, David, for you. And we will never fall out again.'

* * *

And a great big hug. A beautiful story, and a happy reconciliation for the time being.

Travelling On

I have never let my schooling interfere with my education.

MARK TWAIN

I MOVED BACK UP to Argyll, back up to Inveraray. There's not much peat ever gets cut in Argyll. I had no idea that people were still doing it. One day, I was taking a shortcut across the hills, as I always do because in these days it was better; you saved yourself a lot of miles.

Away above Glen Aray I came to an old man. I saw him in the distance. I saw the shirt-sleeve moving when I was coming over the mountain. I hadn't got a smoke all that day and I saw him stop and I saw him light a cigarette. I said, 'Upon my soul if it's the last thing I do, I'm going to ask him for a fag.'

This was to come an experience that I never believed would happen. I met one of the greatest friends that a person could ever have, one of the greatest knowledgeable people in all my days, and that man could neither read nor write. His name was Patrick O'Donnel and he came from Ireland. He was cutting peats on the hill. I walked right down by his little peat bank, and I says, 'Would you spare me a cigarette? I never had a smoke all day.'

'Where do you come from?' he says.

'I come from Loch Awe, over Loch Aweside.'

He said, 'Where are you bound for?'

I said, 'I'm going down to Inveraray, and then I'm going to walk down to Furnace.'

He said, 'What's your name?'

I says, 'Duncan.'

'What's your second name?'

'Williamson.'

He said, 'Are you any relation to big Jock? Big Jock Williamson?'

I said, 'Aye, I'm his son.'

'Oh,' he said, 'I used to work down by the coal boats with your father. Me and him used to empty the coal boats. Bloody good worker!' he said in his Irish accent.

He gied me a fag. I sat down on the banking with him, on the moss, and we smoked a fag.

And he says, 'Where are you bound for?'

'Ach,' I says, 'just back home, see the old folk and maybe take off again.'

He said, 'Would you work for me?'

I said, 'Work for you? You've all what you need.'

'No,' he says, 'I've got two jobs to do. I've got to cut these peats and throw them up from the peat bank (because it was a kind of a ditch), then I've got to climb up and I've got to rue them in fours, let the wind in below them to dry. Now,' he said, 'if you would rue the peats for me, it's quite easy. You stand two together, just as if you're stooking corn, let the wind go in below them so they'll dry.'

When peats are cut they're very heavy, but when a peat's dry, it doesna weigh any more than about ten or twelve ounces, because it's only roots of heather, moss.

'Ah well, I'm no doing very much, now,' I said. 'I've nae place to stay.'

'Oh you can stay with me,' he said. 'Look, there's plenty tea.'

He had a little hut, it wasn't much bigger than an old police box, a wee chimney in it and an elbow came out through the side so the chimney was outside, but the elbow went right in and went into a wee square Queen Anne stove. Outside he had a bag of coal and a bag of peats, broken up peats, heaps of sticks that he collected and a big milk can, one of these dairy cans full of water. It was a wee shed he had, two handles at the back and two handles at the front. Out of the side of the hut was a big hook and on the hook was a rope, and from the end of the rope was a big steel pin. You carried the hut, two people could carry it, and this is where he kept his personal possessions, and this is where he slept. There was enough room for two people to sit, for two people to sleep. He had the wee cupboards in it for holding his food. The water was kept outside, the coal was kept outside. So was the sticks.

He says, 'Duncan, I have to move!'

I said, 'All right.' – I'm 15 year old now – 'Right, Paddy.' I called him Paddy. I says, 'Right Paddy.'

'That's all right, Duncan,' he said, 'Paddy's nice. I like it.'

He took the back, I took the front. We carried that hut maybe, say, a hundred yards and we went back for the water, back for the sticks. He got the big hammer and he took this bolt, and he looped one loop to the west and one to the north, and he took the big steel pin and he tapped it down. He sunk it into the ground in case it was bothered with the wind. A rope on that side with a steel pin, a rope on this side with a steel pin into the ground, just as if you were putting down a big circus tent. So if it got the wind during the night it couldna cowp because the ropes was holding it. Those ropes were tight when the steel pins went down about two foot into the ground. And so we started. We didn't work that afternoon.

'Now,' he said, 'I'll show you around.' He showed me around, he explained things to me, he showed me his peat-cutting spade, showed me all these things. We made tea in a little teapot, little battered teapot. I had tea with him. Oh, he ate a lot of meat.

Over in the corner he had an old sailor's kitbag. It was a really old kit bag with brass eyeholes in it and a rope leading through the holes. This is where he kept most of his personal possessions. It was all stacked away in a corner.

Anyhow, when he went to the shop he'd leave me and walk through the hill path to Inveraray, and he would get messages that he needed, tins of milk. He liked the tins of sweet milk – condensed milk – and it was good for tea. This was during the war when you couldna buy any sugar, and it was good for sweetening up your tea.

I came to like this old man very much. We worked every day and whenever he went to the shop he would always bring back two 20 packets of Woodbine. 'Now,' he said, 'Duncan, try and make that last. I'm not complaining about the cost but we canna just run to the town every time we need cigarettes.' He got 60 for himself and 40 for me. Woodbine. Paid me five shillings a week. Good money.

We'd sit there after the nights were over and we'd discuss many things. You know, he was the most knowledgeable person I have ever met in all my life. Brought up in Ireland, in the rough part of Ireland away back years before my time, back just the time of the First World War. He could not read nor write. He told me he had brothers and sisters but he didn't know where they were. They'd all gone and scattered.

'I had a number of them,' he said. 'Too many!'

He never told me how many.

I said, 'Patrick, do you have brothers and sisters?'

'Aye,' he said, 'I had a number of them but I don't know where they are.'

He told me of his journeys into many parts of the world. He had been a sailor and he'd been in the merchant navy. He had travelled, even China he'd been in. I thought I was clever with nature because I was brought up in the forest with my parents, but here was an old man, not of my culture in any way, not a Travelling man, an old Irishman who had more knowledge and understanding than I would ever gain in a million years, not even till this day, even though I could read and write. He could tell you about the smallest insect in the world, how it was created. He could tell you about the great large fish, but he'd never say 'whale' for some reason. He would say, 'the large blue fish'. I never questioned why he didn't call it a whale. 'Hunting the large blue fish,' he would say, 'on the whalers.' He told many wonderful things, but he never told me any stories. I never had a story from him. He told me about his family in Ireland, he told me about the travels he had done, the places he had been, and the jobs he had done. He had worked with my father on the coal boats, he had worked in the quarry, he had been a wood cutter, he had worked on farms, and he'd done many, many things, like me when I was young, but expertly.

But there was only one thing that really made him happy: after supper-time when the work was over for the day and we had wir wee tea and we had wir wee smoke, and he always used to keep a couple of these old traditional pale ale screw-tops. They were just common big pale ale beer and they had a common cork you screwed with a rubber band to tighten it. He would always have a couple of these in his house and he would fill a wee glass of beer. I wouldn't take any. And this is what he would say:

'Well, Duncan, would you do something for me?' This was the first night.

I said, 'Paddy, I'll do anything for you.'

He says, 'Duncan, I'm ashamed to say this, but would you read me a wee bit of the Bible?'

He went to the kit bag I was telling you about and he opened the rope and he put his hand in and he brought out the Bible. He sat there, I can just see him as if it was yesterday – the wee stove burning and a wee single globe lamp hanging there – he sat there on the floor by the fire, corduroy trousers on him, an old striped shirt without a collar, waistcoat on the top of the shirt, corduroy waistcoat, fags sticking out of the top pocket of the waistcoat, matches on the other side. I'm sitting there – and this was the love of his heart.

'Duncan, it's the only thing I would love to have done in my lifetime. I've done many wonderful things in my life,' he said, 'things I'm proud of and things I'm not proud of. But the only thing I really lacked, I wished,' he said, 'to the Holy One' – he never mentioned, God –, 'I wished to the Holy One that I had learned to read myself.' He would open that Bible, he'd pass it over to me and he would say, 'Read to me. Read it aloud.' And I would read the scriptures and the things that it said on that page. He would say, 'Thank you, Duncan.' He'd close the Bible, put it back in his pack.

We'd work all day, come back in at night-time, we'd sit and do the same thing again. Sometimes we went for a walk if it was a nice evening on the moor and after supper out would come the Bible again. If he opened that Bible, no matter if it was the same place that I'd read that time before, he would just say, 'Read to me, Duncan,' suppose I had read it four or five times over. He loved that Bible.

It was dark, it was a long walk and I knew there's no way that I was going to make home that night, but I travelled, and ran and trotted and jogged, trotted all the way to Melford, down through Melford, up the braes, down the hill, down the glens, down into Ford and then on to Kilmartin. By the time I came to Kilmartin I was completely, completely exhausted. My legs were giving me pain and I knew fine I couldn't go any farther but I had to find some place where I could shelter, where it was comfortable, where I could rest, lie down. I knew in my mind what place I was going to go that night. I'd made my mind up, because my father had camped in the field near Kilmartin on a farm. In the field my father had cut the hay was this very same stone near where I had been sunstruck a long time before.

Near that stone was the Pictish tombs. We had played in these tombs as kids, as children long years before. We even had slept in them as children and our parents knew and paid no attention to them because their tent was nearby. 'Oh the kids are asleep in the Pictish tombs.' We loved it. So me and a couple of the older brothers, we said, 'We'll go sleep in the tombs tonight, see what like it is, have an experience.'

But that night I was on my own. I was a 13-year-old young fellow. I had fags, a couple of shillings left that old Patrick had given me. I walked down to the Pictish tombs, waiting in the gloaming of the dark. Lights on at the farm. Didn't bother the farm and that, dogs would start barking, people would think it's intruders.

I came through the field, over the dykes through the field, made my way towards the Pictish tombs, moon was shining. There was the great cairn of stones from people in bygone times, years, hundreds of years gone by, the little Pictish folk. I wondered to myself, what kind of people they really were. Were they like me? Were they nomads like myself? My father would say, 'These are the bones buried in there.' And mother would say, 'No, maybe just their ashes.'

The Pictish stones, let me explain to you, are a cairn, a big cairn with thousands of stones, thousands of tons of stones, and some of these stones came a long long way because some of these stones are polished by the sea! But now after all those years, bits of moss was growing on them. You could recognise, they were not stones that was gathered off the field nearby. They were washed stones, as at one time, thousands and millions of years ago had been rocks washed with the tide, polished.

The local custom we believe was – we don't know if it was actually true or not, because the're nothing wrote down by the Picts – that when an old warrior or an old chief or someone important in the Pictish clan died, they were either buried in the tombs or they were burned, and their ashes put in the tombs – every little grave, maybe three and a half foot. They're four at that side, two across the top and four down the other side, and there's a space in the middle. The walls are solid rock, built rock like a drystone dyke right up about ten foot high. Then it's roofed with a slab stone on the roof to keep the stones above from falling down.

Here was I with my Woodbine, my box of matches, all on my own. And the wind blows the leaves through the wood, and you know how they gather round and twist and build up and they blew into the tomb! And there they lie on the floor, leaves.

So here's me down in the Pictish tomb, all the little graves, four there, four there. Now at the very back there's a little hole. What the hole was for I don't know, but as if someone left it as a window that a little light could get in. You could see the moonlight coming in through the window. I made my bed, a bed of leaves, my jacket off, boots off, put the jacket atop of my boots and used it as a pillow and stretched out there on the leaves in that place of these ancient people that are gone long hundreds of years before me. I slept peacefully, as if I was asleep in any bed in a great hotel. The next morning I got up early and made my way home.

That was a wonderful experience to be in that tomb. I felt at peace. I felt happy, I had no fear of any kind. I had no fear of ghosts or spirits. I don't believe in the Devil, I don't believe in ghosts, I don't believe in spirits.

I've wandered on my own for years and years and years: I've slept in Pictish tombs, I've slept in graveyards, I used to take the little graveyard shed, put the little picks and spades outside, and sleep in that little graveyard shed. In the morning before I left, put the tools back in the shed, no one knew I was there. I seen me waking through the night and lighting a cigarette and looking out into the graveyard and all these standing stones and the moon shining on them, bright moonlight shining on them.

Characters Galore

DUNCAN AND I WERE ready for an early morning recording session.

'Now David, I'll tell you about some of the strange and wonderful characters I met on the farms. You must have met plenty strange people yourself.'

'Very different no doubt,' I said. 'One day, Duncan, I will write about the amazing characters that I met on my way, the ones that I loved and admired and who changed my life. I've always been lucky; there was a mad politician who drew me into his life of fantasy when I was only 18, a schoolmaster who was reputed to be the best teacher of English in Scotland, my BBC boss who was a wonderful gardener of people and, of course, you.' He laughed.

'You're missing out the women,' he said.

'Time enough, meantime let's get on with your story and your characters.'

As usual, he had taken his early morning strong sweet tea and mandatory cigarette, was preened and ready to go.

* * *

Well now, at that time, work was easy because between Inveraray and Furnace there were five farms, where my father had took me with him as a little boy. We knew the farmer, we knew the shepherds, and of course I knew fine during the clipping time I could get as much employment as possible.

Now we had many strange characters there at the clipping stool time. We had a young chap there, his name was Iain Campbell.

Iain Campbell lived with his mother and his father and his older brother. His older brother worked for the Duke of Argyll, up on the estate. Iain was a shepherd, a good shepherd. He was a very proud man, but he was the most nicest person anyone ever met and he was the handsomest person anyone ever met. And he knew it. He used to say, 'The best looking shepherd on the Duke's estate!' Fair moustache and blue eyes. But funny thing was, I've never seen him with a girlfriend. Now, I was coming up for 14, and Iain at that time, he'd be 25. He was the shepherd in Killean.

What the farmers did then, was, you went to one farm one day and you helped, maybe he had two hundred sheep, maybe three hundred. Maybe it'd take you a day and a half to clip all his sheep, dress their feet, maybe check them for fluke and worms and maybe give them a pill or two. All these farmers, they all carried their traditional gear with them. I did in later years when I was out on the hills with old Duncan MacVicar.

What they carried was a pair of scissors, a file, a leather strap, little piece of string, a rope – and I'll explain to you why these things are needed – and a bottle, a bottle of pills. Maybe two bottles of pills. There would be a fluke pill for fluke, that's a kind of sickness sheep takes. There'd be worm pills, little long pills, a little like some of the pills you get today. And labelled 'not for humans'. They would pick up these things from the local vet in his office in Inveraray. Every good shepherd would always have some of them with him, but also he'd have with him a little pink pill, like an aspirin, and this was wool ball pill. This is true.

A wool ball pill was given to little lambs because these black faced sheep are very woolly creatures and sometimes the wool is close to the udder where they feed their babies. The little lamb standing there under its mummy sucking away and its little tail going like that, as you've seen yourself, sometimes it sucks wool, strands of wool and it swallows them in its little stomach. These wool balls gather and cause a disease called 'wool ball' in its little stomach. It can't pass anything and it loses its appetite. Its wee belly fills up and it just stands there, it cannae suck, cannae eat, there's too many little balls of wool in its stomach.

So all you have to do is check his little belly, cowp him over, put your thumb on the side of his mouth, open his little mouth up, a wee lamb, milk teeth very small, open up, keep your thumb in here and if you think his belly's a wee bit too big, pop two little tablets, and shove them down his throat with your finger, two little wool ball tablets. These tablets are very, very strong. Within an hour, that little lamb should be squirtin from it with the power of that tablet. Not very often do we get cases of wool ball but you were still allowed to carry the wool ball tablets.

Anyhow, we had a man there, a shepherd called Mammy. Mammy had not had a hair on his head in his life. By the time we'd finished the last farm there was about nine of us to end up the last clipping. It was way up, a place called Barraholl. He was the last farmer, he was the biggest farmer, he had the most sheep. We all ended there. Now Mammy was known to every one of us. Malcolm was his name, Malcolm Munro. He was an illegitimate child, which they're many in the world, and he was brought up with his mammy, an old woman. And Malcolm was a mammy's boy.

He'd never had a hair on his body but he was a good worker, strong as a bull. When it came to do other things like building drystone dykes, I saw him lifting stones that we couldn't even move. His arms was red, his face was red, his chest was red as if he was burned with the sun, but he never was. His face was red but there was no eyelashes, no eyebrows. Mammy was the strangest character you ever saw.

There never was one moment if we sat down beside him, had a smoke or a cup of tea; Mammy was telling you what his mammy said he must no do. 'Mammy said this, Mammy says that, Mammy knows better.' If the shepherds were discussing a subject he would interrupt, and say, 'That's no right, Mammy knows, Mammy would tell you what it's all about.' So we christened him '*Mammy*'.

It was the afternoon Iain Campbell and I, Mammy, Cud Johnson (we'll come to him later) and a few of the shepherds, Lachly MacLachlan and one of the old farmers himself was there.

Now when they sat down, they carried these wee tin flasks in a sock because there was no thermos flasks in these days, but Mammy never carried tea. Mammy carried a little flask full of soup. It could be chicken soup, tomato soup, and he would always have this toasted bread. He had toasted bread for his tea, toasted bread for his lunch if we were out on the hills. If we were back the dinner was served on the farm. The farmer's wife took them all in but not me. Even at that time. Never took me in. The maid or the farmer's wife brought me out a bowl of soup. I was kept in the milkhouse or the kitchen out in the shed. I didn't mind about that. After all, I was not one of them. I never wanted to be. But anyway in the holding pen, the yard, the fank as we called it, everybody was the same. It was only because of the farmer's wife that they didn't want me in the house.

There was a lot of good Gaelic speakers among them, and there was a lot of no Gaelic speakers among them. The Gaelic speakers would sit and discuss things in Gaelic. Sometimes they were talking about Mammy, sometimes they were talking about Iain, sometimes they were talking about me in Gaelic. Believe it, I didn't mention I could understand Gaelic. I never mentioned to them, I never do even yet. And I mind Lachlan MacLachlan was discussing something in Gaelic. He was speaking about Iain and he was speaking about Mammy. I was standing and he was after finishing his sheep, and he had left his file for sharpening the shears standing against the side of the wall. He said, 'Duncan, could you pass that file over to me?'

The three of them was close together. And I said to myself when I heard them talking in Gaelic, I'm going to put a stop to this. I handed it over to them, I says, 'Seo, a bhaliach.'

From then on till the end of the clipping there was no more Gaelic.

But back to Mammy. He interrupted everything, would give us no peace. Till one day they were away out in the hills in a holding fank, the nearest trees must be half a mile away, the little birch wood. Iain and me, we'd come back to the fank to collect something. We gathered the puckle that was separated from the rest of the big herd and we brought them back to the holding pen, put them in. The shepherds had left their wee leather bags, they carried on their back with their shears and their tablets. Iain and me sat and we had a Woodbine, a smoke. He was a funny soul and he says to me. 'Duncan, d'ye think that Mammy ever gets wool ball with sucking his mammy's pappy?'

I said, 'D'ye think he's still...'

'Ach,' says he, 'I think he still sucks it yet, Mammy. I think he still sucks his mammy's breast yet. Maybe a couple o' wool ball tablets would do him the world of good.'

I said, 'No, for God's sake.'

'Oh, we'll just gie him a couple.'

He went over to Mammy's bag, opened the sock, a knot on his sock to keep the flask warm. Opened the flask, 'Ach,' he says, 'we'll gie the bugger three.' Now one's enough for a wee lamb, right. We gied him three in his soup.

had the food he would have to have a lick at his plums. He'd lie there and he'd lick them and he'd lick them and he would lick them.

Iain – wait till you hear what a funny guy he really was. He said to me one day and Lachlan was sitting smoking his pipe.

Iain says, 'Duncan, what do you think of old Sam?'

I says, 'He's enjoying it.'

He says to me, 'Do you think that's the only balls he licks?' He says, 'Duncan, maybe he gives Lachlan a lick too. Maybe he'll give Lachlan's a lick tonight.'

God, he was funny. He was really funny. I seen me lying on my bed back home at night-time thinking back and laughing to myself in the bed. The rest of the Travellers thought I was crazy, laughing to myself when I thought back to what Iain would say. He was one of the strangest characters, but he didn't mean no harm with it.

Time for dinner and the two dogs were lying out front and we sat down on a rock. I seen me starving, starving, and Lachlan took maybe a scone and he'd take one bite and he would throw it to the dogs. I mean, ye left that place at eight o'clock in the morning, this is four hours wandering the hill and I didna have any breakfast to start with, I wouldna even have a cigarette, not a dout to my name, and he would sit down there and he would light his pipe up, packed full of Condor bar and he would turn round, and he'd say, 'Oh, and do you like a smoke after your dinner, Duncan?'

I says, 'Lachlan, what dinner did I get? And what smoke do I get?'

'Ach well,' he says, 'it's no fault o' mine if you hadna.' After the dog's eaten a big sandwich. He was a pleasant person, good, never swore in his life, church goer too. Went to the church every Sunday, but would never think a single moment to say, 'Duncan, would you like a piece?' Many of the shepherds gave me a piece. I mean, Iain would share a nut with you and one day he says to me, 'What does he go to the church for, Duncan? To learn to be miserable! My God,' he says, 'he thought more of the dogs as he thought of you. That's the truth.'

These were the things you had to cope with. But believe it, it was a wonderful time. I gained and I learned from it, the experience and the unforgettableness of these characters.

It is 1943. The war has been going for three years. I've just celebrated 15th birthday. I was working with an old stonemason on the hills

Anyway, in they come. We opened the gates for them, you see. Iain stood one side and I stood the other side and we drove all the sheep into the fank, got them all settled down. A few big rams, big horns turned up, big strong buggers, takes a bit holding to get to them. Anyhow, we clipped away. The old farmer had his watch, 'Ach well, time, boys, it's about time we had wir lunch.'

I looked at Iain and Iain's looking at me. Shepherds, they've got a piece and jam. A wee collie, tongue hanging out, it was running all day. They do get hungry because they only get fed once a day. I never had nothing to give the wee dogs. The shepherds would throw a crust, but Mammy said, 'I've got to eat all my toast and I've to drink all my soup."

Iain looked at me, I thought he was going to choke. He turned his back to me. I remember he had on dungarees, belt round his waist. He was a beautiful man, but a pure comic, and the nicest soul you never met in your life, you know, he'd share his last with you.

Anyway, Mammy sat down, stretched out his legs, parked the flask down beside him.

Iain looks at me. Now we thought that the tablets would make a taste in his soup and he wouldn't take it. That's what we thought and it would be okay, see? He would say to hisself, 'Mammy, what's wrong with my soup today, Mammy, it didn't taste very good,' and he'd pour it out. Aye, did he hell!

He sat and he even drained the flask above his head, supped the last grains, put the cork back in, lighted the pipe.

Well, I never thought a human being could move so fast! So we're all sitting and it was just about 20 minutes later, after we had wir break and wir smoke I says, 'Are ye all ready, boys, then? I'll gie ye sheeps and we'll get ye some more.' Iain's looking at me, and Mammy sat down. Mammy said, 'I'm sorry, I have to go!' He got up and he made for the gate. Now when he tried to do his job, we watched him before, he stood half bent and dropped the trousers round his ankles. This is the way he had a shit, that way. Trousers are in the air, and this is the way he shit, with hands on the knees. Mammy says, 'Don't put your arse too close to the ground in case you get germs. And don't wipe your bottom with leaves, keep plenty toilet paper.'

Iain says to me, 'He's going to need leaves today, Duncan, you believe me.'

Oh, I never seen a person go so hard in all my life, he shot across like a stag. He ran to the little birch wood, Oh he was gone for a long, long time. He came back.

'I'm having a little bit of trouble with my stomach.'

I looked at Iain, and we went out of the fank and he said to me, 'He's going to be a week with more trouble with his stomach, when they really takes effect.'

'Right, Mammy, another sheep,' I says.

'No,' he says, 'I'll have to go.'

And he's off again, back to the wood. And the farmer says, 'What's wrong with Mammy?'

And Iain says, 'I think he's got a dose of the skitters.'

I says, 'I think he's got the shits.'

'By Christ,' he says, 'he's running enough, he must have the shits.'

You know, sometimes life at the clipping was a pantomime and you had to have a wee bit fun to keep away from boredom. It was nice that we had that kind of person like Iain Campbell. But Mammy never knew that in his soup was three of the pills that we had given for wool ball for wee lambs. They were harmless, but they would scare the shit out of you, you know!

There's another chap we used to concentrate on, Johnson was his name. I only come across one person in my travels who did this – this man actually chewed his cud. And they nicknamed him 'Cud Johnson'. Sometimes, when we were working close to the farm we'd walk back to the farm and get the dinner.

Dinner in the farm was potatoes and mutton and pudding and scones, good hard food. We'd walk back, it could have been from the clipping or me cutting bracken, we'd all get together for a wee smoke and a wee break, and there would Cud be sitting, but you couldn't sit aside him: it was the smell of his breath. A whiff of his breath; it lasted with you all day. I seen the rest of the men when they used to have their wee flask of tea, they'd turn their back on him in case they got a whiff of his breath; it put them off their breakfast, off their tea break.

What was wrong with his breath I didn't know. I mean I've smelt animals' breath, dogs' breath, horses'; a horse has got the loveliest breath in the world, and cow's breath smells beautiful. But the breath of that man would just drive you insane.

Iain knew about it. He says, 'Duncan, don't you know the man chews his cud?'

I says, 'Iain, a man cannae chew his cud. It's only animals that chew their cud.'

'No, but,' he says, 'he chews his cud. You watch. About one o'clock after dinner he'll bring it up again.'

He would sit there, and I would watch him, he'd go, 'Oop, smack, smack', and start chewing. And he would sit there for another ten minutes, and he'd swallae, 'unhunh', and he'd chew again. This was really strange. We'd sat there and he's bringing it up and chewing away.

Iain Campbell says to me, 'Duncan, are ye hungry?'

I says, 'Aye, I am.'

'Well,' he says, 'ask him for a wee bit.'

'What would you like, tatties, mutton or... how would you like it?' He says, 'Ye can have it in reverse, pudding first.'

And we goes into peals of laughter, the tears are running down our cheeks.

Another strange character was Lachlan MacLachlan, his father was a retired shepherd. Lachlan lived with his father. His mother had die years and years before. Lachlan was as thin as a nail. He had two dog Sam and Goldie. Sam was his favourite. For every day o' the year Sam h a knot, never was combed. You know how a hairy dog gathers in a kn

Now, Lachlan MacLachlan was never seen without these two d I was with him gathering sheep many times.

I says, 'Lachlan, do you no clip Sam?'

'No, I never bother. At least it will keep him warm,' he says.

I says, 'Comb him then?'

'Och,' he says, 'it'd be impossible to comb him.'

It was no only the knots but he was full of these sticky willies f you know these sticky willies and they get into the hair. But he h beautiful things, he had two plums that stuck out the back and w Lachlan sat down to light his pipe or sat down to take a rest, thing was that Sam would come down and lie there. Even in t house, in front of the farmer's sister, Sam loved to have a lick at To tell you the truth, he loved his plums like nothing on this ea was nothing in the world that gave him more pleasure. If you of food down to him, suppose he was out on the hill all da

above Furnace building drystone dykes. I came back one evening, mother was busy making some supper, sat down, had tea. Father was in, the rest of the wee kids was sitting all round the fire inside the tent. And the conversation started.

She says, 'I've saw a cousin of mine passing through Furnace today. My cousin Rabbie and his family.'

My ears shot up like a hare, because I had seen Rabbie before when I was younger and Rabbie had a girl about my age, Betsy. All young men of 15 gets the Spring Fever.

I says, 'When did he pass through, Mother?'

She says, 'Today while you were away working the hill, him and his wife and his family. I was down at the shop, he passed through the village. He stopped, he made some tea in the village. He had a little Shetland pony and a little float.'

I says, 'Where is he bound for?'

She says, 'He thinks he's going to Lochgilphead, and then he said on to Oban.'

I says, 'All right.' This gave me ideas.

The old stonemason, he paid me five shillings every night. So I had no obligation to go back to work if I didn't want to. I was just helping him lifting stones and I was learning the trade gradually. I remember his words to this day, he said, 'Duncan, you know, when you lift a stone up, never let it down. There's always a place for it.' And he learned me many good stories, I learned a lot from him, old Neil MacCallum.

Anyhow, instead of going to work next morning I split the five shillings with my mother, I gave her half a crown. I kept half a crown for myself and I caught the bus to Lochgilphead, but Rabbie must have pushed on that day, or the day before, because I never overtook him. I landed in Lochgilphead. I had a sixpence left. I bought ten Woodbine, which left me tuppence.

I says, 'There's only one chance. If I walk to Oban, maybe I'll overtake Rabbie and the family.'

So, I travelled up my way to Kilmartin and I ran out of matches. I says, 'I'll have to go and get myself a match. I've got to get a box of matches.'

There was an old cottage off the roadside and in that cottage lived a man and his sister, Angus and Susan MacKenzie.

The local people called them 'the doughts' which is the Gaelic word for dirt, because they werena very tidy people, you know. They had a good house. Angus MacKenzie was a rabbit catcher. That's all he did. Mother never passed the door when she went that way, but I had never actually met Angus or his sister. The old sister was a good friend of my mother because my mother supplied her with hairpins and she loved putting hairpins in her hair. She would buy a few things from my mother.

Anyway, by the time I came to the house, which was sat a little bit off the roadway against the wall I saw the rusty bike so I knew Angus was at home because sometimes I saw him cycling in the village in Lochgilphead. Big tall man he was.

I walks up round to the back of the house and I hear someone splitting sticks with a hatchet, heavy chops on the top of the block. I come round and there he was down on his knees by a chopping block. He was splitting kindlings with one hand making rabbit snare pins. He had a big bandage round his thumb and it was dirty and filthy.

I said, 'Hello.'

And he looked up and he said, 'Well, can I help you?'

I said, 'Yeah, I wonder, could you spare me a match?'

I could see he had a pipe in his waistcoat pocket and a box of matches, Swan Vestas sticking out of the top pocket. He reached down and he handed me the box of Swan Vestas and I lighted a cigarette.

He said, 'Where d'you come from?'

I said, 'From Furnace.'

'Furnace,' he said, 'what's your name?'

I said, 'Williamson.'

'Oh,' he said, 'you're one of the Williamsons?'

I said, 'I am.'

He said, 'Are you Jock and Betsy's boy?'

I said, 'I am.'

'What's your name?'

'I'm Duncan.'

And you want to see his thumb, it was swelled up with a dirty filthy rag round it.

'I know your parents well,' he said. 'How's your mother? How's your father? Good, strong, hardworking man,' he said, and he left the hatchet down beside him.

I said, 'What happened to your finger?'

He says, 'I got my thumb caught in a gin trap.'

You know these steel gin traps for catching rabbits? They can cut the leg off a fox, they can cut the leg off of a rabbit. They're banned now, you cannae use them, but they were very popular, because you could put them in front of a rabbit's burrow, cover them with sand and the rabbit came out – SNAP – and the rabbit was caught, and once he was in there he suffered a lot of agony and pain. You had to be very careful to be sure you handled them right because they could take your finger off.

He said, 'I got my thumb caught in one of the gin traps, Duncan. Susan's upstairs asleep and I'm just about to make myself a cup of tea. Would you like to join me?'

I said, 'That would be very kind of you, I could do with a cup of tea.'

'Well, come on in!' and he brought me into the kitchen of the wee house. This was the most roughest place I ever saw in all my life. Everything was in disarray. Over in one corner there was an old paraffin cooker with two burners. Over in the other corner there was a boiler, an old fashioned, traditional metal boiler, and a fireplace below. The table was in the middle of the floor, no table cloth. Things seemed to be scattered everywhere. There was an old chair and its padding coming through it on one side of the kitchen.

'Have a seat!' he said to me.

He was so pleasant! Within a minute with one hand he filled an old teapot and lighted the little paraffin stove, two wee stoves close together. In these days a wee van would come with a tank in the back and you would buy a gallon of paraffin for sixpence. These paraffin stoves were very common back during the war before the days of the electric, because there was no electric in Argyll at that time. Soon he had the kettle boiled and he got two enamel mugs. I remember them just like yesterday: they were all cracked, the enamel was chipped off them. But one thing I must say for him, he made a good cup of tea.

After tea was finished, he said, 'Smoke if you want to smoke!'

He lighted his pipe and he had a smoke.

'Angus,' I said, 'can I have a look at your finger? Have you been to the doctor with it?'

'No,' he says, 'no, I've never been to the doctor with it. Susan put a bit of bandage on it.'

I says, 'You'd better let me have a look at it.'

I unwrapped this bandage and there lo and behold, oh! His thumb was swelled twice to three times the size of a normal thumb. It was as thick as that microphone. It was cut right to the bone. I could see the green fester inside his thumb, and I saw a red strip over the back of his hand.

I says, 'Angus, you're in big trouble with that finger. You'd better let me do something about it.'

'Do you know about these things?' he says to me.

'Angus, I'm a Traveller. When anything happens in the home with the kids we cannae afford to pay for a doctor. My mother takes care of these things, you know what I mean,' I says. 'Angus, that's poisoned.' I went and got the wee teapot and I washed it out, scrubbed it with water, put it on to boil, het it as much as I could. I says, 'Angus, have you got any salt?'

'Ach aye,' he says, 'there's it.'

It was one of thon big old tin canisters of salt he had. I got a wee basin and I put about nearly two handfuls of salt in the basin.

I says, 'Come on over here. Stick your thumb in there,' and I bathed his thumb into the quick. I cleaned it completely.

'Oh,' he says to me, 'that's a big relief, a big relief.'

But, oh, it was in a bad state. His thumb was nearly took off. These gin traps are powerful things.

I says, 'Angus, it looks bad to me, I think there's a wee bit of poison set into it. When do you go into Lochgilphead?'

He says, 'I've got to go for some messages tomorrow.'

'Well,' I says, 'look, I'll bandage your hand for you. And I'll put a salt poultice on it for you. And tomorrow when you go to Lochgilphead, the best thing to do is you go up to the cottage hospital, get it dressed. Definitely, or you can either lose the hand or lose the arm!'

'Is it as bad as that?' he says.

I says, 'Angus, see that wee red strip up here, that's poison in there.'

Anyway, I cleaned it out best I could. I got a bit clean rag, I tore an old pillowslip, I remember it well. I made a poultice of wet salt, I packed it full of salt, even to the cut.

I says, 'It'll nip for a while.' And I put a bandage on it. 'I'll tell ye what I'll do with ye. Ye got an old scarf or hankie or something?' And I put a sling on it, I says, 'You keep that steady there, keep it up!'

'But Duncan, I've got only one hand now,' he says, 'and my snares is all out. And there'll be rabbits in them. They'll rot.'

I says, 'Don't worry about it.'

He says, 'I was going to ask a favour of you. Will you stay a wee while?'

I said, 'Well, I'm really in a hurry.' I was still thinking about Rabbie and the girl. You know how young men are.

He says, 'If you could give me a wee help. Have you ever set any snares for rabbits or traps?'

I says, 'Angus, look, my father's a masterpiece. He bought his own snare wires, he made his own snares, he made his own pins, he made his own hazel holders. We have a few gin traps but we used them to trap pheasants. We wrap the jaws with string so they don't cut the pheasant's leg.'

'That is a clever idea,' he says to me. 'Well, I've got some traps out in the morning, I've over three hundred snares out. Rabbit snares.'

I says, 'I need a wee place to stay.' There was a wee shed outside at the back of the garden.

I says to him, 'What's the shed for?'

'Och,' he says, 'there's nothing in it anymore, we used to have hens, but they died out.'

I says, 'Well, maybe I could stay there for a couple of days, to gie you a bit help till your finger gets better.'

He was the most pleasantest, kindest soul. You couldna go wrong. Although I'd never met Susan yet. She's still upstairs.

'Well, come on then,' he says to me.

It was a wee wooden shed. It was full of feathers, and a couple of hen boxes in it. I says, 'You got a brush?' It wasn't a brush he had, it was a birch besom. I swept it out, wooden floor, and he gied me a couple of black army blankets and a couple of coats.

'Ah! Snug as a bug in a rug,' I says. 'I'll sleep in here.'

'Oh,' he says, 'you can get all your food in the kitchen with Susie and me. You'll be seeing her in a wee while. Come on back in the house and have another cuppa.'

We're sitting there. He says, 'You know, Duncan, I feel I've got relief with my finger. It's not so sore as it was.'

I says, 'That's the salt taking effect.'

He says, 'Youse people are clever.'

Anyway, he made another two mugs of tea. Then I heard, scuff-scuff-scuff coming down a wee stair into the kitchen from the back. Here she comes. His sister Susan.

Susan would be about in her 50s. Her hair was short and grey but you couldnae see because there were hundreds and hundreds and hundreds of hairpins stuck in her hair, and they were rusty! She had a long skirt on her but I could see these old traditional combinations hanging down below the skirt, and I could see the black marks on her legs. And the wrinkles on her face was full of dirt, as if she had never washed her face for many weeks or months or a year. But, her two eyes was as blue as the eyes of a bird. She smiled and her teeth was out the front. Susan Mackenzie, who was to become like a mother to me. She was the most adorable soul I've ever met in all my life.

'Halloo!' she said.

I said, 'Hello, Susan.'

Angus said, 'This is Duncan, Susan, one of the Williamsons from Furnace.'

'Oh,' she says, 'aye, one of the Williamsons. I havena seen your mother or father for a while, since last summer. How are they?'

I says, 'My father's got a wee job working in the stone quarry in Furnace now, breaking stones.'

'And how's the rest of the family?'

I says, 'Well, the boys is away to the army, my sisters is away to the Land Army.'

'Oh dear. Well it'll be a wee bit relief to your mother,' she says. 'How is she?'

I says, 'She's fine.'

He says, 'Susan, he sorted my finger for me, and it feels a lot better.'

'Och, you know, Duncan,' she says, and she was so pleasant, 'I keep telling him to be careful but he's no as young as he used to be and he just gets so careless.'

'Well,' I says, 'Susan, he's got to go to Lochgilphead tomorrow and he'll have to get medical attention for that finger.'

'Well,' she says, 'mind, Angus, do what he tells you. Go up to the cottage hospital and get it properly dressed.'

He says, 'I will.'

And that night we sat and cracked. But this is the fun. Over in one corner of the little kitchen there was a barrel, a wooden barrel. Part of the lid was eaten away at one side; it would be rats or mice, and there's a wooden handle on the top of the barrel. I lifted the lid and I looked in: it was full of oatmeal. I put the lid back down. On the other side there was another barrel. While Susan's and Angus' backs was turned to me, I looked in the other barrel. It was full of flour. But the mice was coming in and eating into the flour and eating into the oatmeal. And you know when mice goes into these kind of things they drop their droppings. I wasn't very happy about this, so I went and got a couple of nails and I hammered and I nailed bits round the lid.

She says, 'What are you doing?'

I says, 'I'm mending your lid, keep the mice out.'

'Oh,' she says, 'we never give it a thought.'

Anyway, we sat and talked and it was a great evening. I sat and talked to them for hours. I had a wee bit supper with them. I boiled a pot of tatties, because he had a garden full of vegetables. Golden Wonders.

She says, 'You'll come in tomorrow and get a plate of porridge.'

'I'll come for a plate of porridge tomorrow.'

I bade them good night anyway. I wanted to leave them alone for a wee while. But my mind was still thinking about Rabbie and Betsy. I wanted to go, but I wanted to stay, because he had promised me five shillings a day, and he'd said to me, 'Do you smoke, Duncan?'

'Aye,' I says.

'Maybe I'll pick you up some Woodbine tomorrow when I go to Lochgilphead.'

'Very well.'

Next morning, I was up bright and early, about eight o'clock, spent a good night in that wee shed, quite nice and warm, comfortable. Had fags, matches, stomach was full of Golden Wonders and cheese. That cheese was good. I came in. She's up, her hair's full of hairpins. She's got a morning jacket on her, and you wouldna take it out of the skip. Ken, one of these morning robes and a string round her waist and old Angus is sitting by the fireside.

'Ye'll be having a plate of porridge, Duncan.'

'Well, to be quite honest with you,' I says, 'I'm not a porridge person.'

'Och,' he says, 'try a wee drop of it.'

I says, 'No.'

He says, 'Susan made plenty.'

I says, 'No, I don't like porridge.'

She had an old girdle, an old traditional metal girdle for making scones, see. And, 'Ye'll have a bit scone,' he says.

I sat down at the wee wooden table with the two of them, and he broke the scone in two. I could see the black pirls in the middle of the scone, and I see on his plate the pirls among the oatmeal, because she boiled them up: mice's droppings. But I was too polite, I didn't want to tell them. I mean it was their life, it was nothing to do with me.

Anyhow, I says, 'I'll no bother, I'll no bother. I dinna eat much in the mornings, but I'll take a drink of tea and have a smoke.'

I says, 'I'll go out to the wee stream. You got a bit of soap?'

She gied me a bar of carbolic soap, 'You keep that one, Duncan,' she says to me. And I went to the wee stream, I washed my face, washed my hands.

A wee while later, Angus comes out and he says, 'Duncan, I'm wondering, could we go and see about the snares? The lorry'll be coming in the afternoon.'

It was a wee lorry called Argyll Transport, it ran from Oban to Lochgilphead to Glasgow, and he had these big wooden hampers made of cane, like basket hampers with lids on them, with belts. No locks, belts. When the man took away two he left two, and these would haud up to 14, 15 pair of rabbits. You gutted the rabbits and put them in the hampers, and carried them away to the roadside and the wee Argyll Transport stopped, put the two loaded ones in and left two empties. Delivered into some poultry place in Glasgow. Oh no, he never skinned them, no, leave the skins on, just gutted them, cleaned the gut out o' them.

Anyhow, we goes up and I says, 'We'll take a few snares.'

'Well,' he says, 'we have a few out at the moment, nearly three hundred.'

'Angus,' I says, 'what we'll do, we'll close the traps and leave them till you get your finger better. Forget about the traps, just concentrate on the snares.'

So we had a good collection. I think we got about 40 rabbits.

'That's what my father used to do,' I says, 'you just take your knife,' – he gied me a shot of his pocket knife – 'split the legs, shove one lug through and go and get a big stick!' I hung a pair of rabbits on the stick and when I had about ten pair on that side, I hung them on the other side and then carried the stick across my shoulder.

He says, 'Duncan, I never seen this before.'

I says, 'That's an old idea how to carry rabbits.'

We reset the snares. He was delighted! He was over the moon. His arm was still in a sling, but that night we gutted all the rabbits, packed them in the hampers, closed the lids. Little lorry came and went away with two baskets, about 25 pair of rabbits. I knew he was getting about half a crown a pair. It was good money. And he was getting paid from the laird for keeping the vermin down. See? He couldna lose.

On the second day, he took his bicycle, you could hear him for miles, squeak-squeak the old rusty bike, and he cycled to Lochgilphead.

While he was away I saw a lot of stuff lying around the floor. In the corner was the big iron boiler and a wooden leg on it, and in below was the little stove. I seen all these things, dish cloths and things lying around the floor. Things that need to be washed. Even the tablecloth was in a mess. After it got too dirty she just threw it aside.

I says, 'Susan, I think I'll kindle the boiler fire.' There was a bag of coal at the corner.

She says, 'You do what you like. I'll go upstairs and have a wee rest.'

I gathered everything I thought was needing the boiler. I put the boiler on. Scrubbed it clean. Filled it full of water. Sitting on the floor was a big tin of washing soda. I put three handfuls of washing soda in the water.

I tidied the kitchen up, oh, I really worked hard while he was away. I made that place like a new pin inside. On the stair, but what did I find? Susie's combinations! They were like you took them out of a dung midden. They were as black and they'd never been washed for God knows how long. She must have got fed up with them. She took them off and left them at the foot of the stair. Well, they were so black that I wouldn't even put my hand on them. I got a stick. I lifted them with a stick and I popped them in the boiler with the washing soda, put the lid down, and the steam was rising. There was a wee hole at the side of the door for the steam to get out. I boiled everything in it. A wee while later, about an hour later she came downstairs. I took everything out the boiler. She had an old basket lying on the floor. Bits was all broken off it, the wee handles was broken. I packed everything in the basket.

I says, 'Susan, you any clothes pegs?'

She says, 'What hae you been doing?'

I says, 'I've been doing some washing.'

'Oh,' she says, 'the place looks really tidy. Place looks really tidy.'

I says, 'I've been tidying up.'

'Oh,' she says, 'you're a good boy.'

Anyway, I went out to the rope you know, the rope was hanging slack. I pulled the rope tight, hung up all that washing on the rope. Wee green at the back, just about the size of the wee hen shed where I lived. Got them all hung up, clothes pegs on them.

A wee while later I heard the squeaks of the bike. In Angus comes.

He always carried an old soldier's kit bag, like my old friend Paddy used to have. He used to have all the things he needed for Susan in the bag. Always hung it over the front of the bike. He came in and he had a clean bandage on his thumb. Still in a sling. He had the bag in one hand. He came in and he put it on the wee table. He looked all around and his eyes lighted up!

And he says, 'Somebody's been busy in here.'

'I thought I would tidy up.'

He says, 'You done a good job,' and he reached in and he brought out a 20 pack of Woodbine. 'That's for you, Duncan, a smoke for you,' he says.

I says, 'Look, forget your scone for the night, forget everything else. Let me make some Golden Wonders for you.'

I boiled them with the skins on.

She says, 'Duncan, have you tried the herring?'

I says, 'What?' My ears sprung up like a hare.

She says, 'Look over there.'

A barrel, a wee barrel, a wee firkin. Pulled the lid. Salt herring! And they were turning yellow with age. About two inches of grease on the top of the barrel. Oh! Oh, Lord, my soul, because this is what we lived on when my mother could afford it. My mother always traded for two or three salt herring and there's nothing more tasty than a salt herring, providing that you boil them with the tatties in.

I says, 'Angus and Susie, I'm going to make you something to eat tonight.'

'Oh well, go ahead.'

I went and got the wee grape and I dug a half a dozen big Golden Wonders, scraped them, put them in a skillet, put six salt herring on the top. Put them on the little stove, turned them. Brought them aboil.

I says, 'Right, supper tonight is tatties and herring.'

Three plates on the table.

They enjoyed that like they never had nothing in their life before.

She says, 'Duncan, we never done that.'

I says, 'That's what we do, my mother boils them. My mother taught me how to boil tatties and herring.'

They really loved it. We had a cup of tea and a smoke and we sat and talked and cracked, and the wind flapping.

Then she got up and she says, 'Duncan, when you were cleaning up, did you see my combies?'

I says, 'Yes, Susan, I saw your combies.'

She says, 'Where did you throw them?'

I says, 'I never throwed them.'

She looked. They were flannel combies. By the time they were through the boiler and boiled for about an hour with the washing soda, they were as white as that paper you have in your hand there.

I says, 'I'll go and get them for you.' I took them in, soft and dry, clean and warm, and I folded them on my arm. I brought them in to her. I says, 'There ye are, Susan, there's your combies.'

Ken what she done? She held them to her cheek, hey! And she smelled them. She says, 'Duncan, you done a wonderful job. I'll enjoy wearing them now,' she says, 'tonight.' She walked over to the mantelpiece and she took an Oxo box that held Oxo cubes. It was full of money. She reached into the Oxo box and she took an old brown ten shilling note, and she says, 'That's for you from me, a present for you.' She closed the box, put it back like that, full of money. Half crowns and shillings, and I wouldn't touch nothing in the house. I folded the ten shilling note and put it in my pocket.

I says, 'Thank you, Susan.' I'm thinking about my mother.

I was there for nearly a week. These two old people were like a mummy and daddy to me. I knew by this time Rabbie would be gone. He would be probably into Oban, back over Crianlarich, and maybe back to Perthshire because they only come on a tour. I thought to myself, I would only stay another few days.

The next morning it was time to go and collect the snares again. They were up making some tea. I came in and said good morning to them, and sat down.

'Would you like a cup of tea, Duncan?'

I says, 'I always love a cup of tea in the mornings.'

'Would you have some porridge?'

'No.'

'A bit of scone?'

'No, I'm no wanting anything to eat this morning.'

Susan was sitting there of course with her old morning jacket on and she had hundreds and thousands of these rusty hairpins in her hair. And I says to myself, they'll no be there tonight when I come back from the hill. I says, 'How's the hand this morning?'

'Oh, Duncan, I forgot to tell you – I got it dressed frae the doctor. After he undid the bandage and he saw the state of it he gave me an injection in my arm, in case of blood poisoning. And he said, "How long had it been like this?" I told him it had been a couple of days. And he says, "Who bathed it for you and who put the salt poultice on it for you?" "Och," I says, "a young tinker boy that's helping me with my rabbit catching seeing as I've only got one hand." "Well," he said, "let me tell you something, Mr Mackenzie, he might be a tinker but he saved your arm. He probably saved your life. You know, your finger was septic poisoning, it was going up your arm, but the salt put a stop to that and that's why you're here today."'

And Angus says, 'Duncan, you know, I owe you a lot. You prob'ly saved my life. Where did you learn these things?'

'Well, my granny,' I says, 'when she had a boil or the bairns had a wee septic finger, my granny's favourite thing was salt. She said, "Salt's the best thing in the world for poison."'

So we set off that morning, didnae get a lot of rabbits that day, set a few more snares and took the rabbits down to the house, and we started to gut them. But one of the rabbits must have been early. It was just after my birthday that I came to stay with them, 22 or 23 April. Angus gutted one of the rabbits, and, 'Oh Duncan, look at this!'

I says, 'What is it?'

'A mother in young.'

'Oh, Angus, you cannae send that away,' I says to him, 'you're better dumping that one with the guts.'

I'd dug a hole for dumping rabbits' guts in.

'Och no,' he says, 'the people that get them'll no know the difference. But I want my foetuses.'

I says, 'What?'

'I want the foetuses,' he says.

Wee unborn baby rabbits. He picked them all out of the wee lung bag, and I says, 'Angus, what are you... ?'

'Oh,' he says, 'they're a delight. Wait till you taste!'

'What?'

'Wait till you taste them,' he says.

'Taste that?' I says, 'I would go to jail before I would taste that. Let me put them in the bucket and let me dump them.'

'No,' he says, 'no, no. I'm going to have them for my tea.'

I says, 'Ye cannae eat that.'

'I'll show you,' he says.

There were about five of them, nae hair or nothing, just the skin, with their eyes closed. They werena even ready to get born. He put them on a plate in the kitchen. I couldna even look at them, but he took an old enamel battered aluminium skillet, and he put them in, he fried them, deep fried them, like chips, then he put them on the plate in front of him on the table.

That was the night I decided I was going the next day. That was the last straw.

And he says to me, 'Oh, would you like a bunny, Dunc?'

'No-o, thank you! Angus, I couldnae eat that.'

'Oh,' he says, 'they're delightful.' And he sat and he ate the whole lot.

'No,' I says, 'I couldnae go that, Angus, I couldnae go that.' I went outside and lighted a fag, still the thought in my head he was eating these wee foetuses, you know.

I went away for a wee walk along the roadway, and I came back and I came in, I had a cup of tea. I says, 'Susan, I'll have to get that hairpins out your hair.'

She says, 'Will you do that for me?'

'Aye, Susan, I'll do that for you. But I'll tell you something. They're no going back in again! You got a hairbrush?' It was one of thon old white – I can remember it just like yesterday – a white ivory comb, wide teeth on one side, close narrow teeth on the other side. I think she probably got it from my mother when my mother used to sell these things in the basket. One by one I picked all the rusty hairpins out. There were some of them rusted into her hair. I says, 'Susan, how do you manage to sleep with that at night-time?'

'Oh,' she said, 'I have to keep my hair in order.'

'You're no keeping your hair in order doing that!'

I took every one out, and I brushed her hair and I combed her hair and I brushed it. And she went to the mirror. That's the first time for the five days I was there, that she went over and put some water in a basin and washed her face.

Angus looked at her, 'By God,' he said, 'Susan, that's made a big improvement to you.'

She couldna help looking at herself in the mirror. I think that was the first time she had her hair combed in her life, since her parents had died. She really looked nice. You see if it had been now, at my age now, instead of being a 15-year-old, and her being a 55-year-old, I could have fancied her now, but not then! She wasna fat or stout or nothing, and she never wore glasses, no, one tooth at the front, one right in the middle, and I remember her just like yesterday.

Anyway, the next morning I rolled up the two blankets, folded the coats, closed the little shed door, had a cup of tea and I bade the two of them goodbye. They stood at the door there and he had tooken the sling off his arm.

He says, 'Duncan, my thumb's feeling fine, getting a little itchy.'

I says, 'When it gets itchy ye have nothing to fear! That's it getting better.'

'Well,' he says, 'I'll tell you something afore ye go; if ye're ever passing by again, please don't pass the door!'

I felt a bit sad as I left that morning and walked my way, hands in my pockets, to Lochgilphead. I took the bus up to Furnace, went up to see my mother and father and the kids.

It was a good job I got there by that time because it was Saturday afternoon and just before the shop shut. I gave my mother a few shillings and she went away to get some messages for the weekend. I stayed over the weekend with the old parents in the tent.

The Hook

THE PROGRESS OF THE recording for this book, one morning, came to another abrupt halt and for me the story of this impediment encapsulated my whole relationship with Duncan.

By the time I came through to the kitchen for breakfast, Duncan was sitting like a lowering November. I asked if he would like porridge. He growled, as if I should know that he didn't take breakfast, though my nose, once again, detected the lingering aroma of incinerated bacon.

'It's all finished for me. There's nothing left. No more storytelling.'

'Dear Duncan,' said I, 'your son Tommy, sleeping peacefully next door in the bedroom thinks you are the best daddy in the world, as does his sister Betsy and all the rest of your family. Wherever in the world you go you are hailed as King of Storytellers.'

'No,' he said, 'that's finished, I'm never going to tell another story. Last month one of my wee grandnieces died and no one took me to the funeral.'

'If you'd lifted the phone there's plenty folk would have jumped.' By now, I was tiring of the broody grumps. 'I have a friend in London who has MS, can't use his legs, his arms have nearly lost their power and he's not complaining like you. You're a grumpy old bear, everyone adores you, you have keys to this house and you are welcome at any time.'

No more was said. I retired to my workroom and a little later the door opened. Duncan had his coat on, threw his bunch of keys on the floor. 'You can stick these up your fucking arse, Mr Campbell,' and he strode out the front door.

I told our mutual friend Lindsay Porteous of this and on my birthday he left me a present, a pair of rubber gloves and a card with the greeting, 'Key Removers'.

It happened that the storytellers were having a networking and workshop day. Duncan was invited to come and tell a tale or two before lunch. He avoided and hated 'bloody workshops'. After his stories we were sitting at lunch and Duncan pointedly ignored me. I came to where he sat, tapped him on the shoulder and said, 'Duncan you don't need to worry about these keys anymore, Lindsay Porteous has given me rubber gloves to get them out again.' He had to laugh.

I went home, larded the rubber gloves with thick sticky chocolate spread, put them in a transparent plastic bag, placed that in a jiffy bag, inscribed a card with the words, 'You can return these to their original condition,' addressed the envelope to Duncan in Ladybank and posted it.

The next time I saw him, he produced the gleaming keys from his pocket and said, 'Look at that, not a bit of shite on them.'

Bless dear Lindsay.

Duncan's own sense of drama required some notable sign of our new reconciliation and he presented me with a silver ring to wear as a token of our renewed 'marriage'. It was either the tropics or the arctic with Duncan.

Our recording recommenced once more for the time being.

* * *

On Monday morning I thought I would go to Campbeltown. I had never been in Campbeltown. Now all my mother's people, the Townsleys, are in Campbeltown. Dozens of them. There'd be young lads about my ain age, lassies, my mother's cousins, my mother's uncles. The Townsleys were camped all right round the tip of Kintyre.

So the next morning, I took off. I walked all the way to Lochgilphead. I had no money left, spent it all. That night I slept in a little shed by the shoreside, a boat shed, and the next day I travelled on to Tarbert. But I didn't go up to see my Aunt Rachel, 'cause I knew she was gone. It was the year before that Aunt Rachel had drowned herself. Aunt Nellie was still around, but old Nellie I wouldnae go near because she just sat and talked to herself all night long and it was boring. So I travelled through Tarbert and I went down to Skipness.

I slept rough that night in Skipness, hungry, had no food or money. And I travelled on to a little village, Grubport. I was really hungry, I couldnae take it any longer! I sees a wee cottage down by the shoreside... and this was my Waterloo.

Maybe it was meant for me to go to that cottage. I don't know, but I walked down to the cottage because I seen a man and he was cleaning the net on the shore. I walked down. He was just a wee man, wee grey moustache, grey hair.

I says, 'Look, I come all the way fae Furnace, and I wonder if your wife could make me a wee cup of tea, give me a sandwich or something, I'm really hungry, starving. I'm looking for work.'

He says, 'Where are you from?'

'From Furnace.'

He says, 'Are you one of the Williamsons?'

I says, 'I am.'

'Hah! Are you one of Jock and Betsy's boys?'

'Aye, I'm one of Jock and Betsy's boys.'

'What's your name?'

'I'm Duncan.'

'Are you the one that played the shinty?' he says to me.

'Aye, I'm the one that played the shinty.'

'And,' he says, 'you played against Tarbert.'

'Aye, we played against Tarbert, we beat them three nothing in Tarbert, top o' the green.'

'I remember it well, I was at that game, and my boy Angus,' – Angus would be about 17 – 'he played for Tarbert. It was a disgrace. Come in, see the wife!'

He took me over to the wee house and this wee woman came out, short grey hair, freckled face, and he says to her, 'Mary, this is one of the Williamsons, one of the boy Williamsons from Furnace, Jock and Betsy's boy. I used to work with your father when they made the new road bypassing Furnace, the new cut. My name is Donald Mcgillivary, and this is my wife Mary.' He says, 'Are you busy at the moment?'

The woman took me into the house. Oh, she took me into the house right enough, into the kitchen.

She says, 'Have a seat.' She gave me a cup of tea, made me a big sandwich, cheese. I sat there.

He said, 'Where are you going to?'

'I'm going to Campbeltown.'

He had a wee Ford Eight van, green one. 'I take the wife down sometimes to Campbeltown, seen some of your folk sitting on the green there with their shawls on their shoulder, sitting around on the green with their pitchers of beer, cans of draft beer. Poor folk never trouble anybody, never bother anybody. You see them, their bonny weans, bonny kids. If you're not too busy, maybe I could give you a couple of days' work. I'm needing a wee bit help, Angus has gone off to work somewhere. I've got these nets to clean and my lobster creels to fix and things like that. Have you got a tent?'

I says, 'No, I dinnae hae a tent.'

'But,' he says, 'youse people are good at building tents.'

I says, 'Aye, we build wir wee summer tent, wee bow tent.'

'Well,' he says, 'come on with me!' and led me over to the wee shed. 'Look at that? Would that make a tent?' An old jib sail for a boat. White canvas. 'Could you make a tent with that? Do you see down there on the beach by the shoreside, see that wee stream there? That's where some of the campers camp. If you could build yourself a wee tent down there on the shore you could have a bite with me and the wife and I could give you a couple of days' work.'

He gave me the sail. I says, 'I havenae got a knife.'

'Oh, I'll give you a knife.'

There was a strip of hazel wood. I went up and he came with me and he watched me. I cut a few hazel boughs, long hazel saplings and he gien me some string. I stuck them in the ground, bound them over, threw the tent cover over, stoned it down with some stones. He looked into it.

'Man,' he says, 'that's a comfortable wee nest in there.' He called it a nest. I went and gathered some brackens, dry bracken, spread them on the ground.

He says, 'Maybe I'll get you something to sleep in. He went up to the shed and it was two big army coats he gave me, soldier's army coats from the 1914 War, and a blanket, a grey blanket. 'That'll keep you warm,' he says to me.

'Anyway,' I says, 'I'll be like a bug in a rug.'

In the morning we started to clean the net. He gave me a wooden needle and I mended the few holes, maybe from a ship, passing shark or something, and we went and mended the lobster creels. I spent the whole day with him.

The next day he says to me, 'Duncan, have you ever done any fishing?'

'Ah,' I said, 'fishing was our life! Not the kind of fishing you would do, commercially. Fishing was our life, Donald. We fished for fish to eat. I poached a few salmon forbyes.'

'Ach aye, well,' he says, 'it's all in the game. One for the pot.'

'One for the pot!'

'Well,' he said, 'I drag line fish. Have you ever done any drag-line fishing?'

'No, I haven't. I heard about it though.'

And this was to be my Waterloo.

'Well, I'm going to set a drag-line today for cod.'

Now, to let you understand about a drag-line. You have a 28 pound lead weight and you have a line as thick as that cable to your recorder, and that goes for about half a mile. Then every six foot, there's a piece of gut and a hook and it's all coiled in a basket in the back of the boat on one side. On the other side, at the back of the boat, there's a basket of shelled boiled mussels. We had a good four or five hundred mussels, two to a hook.

On the back of the boat is a wooden block, and a little hatchet. He explained to me, 'If a hook catches in your clothes or your sleeve or your hand, cut the line. You must cut the line! Otherwise it'll tear you to pieces with the weight. I'll row the boat. You sit, throw out the weight.' There's a ring on that weight to the end of the line and every six foot that that line runs out, a hook passes by; as the line goes out, you click two mussels on and off it goes. When that line's hanging out like a long strip all these hooks hang down the way with two mussels, and the cod comes along and swallows them. Then he gets caught by the hook!

'But for the love of your life,' he says, 'if a hook goes into your hand or your finger, cut the gut, not the line that the hook's on, and then we'll get the hook out of your finger.'

So we flung out the line. I must have baited about 50 hooks when all in a moment he said something to me. I turned round... and in it went! In there, one of the big hooks right in my hand! And with the weight of the line and the weight of the sea, it just ripped everything apart. I hadn't time to grab a hatchet in my left hand and cut it. It tore everything apart, and that finger fell that way, and that finger fell that way.

He looked at me, he said, 'Oh God, Duncan, you're in trouble.' And he reached over the boat and he took a hatchet and he cut the lines.

You see that hole in my thumb in there, and I cannae move these two fingers, these two are paralysed completely to this day. Anyway, he rowed into the shore, forgot about the line, never put a buoy in it or nothing. What you usually do when all the hooks were out, you put out a red buoy, so youse ken where to pick your line up.

'Let the bloody thing go, you're in trouble, boy,' he says to me. Rushed in, went to his wife and got a bit of rag. Blood was pouring from it. He started his van and he rushed me to Carradale to the doctor.

The doctor says, 'What's the problem?'

'Boy's been caught in the hook.'

Doctor says, 'He's in a bad way, but I cannae stitch it. I'll have to put a clip in it.' He put a steel clip in it, to hold it together, bandaged it up.

Donald took me home.

I stayed that night in the tent. Sat with him for a night and next morning I went away at breakfast. When I was leaving, I said, 'I have to go home, this hand's in a bad way.'

He walked into the house, 'Wait,' he said, 'I'll get you some money.' He handed me a five pound note, the first five pound note I ever had in my life. It was one of those with the plain paper back, the old five pound notes in the '40s, big! 'There you are, Duncan, that's for your damages, and that's for your help, that'll help you out aways. If you're ever back this way again, look in on me.'

So I walked on my way. I said, 'The best thing I could do is go to Campbeltown. If I dinnae see any of my mother's people, I can always take the bus.'

My hand was really sore, really bad, I had it in a sling. Doctor told me to keep it in a sling. I stopped off in Carradale and I walked into the little post office. I asked for 20 fags and the woman looked at me. Now I was clean and tidy, my arm in a sling. I handed her the five pound note and she looked at me. She looked at the five pound note, and instead of going for cigarettes, she went into the back of the post office. She went and phoned. I'm waiting because she took the money from me. I'm waiting on fags; fags was on ration, but she said she had a few. Tried to hold me. What did she do? She phoned the police! The local constable; he came with his bicycle. I was surprised to see the policeman, I never did any harm in my life.

He says, 'Hello, what's your name?'

I says, 'Duncan Williamson.'

'Where are you from?'

'Fae Furnace. My parents live in Furnace.'

'And what's wrong with your hand?'

'Eh, I got it caught in a drag line with Donald Mcgillivary.'

He said, 'Where did you steal the five pound?'

I says, 'What are you talking about? To steal five pound! I didnae steal nae five pound. That's for two days wages, forbyes that's to help pay for this. Donald Mcgillivary gave me that.'

'We'll soon find out,' he says. He went to the phone. Came back out, put his bonnet on his head, says, 'Give the young man his fags, give him his change!' He walked out.

That woman looked at me as if I was come from some other planet, as she counted out the change for five pound to me and gave me 20 Woodbine. That was the first and the last time I've ever been in Carradale.

I went to Campbeltown and stayed with my mother's people a wee while. They spoke a funny kind of language. The accent was kind of strange to me because they were brought up round about Campbeltown and Kintyre and some of them I couldna understand. Some of the lassies were nice.

Some of the young men my own age were a wee bit terrified about me because my father was supposed to be a hardy man. They would never come up the length of Furnace because my father had got the name, Big Jock Williamson, big wild man! My Uncle Duncan was married onto my father's sister. He was terrified. He had said things about my father that wasna true. That was because my father had hit him one day for slapping and kicking his wee boy. Then he'd said that my father was a big ugly beast of a man, would cause trouble with you in a moment, and me being his son, they didna make me welcome. I wasna even made welcome with my mother's own people.

From Campbeltown, I got the little bus up to Tarbert and spent a night with my Aunt Nellie.

Now for the first moment when you went in, Aunt Nellie knew who you were, would say, 'Hello, how's your father? How's your mother? Would you like a cup of tea?' But the moment she stopped speaking to you she went off on her own wanderings in her own mind. One night she says to me, 'If the snake hadnae crossed the road the man wouldnae been terrified of the snake.'

This is out of the blue. Ramblings! 'If the snake hadnae crossed the road, the man wouldnae hae been terrified, and the man wouldnae hae been knocked doon wi' the car. The snake managed to escape but the man was hurt. Whose fault was it? Was it the man's or the snake's?'

She gave me some tea and some food but she sat and talked to herself all night, and the most thing was about Rachel, her sister. 'She's happy noo. That's all she wanted. She's away swimming now in the sea, and I have to sit here, comb her hair while she swims away with the seals. What did she dae it for? Was she no as weel tae stay here with me? Why does she want to go away and droon herself?'

'Aunt Nellie,' I says, 'be reasonable. Maybe the woman had something wrong with her.'

And she says, 'Oh, you're here. I forgot you were there.'

I says, 'Aunt Nellie, come on, we'll go and wander for a way, get some sticks for the fire.'

If you went for a walk with her for some sticks she was sane, completely sane. But when she sat down, spent any time by herself, I could be outside the door doing something and I guarantee you'd think there was about 20 people in the tent with her. I couldn't stand any more of it so I went back home to Furnace.

It was 25 years, a long time, since Nellie's husband was killed. I wasna even born. He was killed up by Aberfeldy. She went back and lived by herself near her sister Rachel at Tarbert. Nellie lived there for the rest of her life. She was found dead through an overdose of drink. She was in her 70s. Nellie was the last of the old Williamsons; my grandfather was gone, my granny was gone, Rachel and Jeannie were gone, her sister Bella, my Uncle Duncan's wife; and Nellie was the last of my father's sisters. No, my father saw them all away, every single one of his sisters and brothers and he was the last of them. Nellie never had married again, she lived on her own but stayed within camping distance of my granny and grandfather; after my granny and grandfather split up over that carry on with Mrs Campbell's umbrella. Aunt Nellie was found one night... she liked a wee drink. She'd walk to Tarbert and buy herself a half bottle of whisky, which wasnae very much then during the war. The doctor said that they found her lying dead in the tent, choked with whisky. She was buried beside her father and mother and her sister Rachel in Tarbert, they're all in the same grave.

The next day, that was the bandages on my hand for three days. I never looked at it. I took my bandage off and my older brother George went to my father's tool box. He took the clip out with a pair of pliers. They were full of pus and green. I threw them away and my hand healed up. It left me with a paralysed forefinger and thumb till this day.

That very same cut was to stand me in good stead many years later when I was 17, because when I went for my medical (after the war you were supposed to do two years National Service) they wouldnae accept me in the army so they gave me a Grade Four.

Well after my accident with Donald Mcgillivary, I came back to Furnace again, back to the old tent in the forest in the woods where we lived with my parents. It took my hand a long time before it actually healed up and I was probably one handed for a long time, for at least a month. I couldn't use it properly because I lost the power of both these fingers. Oh, I could use a scythe, I could still cut with a scythe and I could still tie corn. I could still do a lot of things but a lot of things I couldnae do from then on. I couldna hold a pen to write, finger and thumb, canna hold a pen in that hand yet unless I stick it between the other two fingers. I had only the power of three fingers. I couldna catch nothing, building drystane dykes was past, out of the question. I couldn't clip anymore, couldna clip sheep because I couldna hold scissors in this right hand. And of course, you needed to do something to keep yourself alive.

Now during the war when food was on ration, there was always plenty of fish round the rocks because the quarriers had tipped up all the stuff from the quarry and made a bit point away into the sea at Furnace, and it was rich in fish. You could catch fish galore, but you needed to have bait. Of course if you went to the quarry to work in the morning, when you go home at night there was a long summer evening to fish. But what was the point, because probably the tide would be in and you couldn't dig any bait, and if you couldn't dig any bait you couldn't catch any fish.

Here out of the blue an old man came to me one morning and he says to me, 'Duncan, will you do something for me?' Old man, wee Donald, Gaelic speaker.

I said, 'Aye, what is it?'

He worked in the quarry. He said, 'Could you dig me some worms when the tide goes out?' Now on the beach you dig these big what you call rag worms, some of them was about two feet long. They have hundreds of feet on each side and they can bite you. They nip you like a crab, you've got to be careful. And he says, 'You can borrow my grape and put it back in the shed when you're finished, and I'll pay you for my worms.'

I says, 'Very good.'

So I went down and the tide was full out right on the beach, ah, worms galore! I dug a nice pail of worms, filled them full of sand, some salt water on the top, some seaweed to keep them fresh. I take them up, puts the wee grape back in the shed and I put the pail of worms in the corner where it was away from the heat, the sun. I left them there, went home. About half past four he came back down and he came up to me, 'Duncan, did you get me the worms?'

'Aye, I got you a pail of worms.'

'Oh,' he said, 'that's wonderful.' He put his hand in his pocket and he handed me half a crown. Oh, two and sixpence then was a lot of money! 'Ah,' I said, 'thank you very much.'

Then the word spread to the rest of his workers because he went that night, with his pail of worms to the tip. Now the way the fish goes, a big bamboo rod and you just tied the line on the point. About six foot from the point you had a big float, a big cork and from the cork downwards, a piece of cat gut and a big sea hook, and you put a big worm on it. You cast it out and you let the cork float in the deep about six feet from the hook. Then you sit and watch it. You just sit and smoke and watch your cork and you see the cork bob-bob-bob-bob-bob, wait and watch it bob, and you ken that there was something when down it goes, the cork float. You pull it up and it was rich and live, cod, rock cod. Of course, word spread that I was digging worms. One by one, all the men that wanted to fish that evening came to me and said, 'Could you get some worms?'

This became a trade to me, eh! Out of the blue. I could spend the whole day on the beach and fill a big monster pail of worms, a big pail of worms, and then I would divide them into different wee tins and canisters, some for you and some for you. That night you seen them all going away to the tip in the evening after their tea, the men from the quarry with their fishing rods. They're all sitting out on the tip full of worms. I was doing all right with my worms because the tide was out full when they were working, and when they came home at night the tide was full in.

But life gets kind of boring. It doesna matter what you are doing, especially if you're only 15 and you want to see a bit of the world.

The Ceilidh

AFTER THE STORYTELLING SESSIONS, during the Edinburgh International Storytelling Festival, we would often adjourn to my house for a ceilidh. Duncan would assume the mantle of *Fear an Tigh* and with equal measures of insistence and charm, persuade a song or story from everyone in the circle. At one notable such gathering, he gave his customary introduction.

'Tell a story, sing a song, show yer bum or out ye gang. And we don't want to see any bums here tonight.'

The sonorous reply of Hamish Henderson, the great folklorist, came from the doorway where he stood. 'And why not?' A response which amused Duncan sufficiently, knowing Hamish as he did, to recount on many subsequent occasions.

'The nicht drave on wi' sangs and clatter
And aye the *drams* were growing better.'

It was, that night, a glittering assembly: Old Willie McPhee, Traveller and gentleman of the road, his wife Bella, nut brown and wrinkled with beauty, Stanley Robertson, fey and pacific, Paraig MacNeil in philamore and his partner the consummate natural storyteller, Alison Millen, my wife Linda and many others. All contributed songs, piping and rivers of whisky talk.

I sat in deep conversation holding Stanley Robertson's hand, my frequent custom particularly after a few drinks, when I saw Duncan gaze with undisguised jealousy and affront at this betrayal. He looked as if he would burst into flame. It reminded me of another inflammatory night in this same room but like another time, another place, and I realised that I too travelled in two worlds.

Duncan with characteristically intense gaze

I belonged to, and was a founder member of, a group instigated by a man called Stuart McGregor, described by Sorley Maclean as a man of 'great vividness and great warmth'. This group, the Heretics, held monthly meetings with weel kent poets, writers, musicians and singers along with such fledglings at the time as Liz Lochhead, Donald Campbell, Bernard Maclaverty.

On this particular evening after a reading the company returned to Dundas Street. Amongst them were Hugh MacDiarmid, his friend and admirer, Norman MacCaig, Hamish Henderson, Douglas Gifford, then a lecturer in English, and an unanticipated protagonist of the evening to come, and Barnaby Hawkes, a friend, bon viveur, witty racounteur, quintessentially English, proud of it and simultaneously a lover of the Scots.

Barnaby, conscious of the great man MacDiarmid's anglophobia and consequently meaning to delight him with a rendition of the poet Willie Neill's satiric poem, 'The

English Politician', burst into a recitation with his strident Oxbridge voice.

> I'm an English Politician, Economic statistician
> And prognostication is my speciality
> And 'though I've always been mistaken
> England's God has saved my bacon
> By planting oil beneath the Scottish sea
>
> Now we all know that the Scottish
> Are a people dull and sottish
> Who dwell upon a rocky knuckle end
> And imprison all their art in
> Scots, gaelic, bagpipes, tartan
> But always do what Englishmen intend.

Barnaby did not have the chance to finish his rendition. MacDiarmid was sitting almost somnolently by the fire nursing a favourite Glenfiddich of which he was the patron saint. Being rather hard of hearing our anglophobic poet took Barnaby's outburst to be the invasion of the company by an arrogant English upper crust voice. The effect was as of igniting a lorry load of nitroglycerine, transforming benign saint to fire devil.

With his own penetrating vocal sharpness, and burning with non celestial fire, Mr MacDiarmid sat up and, at the startled Barnaby, blazed a volcanic tirade at all the 'touts and toadies and lick spittles of the English ascendancy.'

After this, in retrospect, comical fracas had subsided, the drama of the evening had not finished. The animosity that simmered between Norman MacCaig and Hamish Henderson somehow reached a steamy boiling point and Hamish hurled his whisky glass which smashed against the wall. Douglas Gifford stepped between the two to quell the battle, whereupon a lanky visitor, whose indentity I don't recollect, aimed at Douglas a drunken but misdirected punch which hit thin air and overbalanced the pugilist onto the sofa.

Dolina MacLennan who was sitting at MacDiarmid's knee, with an intuitive flash, burst into a beautiful Gaelic song. This induced a startled appreciative silence upon the company, which thereafter resumed the usual robust but congenial flytings.

At least Duncan's ire at this subsequent gathering was confined to the blaze in his eyes.

* * *

Sitting in the camp round the fire and the wee cruisie light above our head and the wind outside, father and mother would say, 'Where are you going to travel next to?' My father brought up the subject of Islay and where his father was born, in Bowmore. Old Willie Williamson: Uillium MacUillium.'

I said, 'Grandfather was born in Bowmore?'

'Aye, my father was born in Bowmore, Islay. Me and your mother used to spend some time there. I think there're some distant cousins or distant relations o' your own in Islay at the moment, the Williamsons.'

'Ah, ah.'

So, I got kind of itchy feet and I says to myself, 'About time I was going for a trip to Islay.' I had been in Arran and Gigha before I was 15 but I had never been in Islay in my life. Now you've got to go to Tarbert, and up past Tarbert to West Tarbert, and you get the boat to Islay, what takes about 45 minutes. I think it was twelve and sixpence at that time. I had saved a few pennies for my trip.

When we were in the tent the way to pass the evening was with songs and stories and singing, but I never actually ever did anything in public in my lifetime, apart from reciting a poem in school. I got the boat to Islay and I landed in Port Ellen, walked through Islay, and I was in the street one day and I seen this chap standing. I thought he was a Traveller man and I came up to him.

I asked him for a match, 'Can you give me a light?'

'Aye,' he said, 'I'll gie ye a light.' So he took out an old fashioned brass lighter. He gave me a light and says, 'Where are you from, boy?'

I said, 'I'm over from Argyll, from Inveraray, from Furnace.'

'Oh yeah, Furnace. What are you doing down here, you looking for work?'

'Aye,' I says, 'I'm looking for work.'

'Ach well, no much doing about here, but I'll tell you, have you ever been in Jura?'

'Nah,' I says, 'I never been in Jura. Where abouts is Jura?'

'Just the next wee island to this one, Jura. I've got an uncle over there in Jura. Have you ever cut any brackens?'

I said, 'Aye, I've cut brackens all my life, with my father, with a scythe. Ye dinnae need a very good scythe to cut brackens!' He laughed at me, you know.

'Well,' he said, 'if you would like to go over to Jura and cut some brackens for my uncle, Sandy Maclean, I could get you a job.'

'All right.'

'Anyway,' he says, 'I'll get in touch with him. I'll meet you tonight here.'

I said, 'What's your name?'

'Donald Ferguson.'

I wandered about there, got myself a cup of tea and that, but I did go back and I met Donald Ferguson that night.

And he said, 'I got in touch with my uncle. He said he'd be awful pleased you're coming to cut some bracken for him. What do you get?'

I says, 'Ten shillings a day.'

'Ten shillings a day!'

'Aye, I get ten shillings a day.'

I never got ten shillings a day for working in my life, it was only five shillings a day, ken. I never told him that.

'What are you doing tonight?'

I said, 'No very much, I should go and look for a place to stay, find myself an old shed or an old barn or something to pass the night away.'

'Well,' he said, 'I'm going out to a ceilidh tonight. Would you like to come along?'

'What is a ceilidh? I heard the word. Is it some kind of a sing-song or something?'

'Aye, it's a few friends on the farm, friend Jimmy MacTaggart and he's got a farm out there. I'll pick you up.' I didn't know he had a car. 'Anyway,' he says, 'you meet me here tonight and I'll pick you up.'

I met him and he had an old Ford van, an old blue Ford Ten van. There were about five or six young people. He put us all in the back of the van. I hadna a clue what we were going to do. What was I doing in here in the first place? I was a stranger, I was a Traveller. What am I doing among all these young folk, well, some of them young, some of them old? There were about six or seven of us in the back of this strange van and he drove up this old farm road into this farm square. There was about five or six old cars lying on the farm square when we got there, maybe about seven o'clock, and we went to the door. This man came out, big tall guy.

'Come in, boys, come in!'

I didna want to go in, I couldna go in! I stood till everybody else went in, you see. Donald Ferguson was standing cracking to him. I'm still standing at the door because I had never been invited, see? They had come, they were invited, they'd been there before.

And he says, 'This is Jimmy MacTaggart.'

I said, 'Yeah.'

'This is one of the Williamsons,' he said, 'fae Furnace, over fae Loch Fyneside.'

'Well, you better come in, young man!'

'I can come in, but to be quite truthful, I've never been at this kind of thing before. What is it, a sing-song, a story or something?'

'Ah well,' he said, 'a bit of both. Do you sing yourself?'

'Ach, a wee bit,' I said, 'I sing sometimes.' I telt him I was a Traveller.

'Makes no difference what you are, we're all friends here, everybody's the same here in my house.'

He brought me in. Everybody's sitting all around the house, big fire burning, big old fashioned grate, big iron kettle sitting on the top of the stove. But the thing that took my eye to start with, right on the table was a big bowl, like the women use for baking in, big monster bowl. And that bowl was full of hard boiled eggs with the shells off. I never seen so many boiled eggs in my life before. War was still going strong, things was on ration. Then the woman came in and she placed a big plate of scones, homemade scones on the table. I thought we'd come for a meal, but naebody seemed to never touch nothing, you see what I mean. This was very strange to me, this was a new world to me, I never knew this kind of thing before. Jimmy MacTaggart and his wife, Mary Ann I think was her name, big tall woman, dark hair.

He stood up. 'Well,' he said, 'ladies and gentlemen, it's a great pleasure to have you all here.' He had this Highland accent. 'Tonight, I hope that everybody enjoys theirself. I hope we'll be able to hear youse all tonight, and get a wee song or a story from you or a poem or something, keep the ball rolling, we'll make sure the radio's turned off.'

I said to myself, 'This is fine, eh!'

He says, 'There's not much for to eat as far as the food goes, but if anybody's hungry, there's plenty eggs and scones there.' He went to the cupboard and he brought out a full bottle of whisky and his wife went round and she got glasses, bonnie wee glasses, and she put them all on the table. And then she went and she filled a jug of water, poured a big jug of water and she put it on the table. I didnae drink at the time, I never took any drink of nae kind. He offered me a drink.

I said, 'No.'

Then this woman she started to sing. Oh God, Gaelic. I wish you could have heard her: it was the most beautiful voice of a woman I've ever heard in my life. Anyway, they all took a shot of singing, but they never bypassed me. I'm sitting at the end of the table, a wee bit, ken, a wee bit feeling strange, ken, I feel out of place, because this is my first time here, first time I get in this kind of thing.

And it was Donald Ferguson said, 'Duncan, are you going to give us a song?'

And everybody was quiet. I felt a wee bit embarrassed, you know. I was only 15 past and I still had this bad hand. I had to keep it shut to keep people from seeing these two fingers.

I said, 'Yeah. We do a lot of singing in the tent.' Of course, by this time everybody knew I was a Traveller and I told them about getting my hand cut and things, had a bit crack to them. Everybody seemed interested.

They said, 'Will you sing us a song then?'

'Well I'll sing you a song or tell you a story, my granny tellt us plenty of songs and ballads and stories in song, and eh, I'll sing ye a song.' And that was the very first song I sang to them, 'The Cruel Grave', I remember it just like yesterday, one of my granny's favourites.

'The Cruel Grave' was the story of a young sailor man going off to sea and he left his girlfriend behind him, and she waited and waited and waited, and she waited for seven years, but he never came back. She never got in touch with anybody else. She never had another boyfriend, she never did nothing, she stayed with her parents. But every night when she went to her bed she would lie there praying, praying and praying and praying that God would send him back to her so she could have him once for all. Because of her such a-praying his soul could not rest because he had been drowned at sea, and they just wrapped him in a piece of burlap sack, what they used to do with the sailors, and just dropped him over in the sea, buried him at sea. She didn't know about this, 'cause to them, the sea folk, he was just another sailor. Anyhow, she kept praying, she prayed for seven years every night. Then one night when she went to her bed she heard a knocking on the door. Couldna be her father and her mother, no, must have been somebody late at night. Who could it be? So she went and there he was standing at the door, pale as a sheet, soaking to the skin. She was a bit startled, she said, 'What do you want?'

He says, 'I want you, I've come to visit you.'

She took him in, she looked at him and she saw that his colour had changed. He was white, pale. He told her to open the door, 'Let me in, I'm cold and I'm wet and I'm soaking.'

She brought him in but she was a wee bit strange, and she sat a wee bit apart from him, but then when they begin to talk she realised that it was her sailor boyfriend that she'd never seen for seven years. So they sat talking for a while, and then they went for a wee walk outside because the early morning was coming in. It was a summer's morning. They sat down outside and she coaxed him.

He says, 'Look.' The cock started to crow, just the cock crowed once, small little cockerel on the farm where they lived crowed. He stood up and he says to her, 'Look, I have to go,' but she begged on him, she preached on him, begged him not to go. He told her straightly, 'I have to go, there's no way I can stay. But do one thing for me. When I'm gone I won't be coming back but don't pray anymore for me. Stop praying because it's no matter though you pray to the end of your life I can never return.' And he was gone.

You see, you're supposed to love a person when they're alive, let it be your sister, your brother, your father, your mother, you love them dearly, or your wife. But once they are dead you're not supposed to love them the same way. You're supposed to let them lie in peace because if you worry about them, if you think too much about them, if you still love them after they're gone, then their soul can never rest. So I explained the story, everybody listened carefully. Some of them had never even heard it before, and I sang the song. I'll sing you the first verse.

O it's seven long years since my true love left me,
It's seven long years since he went to sea,
But another seven I will wait his pleasure,
Till he comes home and he marries me.
Now I lie in my bed and I often wonder,
I lie in my bed and I often pray,
I pray to my dearest God in heaven,
Would he send my true love back home to me.

This was the song I sang in that ceilidh, the very first ceilidh in my life. Everybody seemed very impressed. That was the ice broken, and that night when the whisky went round I didn't take any drink, I had a couple of boiled eggs and a scone and that. I remember it fine. MacTaggart's wife gave us all a cup of tea. I must have sat there till about ten o'clock and one by one people had a dram and they brought out some more whisky. I can remember just like yesterday. You'd prob'ly remember the bottle he had put on the table, it was Haig's whisky from Markinch, thon three cornered bottle with a little net round it, like a rabbit's snare, you know, wire round the bottle, Haig's whisky. I didn't know what Haig's was. I'd never been in Fife: it was just a name to me, but it was to become well known to me in future years. So anyway, we all piled back into the old van.

Donald Ferguson says to me, 'Duncan, what are you going to do tonight?'

I said, 'I'll sleep in the van.'

'Well, I'm no working in the morning, but I want to take you over to my uncle's. He's got a job for ye, he needs you to cut some bracken to let the grass up for the sheep.'

I slept in the van that night. He gave me a couple of blankets. The next morning, he gave me a mug of tea in front of his wee house. We crossed to Jura on the little ferry the next day in the van. He took me out to old Sandy's. He dropped me off at the farm, it was all rocky and hilly, but it was covered and buried in brackens.

Sandy pointed out to me, this is true, 'You see that wee cottage over there in the distance?'

I says, 'Aye.'

'That's the house where George Orwell was inspired to write his books out there.' You could see it in the distance. 'That's his cottage,' old Sandy told me.

It was late in the year that George Orwell was there at that time. In the film they used the same cottage – I knew it well because I cut bracken not far from it.

There was an awful lot of deer on Jura. So I says to Sandy, 'You ever get any?'

He says, 'I dinnae need to go look for the deer, Duncan. I just wait till one comes walking by and can pop 'em with a rifle from my window. I don't need to go hunting for deers. They come to me.'

Anyway, he gave me an old scythe and I slept in the stable. There was nae hay. He had nae horses, the horses was all gone by that time. I slept in a stall in the stable and I cut all his brackens to him, took me three days, cut them all, big green brackens. Scythe was sharp, I could grip the scythe with my hand because the hand had healed up. Two fingers were paralysed, but I could still grip the scythe.

He said, 'You're a good hand with the scythe.'

I said, 'Ach aye, you got to watch for stones though, that's the problem. If you hit a stone you're ruined.' He gave me a sharpening stone for the file.

'Come down during the day,' he said, 'and get a bite to eat, aye.'

'Be fine, I'll be back later on.'

But it was good. I never met anybody else there. I never met anybody else excepts him hissel.

But the ceilidh was very good, I really enjoyed the ceilidh and that was my first experience in singing at the ceilidh. I came back from Jura, I went back then to Donald Ferguson's again. I wouldna go and leave without saying goodbye. I did have a wander round, but it wasna for me. No it wasnae for me, but I wanted to have the experience of being on Islay where my grandfather was born, in Bowmore. I went there, and that's where I had the first ceilidh. I did sing a couple of other songs that night and I did tell a story. I told the Traveller's story about the tinker and the fairies, and they really enjoyed it.

They said, 'What kind of stories do you tell in the tent, Duncan?'

They all gathered round, I felt at home then with the people, you know, they're so friendly. I said, 'Granny tells us stories and we all tell stories.' So I told them this story.

'There was this Traveller man, tinkerman, and his wife, and two wee boys. They had a wee handcart. He was a piper. He piped at all these guest houses and that. That's where he made his living, playing the bagpipes and his name was John MacDonald, well known piper among the Travelling folk. Anyway he came to this little camping site one night, him and his wife. It was a camping site for Travellers, used frequently, because in these days back in the '40s any old quarry and old right of ways, old roads – the places were left open for the Travelling folk providing they didna make too much a mess. The land owner didna seem to mind because they didna stay very long, maybe a night, maybe two nights and they moved on. But it was always provided they left the place clean, left no rubbish behind them, then they were okay. Otherwise, they would have closed it. The Travellers began to realise this, so therefore they kept the places tidy as possible, left no sticks, left no rubbish around. In these days things was so hard they didna carry very much with them and they were there, then gone.

Anyway! The old man and his wife and two wee boys came to this campsite, and he'd been there before, before the kids were born. Two wee boys he had, maybe a year between them, and his wife. A Traveller woman can put up a tent as good as a man, you know. They were very clever.

So he says to her, "Mary, you put up the tent and I'll go over to the big house over there. I'll play the pipes in the big house and I'll go round to the cook at the back door, maybe get a bit o' meat for the bairns, the weans." See! She had a few things, like tea and sugar and that, but she didna have very much food. Things was very hard for Travelling folk.

Instead of going round the road he crossed the field. The woman put the tent up, good job of it she made, stoned it down, went and collected dry grasses for the bed for her two wee boys and herself, hung the door close on, kettle on the fire, made a wee cup of tea, black tea without milk for the wee laddies, maybe gave them a wee bit o' bread or something, whatever she had. But she waited and she waited and she waited and she waited. Nah, John MacDonald never came back. She couldna wait though she waited a week. He was gone. She had to leave the next day.

"Ach well," she said, "I have to go. I cannae keep the weans sitting here. I'll have to go and look for something to eat for the wee bairns." So she packed her wee tent, she had a little pram, she packed her wee tent in the pram, put the youngest boy on the top and she pushed down to the village.

That wee Mary MacDonald lived herself with her two boys for 20 years! The two boys grew up, Sandy, and John, called after his father. They grew up young men but they never married, they never took a wife.

They wouldn't leave their mother for nobody breathing. And the woman now began to get kinda old, up in years. The boys worked and they bought a wee pony and a wee cart, so they could gie their mother a hurl, what was the popular thing to dae.

But, 20 years later, they came back to the same place, two young grown men in their 20s and their old mother. Boys put up the tent quickly for their mother and one for theirselves, kindled the fire, made their mother a cup of tea. This old woman now was up in her 70s. And lo and behold, out of the blue the pipes start to play, and the old woman listened, and she listened.

She says, "Boys, listen!" And the two lads listened.

They said, "Mother, somebody's playing the pipes." They'd never learned to play the pipes.

"Boys, I'll tell ye something," she said, "if I'm no mistaken, that's your father that's playing the pipes."

"But, Mother," they said, "my father's been gone for 20 years."

She says, "That's the house your father went to 20 years ago over there," and she said, "he never came back, but that's his piping." The pipes came a bit closer and closer. Then they watched.

And in he walked. The pipes stopped. In he walked with the pipes under his arm. "Are you there, woman?" he said, and he looked at the old woman sitting there. He was not one day older since the day he left, but she was. He says, "I'm looking for my wife and my two weans."

She says, "I'm your wife."

He says, "You're no my wife. My wife's a young woman, what are you doing here, and whaur the horse come fae?" The boys got a horse.

She says, "John MacDonald, sit down and tell me where you've been for the last 20 years!"

"What do you mean, woman?" he said, "I went over there five minutes ago, or ten minutes ago, and I got to the house. I blow up my pipes and the old man came out to me, an old gentleman, and he said, 'For God's sake, man, for God's sake, would you stop, would you stop that noise? It's driving me crazy! Is it no enough that I've got to suffer it all day long, that you come when I've got to suffer it inside the house.' So I stopped my pipes.

'What's your problem?' I said.

He said, 'Them, them, down the stairs in the basement, them, never give me peace. They're driving me crazy. I'll give you anything to get rid o' them.'

I said, 'Who you want rid of?'

'The wee folk,' he said, 'the little ones. They play and they dance and they dance and they play all day long and it's driving me mad.'

'Where are they?' I said.

He says, 'Down the stairs in the basement.' And the old man led me to the steps of the big house, down to the basement, and he lifted a trap door.

'Now,' he says, 'down there.' And he closed the trap door behind me."

Afterwards, John MacDonald swore he went down into that trap-door, it was a cellar below, and it was lighted with flares on the walls that never seemed to go out. There were dozens of them, little folk, and they're all playing the pipes, bagpipes. They're singing and dancing and drinking. They invited him down, and he sat with them, and they made him play, and they gave him drink and they gave him money, gold coins. He played and he drank and he played with them, till at last he fell asleep and when he awoke they were gone.

He climbed up the steps, pushed open the trap door. It was creaking and full of cobwebs and when he came up the old steps the old house was in ruins. Out to the front door everything was overgrown with grass. He walked across and the one thought he had in his mind was his wife and his two wee boys. Where in the world had he been?

John MacDonald had been with the fairy folk for over 20 years and when he came back and told his wife the story of where he had been, she sat there an old woman, and he said, "If you don't believe me," hand in his pocket, and he put a handful of gold coins in her lap, "I didnae get nae food, but I got enough to buy food with. Who's the two men?"

She says, "Two men? That's your laddies, that's your weans."

John MacDonald never left his old wife again till she was an invalid, till she died. The two boys got married and went their own way.

John MacDonald told that story to many many people. People remember seeing the old widow wandering with the two children by herself because she never took another man till John MacDonald came back to her 20 years later.'

That's the wee story I told in the ceilidh. It's called 'The Tinker and the Fairies'.

Hitler

WE WERE IN MY campervan, a cold night outside Mintlaw in the North East, but with a wee dram for me, a super lager for Duncan, we warmed up and took out the tape recorder. Duncan announced. 'I'm going to tell you about the time I buried Hitler.'

I supposed this was going to be a joke and, as the recording continued, I wondered when and if he would get to the point, or if the super lager had dictated a different narrative.

* * *

One day I was down in the village. I went for something for granny. The war was still going strong and of course sugar was on ration.

One thing granny liked was these big Granny Sookers, lozenges, and you would get about six for a penny. If you bought a sweetie you couldna buy the sugar and if you bought the sugar you couldna buy the sweetie. So granny was allowed half a pound of sugar per week and instead o' buying the sugar she used to give her sugar coupon for this big poke of lozenges, still called today Granny Sookers. When she made a wee drum of black tea she would pop one of these things into it: it would keep her going for a week.

One day Jimmy Munro in the post office beckoned to me.

I said, 'What's he wanting?'

'Duncan!' He knew who I was 'cause I played shinty with his son. He said, 'Duncan, the're a postcard here for you?'

'A postcard? For me?' Penny stamp on it, a green penny stamp, and writing: 'Dear Duncan Esquire, I was wondering if you'd come up and give me a wee help, I'm really stuck with the dipping. Yours truly, Duncan

Macvicar, Achnagoul.' The first postcard I ever got in my life. I'm going 15 past, my first postcard.

So I went up. Of course my mother couldnae read, my father couldnae read, my granny couldnae read, so I read it to them. Now it was four miles from Furnace to Achnagoul, on the road to Inveraray. I'd worked with my father with old Duncan before, I'd clipped his sheep before, I'd done a lot of odd jobs for him.

He used to live with two old sisters, his aunties, Morag and Chrissie. He had a wee farm up on the hill, called Achnagoul, in Gaelic it means the field of the foreigners. It was only five shillings a day, that's all you got: he never paid any more, but he paid you every night, two half crowns every night and he gien you all your food and you ate in the house with him. Oh aye, I used to cook boiled tatties for him, and he would let you do the cooking. He'd just sit in an old chair. Upstairs in his room he had a lovely bed. You know he never slept in that bed up the stairs since one old auntie went away to Inveraray, and she died, and then Morag, she vanished completely. She never was found. People searched the hills for her; they searched the River Douglas for her, they searched everywhere, but till this day nobody can tell you what ever happened to old Morag Macvicar.

From the day this old sister went amissing, Duncan never again went upstairs to that front bedroom. He would never go upstairs to that bed. Oh no, he had there two big fireside chairs and at night-time he'd put them together and sleep in front of the fire and the two dogs would sleep on the floor by his side. He'd never bring up the subject of Morag, his auntie. Some people said that he'd done away with her, but nah, I don't think so. I did get him a wife in later years that he spent his entire life with, but that's another story.

So the next day, I made my way up to Achnagoul. He would be in his 60s. I would be 15 past. He was pleased to see me.

He said, 'The police was up. They're coming back again.' In these days, when a farmer started dipping the sheep they had to have the presence of a policeman to certify that they really dipped the sheep for fluke and all these diseases sheep takes. He says, 'I need a wee help to gather the sheep and get them penned. It's only me and Lachie and you ken what like Lachie is, he's that slow. It'd take Lachie a week.' (That's Lachlan, him that I was telling you about, him with the dog Sam that loved his plums.)

Anyhow, we had a cup of tea and he got his bag. He always carried a bag with him, a pair of shears, a sharpening stone, a file, pair of pliers, and he put it all in his bag. We'd walk up the hill and he had one old horse and it was as old as the hills, but it was a good worker, quiet as a sheep, and the name of this horse was Hitler. Hitler was his name. And you know, the sorriest thing was, I worked old Hitler many's a time, but one day I had to go and bury old Hitler and I buried old Hitler out in the field where he fell. I went out one day to get him, a halter in my hand to bring him in. I think he was going to use him for the cart or something and I went up to him. There he was lying, two eyes closed. I gave him a touch with my foot, nah, stiff as a bone.

So I hurried back, I says, 'Duncan, old Hitler is deid.'

'No, Duncan,' he said, 'he cannae be!'

I said, 'He's deid!'

Him and I walked down to old Hitler, 'Aye,' he said, 'he's gone, poor old bugger. We'll have to bury him.'

'Well,' I says to him, 'best place noo is to bury him where he is because we cannae drag him.'

'No,' he said, 'that's true. We've no way of moving him.'

'I'll tell you what I'll do,' I said, 'tell Lachie to come down with me and bring the picks and spades and we'll dig a hole right at his back, up close to his back. We'll dig a big deep hole. Me and Lachie'll coup him over into the hole, and we'll put him in.'

He said, 'Duncan, you would maybe break his leg with an axe before you put him in.'

I said, 'No, we'll no break his legs. What do you want to break his legs for? Dig a big, wide enough hole.'

'But, I mind my father telt me when you bury a horse or a cow, it's far better to break their legs because you dinnae need to dig such a big hole, and you bend their legs up close to them.'

I said, 'Duncan, Lachie and me will dig the hole, we'll bury the old bugger.'

So Lachie came down, and Lachie stepped out to measure him. Lachie tried to measure the horse, the same thing as a sheep.

'Lachie!' He wanted to dig a track for his feet, a track for his hind feet. I says, 'Lachie, for God's sake, we dig a square hole.'

Lachie said, 'But we'll no need to dig a square hole, if we just dig him the shape of the horse's body and we can roll his legs in. We could dig a bit for his front feet, a bit for his back feet and then a wee bit for his head.'

'No, Lachie, that's nae good! We must make sure that the hole is deep enough, because if we put him in the hole the're no way we're going to get him back out. We'll just dig a big hole right up close to his back and cowp him in!'

So we dug a hole four foot square, and, 'Do you think it's big enough, Duncan?'

'Well, no, it's no big enough yet. We'll need to go another bit yet.' So I and Lachie went down into the hole and we dug and we dug and we dug, big four foot square hole, right at old Hitler's back.

'I think it's deep enough now, Duncan,' he says, 'it's deep enough now.'

'Ah well, we'll see anyway,' I said.

And he says, 'We'll birl him over.'

He got his front legs and I took his back legs. There wasna much on old Hitler, he's as thin as a nail and we bended him in a bit, but when we got him in, his head was out still sticking out, and he's lying in the hole but his head's sticking out of the hole.

'Duncan,' he says, 'do you think we could bend his neck a wee bit?'

I said, 'Aye, you bend his neck a wee bit.'

So he jumped back in the hole and he got his arms round the wee horse's neck and he's pulling its head down between its front legs, and then he put his foot to it and I heard its guts going, 'wheeagh', and at last he put his big tackety boot down and he pressed his heel down and got its head between its front legs. Then he wanted to make a wee cross above his head.

I says, 'Lachie, it's not a human being you're burying.'

'Ach,' he said, 'I'm goin to make a wee cross, a wee cross for Hitler.'

Honest to God! He went down and he got a bit rope and two bits of hazel stick. He made a wee cross and he stuck it above Hitler's grave, and he said, 'Ach, in case Duncan comes in, he'll know fine that we made a good job o' him.' And that's what he did.

I used to walk past that wee cross months after that and it was still standing there. You could see it in the middle of the field. Lachie's Cross, they called it.

The Jackdaw

DUNCAN LOVED TALL TALES and practical jokes and I have been accompanied, more or less since childhood, by an elf of mischief. I inherited this trait from my mother. I gloated at Duncan's outrage when he realised I had him hooked with some far fetched tale. It was one of our games.

During transit on a story trip we were making to Toronto a boarding official informed him, 'Your wheelchair will be coming, Mr Williamson.' For once he was speechless. A little joke I had arranged. I told him he was a fool not to accept it and have me hurl him through the busy airport.

He loved this kind of mischief.

One evening, when we returned from a school's story-telling day, Duncan and I were sitting in the kitchen in Dundas Street with a visitor from New Zealand who had been sightseeing in Edinburgh's Old Town. He remarked on the number of one-legged pigeons he had seen in Waverley Station.

'How can there be so many of them?' he asked.

Up jumped the elf. 'You don't know the story?'

'No.'

'Have you heard it Duncan?'

'No.'

The hook was baited.

'Well,' said I, 'in the 17th century a great famine devasted the city of Edinburgh. People starved, people died and a city councillor suggested pigeons should be killed to provide food. "No," said the Lord Provost, "if we kill them they will be gone forever. Let one leg be taken off the birds to make soup. The people will get a bowl of one-legged pigeon soup and the pigeons will be free to fly around the city and produce in their likeness." '

'What an amazing story, David,' said the visitor. 'And these pigeons in the city today... '

'These,' said I, 'are descendants of the old pigeons. Their reward to this day is free crumbs. The custom, if you walk in the station, is that you should give a few crumbs, a token of gratitude.'

By now, I could see that Duncan had rumbled my nonsense and I sometimes wonder if our antipodean friend took that tale home with him. This mutual tale stretching shortened many a journey Duncan and I took in my van.

* * *

Old Duncan Macvicar was the strangest you ever saw in your life. Out of the blue he would say, 'Duncan, what do you do in the tent at night?' And ask question after question. I would try and give him the most far-fetched answers in the world and he'd believe me. And then he would say, 'Duncan, how do you eat tatties in the tent at night-time? How do you eat them?'

I said, 'We eat them just the same as anybody else eats them.'

'But how do you cook them?'

'Ah,' I said, 'you want to know?'

He says, 'Yes, I would like to know.'

'Well,' I said, 'my mother puts a big pot of tatties on.'

'Yes.'

'And she puts some salt on them. Bring them aboil. And my father goes into the wood and he cuts us all a sharp stick and you stick the stick into them and eat them like toffee apples.'

'Amazing,' he said. 'I never seen tatties eaten like toffee apples before.'

He believed everything you said. He was an inquisitive old man, but he was the heart of corn, he was a gentleman at heart. He said to me, 'You know, Duncan, I was up on the hill the day afore I wrote you the postcard.'

And he said, 'I took the gun with me.'

He had an old shotgun. There's a story about that shotgun you'll be hearing in a moment and I could take it any time I wanted and go and shoot a pair of rabbits for my mother. He had a box of cartridges sat above the fire – I was always afraid they would fall in the fire and explode. I used to keep shoving them back from the mantelpiece.

'Anyway,' he said, 'there's a wee loch on the hill and I shot this bird, thought it was a goose, but it was a swan and I shot the bugger.'

I said, 'You're not allowed to shoot a swan, Duncan.'

'I didn't know it was a swan, I still have it. It's hanging on the back door.'

I said, 'What are you going to do with it?'

He says, 'That's what I'm asking ye, how do you cook it?'

I said, 'I'll tell you what I'll do with you, Duncan.' I says, 'You go down to the beach and you get two pieces of wood.'

'Aye. But what am I going to do with two piece of wood?'

'It's got to be driftwood, wood that comes in with the tide, saltwood that's been in the sea a long time.'

'What would I do with that?'

I said, 'You take two nice pieces of it, then you put these each side of the swan, and you tie a bit string round it, the swan in the middle and you put it into the oven, big old iron oven by the fire. And you roast that for three hours.'

'Oh, I see,' he says.

'Let it cook with the wood on it,' I said. 'Aye, it cooks fine with the wood on it, and the flavour, you've no idea of the flavour.'

'And what do you do then?' he says.

I says, 'You just throw it away.'

'What do you mean,' he said, 'throw it away?'

I said, 'You throw away the swan and eat the driftwood. The flavours of the swan goes into the driftwood.'

'Ah,' he said, 'would it no be hard on your teeth and your stomach?'

I said, 'No, that's the only way you can do it. You're no allowed to eat the swan.'

'I never knew that,' he said.

He was so simple.

I said, 'We've got a pet jackdaw in the tent.'

'A pet jackdaw?' he said.

'Aye,' I said, 'aye. Jackie, we got him out the nest when he was a wee baby without any feathers on, we brought him up for the kids for a pet. He's a lovely wee bird and we love him dearly.'

'A jackdaw?' he said. 'It's a kind o' skittery bird,' he said, 'are you no afraid that they'll skitter in your tea?'

I said, 'That's what we keep it for. I love when a jackdaw squirts in your tea, it's the best.'

'Oh no,' he said, 'you don't tell me that you like the jackdaw's droppings.'

'Oh,' I said, 'Duncan, it's the best in the world. You never tasted jackdaw's droppings in your tea?'

'No.'

And you could go on with him like that for hours.

I said, 'In fact we fight about it to see who's going to get the next dropping in our tea. Me and the lassies and the boys we fight about it.'

'Oh, I don't believe it.'

I said, 'That's the way it is. We fight over the jackdaw's droppings. First come, first served!'

Anyway, I had great fun with him and I stayed with him many, many times before I left school and after I left school.

One day after dinnertime, I looked out the back window, and here's a big brown hare sitting, popping away out of the grass, two big ears up, big brown hare! Now, I've seen many mountain hares, white hares or blue hares as they call them, but very, very rarely do you ever see a big brown hare. It was right up the back of the kitchen window and sitting crumping away this big hare, and I knew fine it was within shooting reach, you see!

Old Duncan's sitting smoking his pipe by the fireside, a fire of sticks on. I reached over, the gun was in the corner. He'd always keep it in the corner. I picked up the gun.

He said, 'Where are you going? To look for rabbits?'

I said, 'No, I'm no going to look for rabbits, I'm going to shoot that hare.'

He says, 'What?'

I said, 'I'm going to have a shot at that hare.'

'What hare?' he said.

He got up and he looked out the window, and I never saw a man go in a state that he went in my life. I knew Duncan since I was a wee boy sitting on the reaper with my father and I never saw a man get so angry in all my life. He seemed a complete different person. He rose and he came over. He put his pipe down and he snapped that gun out of my hand, and he reached over to the mantelpiece where he'd a box of cartridges.

I said, 'What's wrong, what's wrong with you, Duncan?'

He said, 'Dinnae tell me you were going to shoot that hare!'

I said, 'That's only a hare.'

He said, 'From now on, never you ever lay your hands on this gun again as long as you live. Now keep away from it. And don't ever even *think* of shooting that hare, if you ever see it again.' He sat there for about ten minutes, he wouldna even speak.

I worked with him all that winter and I dinna ken what happened to that gun. He hid the gun and he hid the cartridges: I was never allowed to get my hand near it again. That hare never came back. After that, about half an hour later he was as pleasant as ever.

I telt my father and my granny the story about Duncan and the hare.

And my granny says, 'Maybe it was old Morag, his old auntie that went missing. That's who it was. That's why she never was found.'

Morag was the subject of the talk with the people for a long time, you know, because after she disappeared, they searched for her for two years. An old farmer's sister disna vanish for no reason. I mean, if her body had been found, if she'd been battered to death and her grave had been found or her burial, somebody would be accused of killing her. But – just to vanish off the face of the earth. She never even took her hat, she never took her handbag, she took no money. All her money was in the bank in Inveraray, the story tells you. She wasna poor.

I remember her well, an old tweed skirt, a man's sock round her neck with a safety pin. You could see her: she used to go out among the green corn, out in the field where the young corn was coming up, pulling skellies, dandelions and stuff to keep the corn clean. When the corn grew up high because it was very fertile land up there, up in the hill, you could see the smoke coming up among the corn because she smoked Woodbine. You saw the smoke before you saw her. She smoked Woodbine non-stop. That was Morag.

Granny was the only one who thought that old Morag had turned into a witch. Granny said that old Morag turned into a hare. She was a witch and she had supernatural powers.

But I never asked or questioned old Duncan about the hare after that. It was so embarrassing the way he lost his temper, because I never seen him angry. I never seen him raising his voice the whole time I was with him, and I started going there with my father when I was about four, and I was still working with old Duncan when I was 17 off and on and he'd give me five shillings every night, and a puckle tatties and a big bottle of milk for my mother. He was a good old man!

I worked with him again after I came back from Perthshire many years later. I got him a wife... well he didnae marry her but she came as his housekeeper, and she stayed with him till he died. She was Chrissy Campbell, a Campbell come from Skye. I used to work on a farm in Inveraray to Donald MacIntyre, and Chrissy was Donald MacIntyre's housekeeper, but her and Donald fell out.

I was up in Inveraray when I came on Chrissy and there she was sitting with her wee bundle and her wee case by the roadside.

I said, 'Chrissy, what's happened to you? Where are you going?'

She said, 'Donald and me fell oot. And I've got to go back to Skye.'

I said, 'Look, I could get you a job.'

She said, 'Where am I going to get a job?'

I said, 'I could get you a job with old Duncan Macvicar. He needs a housekeeper.' Duncan was coming up in his 60s and Chrissy would be in her 50s.

So me and her went to Achnagoul. I carried her things, all the way, and I took her in and introduced her to Duncan.

I said, 'Duncan, I've got you a housekeeper.' This is true! She stayed with him, till the day he died.

I went up to work with him one morning. The outside door was never shut. I came into the kitchen, the two dogs was lying on the floor. The kitchen was empty. Duncan's chairs was empty. They were aye pulled together: they used to be his bed. I walked upstairs to see what happened. Where were they? I didnae shout. I walked upstairs and opened the stair door, and there, two of them lying in bed together, the bed he'd never slept in all these years. He was back upstairs in bed with old Chrissy Campbell, and from that day on they were inseparable.

Chrissy was good to me. She became the housekeeper, she made all the food, she cleaned the house, she did everything, she did all the shopping when the van came in. She was really good and she smoked fag after fag. Every time I came back to Argyll, even when I got married with my first family, I would go back up to Achnagoul. Chrissy would give me a can of milk for the bairns. She would always slip me a pound.

One day I came back in my late 20s. I had about four kids at that time. I said, 'We'll go up to Achnagoul.' But Achnagoul was sold. Old Duncan had died. He died in the Royal Infirmary in Glasgow with cancer.

Chrissy was left the farm, the sheep, everything, he left the lot to her. She moved down to Furnace not far from the shore where I was born, the wee white cottage down the lowside and she bought that wee house there for herself. Somebody said that an old uncle came to live with her. Well, she said it was her uncle anyway. I think it was another fancy man. I was passing by one day and I found out from some of the old mates in Furnace I was talking to that Chrissy was there. I walked up to the door, knocked on the door, and she came out. Nae difference in her after all these years.

'Hello, Chrissy,' I said, 'how are you?'

'Oh Duncan, it's you,' she says. 'I'm sorry I cannae take you in, my uncle's just having his tea. But here ye are, oh wait a minute,' and she put her hand in her apron pocket and she brought out a single pound and a Woodbine, and, 'There ye are now,' she says, 'I cannae talk to you at the moment.' She closed the door. And that was the last time I ever seen old Chrissy.

She was supposed to be with her uncle. But I don't think it was her uncle.

The Lang Sang

Duncan is a great artist first, and an extraordinary one.

GEORDIE MACINTYRE, singer

He was a professional in the way he went around collecting songs.

HELEN FULLERTON, lecturer, folklorist

MANY TIMES DUNCAN told me of the evening, aged 18, that he walked into a quarry in Aberdeenshire. It was a pivotal evening in his resolve to further prepare himself for new worlds, so it surprised me and didn't surprise me when he said to me:

'David, I was not ashamed of my ability to do things, I was not ashamed of my appearance. I was sitting with these Aberdeen Travellers and I was ashamed of my heavy Highland accent. This Highland accent, I had to get rid of it.'

So it was, that late, hungry and tired, he saw horses, carts, old and young folk around a fire, Travelling people, singing, chattering, drinking. Into this Travellers' ceilidh he walked amongst folk he'd never met. A young fellow Traveller, they welcomed him in and introduced him to the oldest woman there, 'smoking a clay pipe' and then the usual greeting.

'Whaur ye fae, laddie,' she said in Doric.

* * *

My brother Sandy, the oldest one, got discharged from the Navy after four years. He disappeared twice. I think he was longing for his wife and other things. I mean people get problems, very simple problems. He was a great swimmer and, you know, he drowned himself, commited suicide. Though that was many years later.

He was the first person I left home with completely. I'd always treated the old camp and place where my parents was as a kind of a base. I would be gone for a week, gone for two weeks and back. Off in the next direction, and go on up to Oban, down to Campbeltown, down to Skipness, down into Islay, back again. I always came back. When Sandy came over for a visit to see my parents he persuaded me to go back with him to Cupar Angus where he was living with his wife and two kids. He said, 'See a bit of the countryside!'

I stayed with him in Balbroggie for about a week. Him and the wife, after the kids went to bed, cuddled and kissed for hours and it was so embarrassing to me. There was nothing there for me so I told them I'd be leaving.

I left them. I walked to Perth. Wandering feet took me again. I was needing to go away further afield. And this is when I landed in Aberdeenshire.

Now, I'm 18 years old and I'm travelling on my own from Perth and I was away up into Aberdeenshire. I had spent some time in the Western Isles, I had spent some time in Mull, I had spent some time in Islay, in Jura, in Arran and I had wandered Campbeltown to Kintyre when lo and behold night approached. Hungry, I needed some place to stay when I saw in the quarry – fire. Now fire meant people. I left the roadway and I walked in the old road to the quarry and there was a group of Traveller People, horses and carts, young people, old people, all round the big fire. I think they were Stewarts, a big family. They were having a kind of a Travellers' ceilidh. I was made welcome – you never turn a Traveller away from your fire – and they brought me to the oldest woman. I remember her clay pipe. She smoked a pipe.

'Whaur are ye fae, laddie?' she said in Doric.

I said, 'I'm from Argyll.'

'Och aye, are you a Traveller?'

I said, 'Yes, I'm a Traveller.'

'And what's your name?'

I said, 'My name is Williamson.'

'Oh, you're a Williamson. What's your father's name?

I said, 'Jock Williamson.'

'And your mother's name?'

'Betsy Will...'

'Oh, you're Jock and Betsy's boy, come in!' She said to some of the lassies, 'Give the boy a bowl of tea.' They gave me a bowl of tea. Gave me a sandwich. 'Come and join us by the fire.'

This is the first time I had contact with different types of Travelling folk. Aberdeenshire Travelling folk. They all gathered round the fire and they were singing, drinking and playing the pipes, playing the chanter and singing songs that I'd never heard.

Then, the old woman spoke and there was a hush. 'Noo laddie you've been sitting there a lang while and ye haenae told us a wee story or sung us a song. Ye ken,' she says, 'if ye join the company you're supposed to sing a wee song or tell a wee story.' She was respected.

'Well, to tell you the truth,' I said, 'I could tell you a story. I could sing you a song.'

'Oh,' she said, 'I know you come from a long line. Your father's a piper isn't he?'

'Aye, my father's a piper.'

And she says, 'Your granny is a great singer. We've heard about your grandmother.'

I says, 'Yah.'

'Well,' she says, 'would you sing us one of your songs?'

I said, 'No, but I'll tell you a story.' And I begin to tell her a story.

And just in the middle of a wee bit of the story, she says, 'Wait a minute, laddie,' she said, 'that's nae a story, that's a lang sang.'

I said, 'A lang sang?'

'Aye, laddie,' she says, 'that's what we call a lang sang.'

'Well,' I said, 'I've heard it told as a story. But I've never heard it sung as a song.'

'Now, ye ken laddie I'm no much of a singer, ye ken, but I'll gie ye a wee bit of it.' And she sang 'Lady Margaret.'

Lady Margaret sat in her high chamber
She was sewing her silken seams
She looked east and she looked west
And she saw those woods grow green, grow green.

I knew the story about the two lairds my father had told me, one in Newcastle, one across the Borders o' Scotland, who were great friends to each other. I knew of the family betrothing the two children to each other as a story. One little boy whose name was William and the other, a little girl, was Margaret. The estates bordered each other. They were great friends, played together, little Margaret was three, William was only a baby.

Then my father had said, 'For a strange reason little William was gone, he vanished.' This is the story I'm telling them. The laird offered a large reward to find his little remains. But no, he couldn't be found. The couple's heart was broke. Meanwhile over on the estate in Scotland, little Margaret grew up. The couple in Scotland had no more children. She was an 18-year-old young woman. She had a great love for one thing: when it came to Halloween she asked her parents to take her to the Scottish border, because there in the Scottish part of the estate of mother and father's friends, was hazel trees. She loved to collect the hazelnuts on the trees.

So one evening, she sat there looking out the window (see this is how my father told me the story). It was Halloween and she wanted some nuts for Halloween. She hadn't far to go to the forest on the Scottish estate. And she lifted her petticoat and walked over; started pulling hazelnuts in her apron, as a young lady would in bygone days – this is the 15th century – when all in a moment out of, it seemed, nowhere, came this rider on a white horse.

And he says to her, 'What are you doing here, young lady?'

She said, 'I'm collecting hazelnuts, of course.' She said, 'Where are you from?'

He says, 'From England,' and he explained to her who he was. He climbed off his horse and he took her gently and he laid her down and he had intercourse with her for the first time in her life, under the hazel trees. And you knew fine in these days, the're no protection against intercourse.

And she says to him, 'What if I should have a baby?'

'Well,' he says, 'if it's a baby just call it after me.'

But she said, 'I don't know who you are, sir.'

He said, 'I'm an Earl's son from Carlisle and I own all those woods green and,' he said, 'I was taken when I was small by an evil fairy queen.'

Aha! Margaret remembered the story her mother had told her of a little William. Things began to collect in her mind. Could this be William, the man she was supposed to marry when she was a child, betrothed by her father and mother to him? She says, 'Tell me a little more.'

He said, 'I've been taken with a fairy queen. But,' he said, 'tomorrow night is Halloween and if you will come to the five mile gate on my estate, there you can set me free because the fairy queen with all the young men she has captured through the years sets them free for one night. I have discovered secretly what'll set me free from the powers of the fairy queen.' He said, 'First, there'll come some dark' – meaning dark horses – 'then there'll come some brown horses. You make your way,' he said, 'to the gate, the five mile gate and you wait there. When you see this white horse coming, you pull me down from the horse. Then I'll turn into a snake, a wicked snake, but don't be afraid. Just hold me tight, I won't touch you. And then, I'll turn into a lion wild, but I won't hurt you. And then,' he said, 'I'll turn into a naked man. Throw your cloak over me to cover my nakedness and then you'll have me free. Now,' he says, 'you do that for me.' And off he went.

She never mentioned a thing to her mother.

So that night at the midnight hour
Lady Margaret she made her way
And when she came to the five mile gate
She waited patiently.
First there came some dark, some dark
Then there came some brown
But when there came a milk-white steed
She pulled the rider down.
First he turned to a wicked snake
And then to a lion wild
She held him fast she feared him not
He may be the father of her child.
Then he turned to a naked man
O an angry man was he
She threw her mantle over him
And then she had him free.
And then cried the voice of the fairy queen
O an angry queen was she
Sayin', 'If I had have known yesterday

O what I know today
I'd took out your very heart's blood
And put in a heart of clay.'

And if he had a heart of clay, if the queen had given him a heart of clay, he would never have fell in love, he would never have had sex, he would never have got the young girl to break the spell. So, she broke the spell and she set him free, and he took her back and he married her.

This was a story told to me by my father round the campfire in front of my granny that he had learned as a story from his mother. But, when I tried to repeat that as a story in Aberdeenshire in that quarry before that bunch of Travelling people, the old woman said, 'Laddie, that is a lang sang.'

The funny thing was I was to bring that subject up to my father the next time I went back home. And I said, 'Father, see that story you used to tell us. I got an old Traveller woman, old woman Stewart, she said it was a song.'

'Ach, my sister used to sing it for years, my sister Rachel sang if for years and so did my mother.'

I said, 'How did you no tell us?'

He said, 'I thought it was better telt as a story.'

Then, I realised that my father all these years had been telling me ballads as stories. That's why I became interested in collecting ballads. I set out to find and ask about ballads from people in Aberdeenshire, people in the Hebrides, people in the Western Isles, in my years in my travels. I'd be travelling for another three years after that on my own before I got married at the age of 21.

I could sing the ballad because I knew it as a story. I mean it was not something that was new to me. I mean you could learn a song but if you're brought up with a ballad told as a story it's a different meaning, because you're actually in the ballad, you're in there, because when someone tells you a story you feel that they're painting you a picture and carrying you with them in the story.

It was ballads, man! Long traditional ballads, and the old Travellers, the old Travelling folk like my granny, and my father and mother, they never had a clue what a ballad was. I'm 17 years old and I didna ken what a ballad was. I had the story. I could sing, I could carry a note, and I had music, I could play the chanter, I could play the pipes. I could play the jew's harp, mouth organ, I used to busk with a mouth organ when I was down and out for pennies.

It was a lovely evening that evening in the quarry with the old Travelling folk on my way to Aberdeenshire that night. I think if I had hae been more accepted in Islay where my grandfather was born, I would have maybe stayed a little longer. The people were sociable enough but they were just, as if, you felt you were always out of place some way, you know? But that night in the quarry there among the Travelling people, five or six tents, ponies, horses, dogs running around, kids playing, crying children, you felt differently, as if you belonged here.

But sad to say, I knew I couldn't stay because I had to go on my way the next morning. It's the custom of Travelling people if it's a nice morning, they're always up early. Got some tea from them and went to the river and washed my face. Some of the girls came over, young lassies came over:

'Are ye going away today?'

I says, 'Aye.'

They would have liked me to have stayed on. So would I, but you don't like to overstay your hospitality anywhere.

I said cheerio to them all. I think they were staying there for another two-three days and then they were going to move on. They would be splitting up and going their own ways. There'd be uncles and aunties and friends with each other, so probly never see each other the rest of the year. But I was heading further up; I wanted to see a bit of Aberdeenshire.

* * *

> The epiphanal meeting with the lang sang in the quarry had made Duncan more aware of the rich legacy he was to carry into the non-Traveller world, where the depth of his insight and artistry were applauded by such folk scholars and fine singers as Geordie MacIntyre, a huge admirer and friend. In my recording with him he had this to say about Duncan.

* * *

> 'The value of Duncan, as I see it, he is an individual who has a great respect for the past, for the positive values of the past, the realities of the past, and how he can link. With Duncan you are getting the authentic voice of a living tradition.

Duncan singing 'Jock o' Monymusk'

He thought about what he was singing. He could talk about it in ways that any drama college would be proud of. I have a recording; Duncan explaining to me 'The Braes o' Gleniffer', everything that is happening there, the season of the year, what was in a person's heart, everything is explained. No method actor could have articulated it more vividly. All the things that he knew from beginning to end, from before the beginning and after the end that he knew, he was putting into this song. You think, oh well, you just gather this song, take it out of the tradition, and sing it. Duncan had thought this song in and out. He is a creative artist first and a very extraordinary one.

And Helen Fullerton said, 'He was very professional in his approach to things; in the way that he went round collecting songs and collecting stories, even before it was the thing to do. I know that this is what Hamish (Henderson) was doing, and Ewan (MacColl) was doing, and so on and so forth, but he didn't know that. Duncan was doing it because he knew the value of the Travellers' tradition.'

The Minister

ONE NIGHT, DUNCAN and I were sitting by the fire, in my front room, drinking a whisky or two.

'Tomorrow I'll tell you about my time in Fraserburgh,' he said.

We reckoned that I'd have been an 11-year-old pupil, in the Central School, when he aged 18 had been seeking out his mother's cousin Sandy, whose teenage daughter had put spring fever in his feet and elsewhere.

'You know what that's like, David? When did you first fall in love?'

'In Fraserburgh,' I told him.

'Do you remember her name?'

'Nadine Soutar, Vivienne Stafford and Norma Buchan.'

'That's three!'

'Yes, and I was only five! They were in primary one and I secretly loved each one.'

'You haven't changed,' he said, 'except it's no secret.'

Duncan didn't find Sandy or his lovely daughter.

'What did you do then?' I asked.

'I slept on the beach, and remembered Aunt Rachel's words, "As long as you know what you're doing you'll never be stuck." I made a stripper, sat in a wood, gathered, cut and pulled willows and went into a Fraserburgh backstreet shouting, "Baskets to mend. All types. Neatly and cheaply repaired at your door."'

A baker took him up on the offer. I wondered if the baker was John Pirrie who visited my mum and dad and brought us mouth-watering butteries and other delicacies in the frugal war days. After working for the baker, Duncan had a packing job in McConnachie's food factory.

I wondered if his eyes had ever fallen on my sister, ten years older than I, who briefly worked in the offices there.

'If I had, maybe I'd be your brother-in-law.'

'It's bad enough as it is.' I said.

He told me of his Furnace school teacher who made liberal use of the belt. I told him of my first school teacher, Miss Petroshelka, a young Polish lady, who gave me the belt for talking. I returned to my seat and continued to talk to my little neighbour.

'Why are you still talking?' she demanded.

Apparently, I replied with five year old innocence, 'I hadn't finished what I was saying.'

'Nothing's changed,' replied dear Duncan.

Fraserburgh was a great meeting place for our conversations and our different worlds. I was a kid at school during the war. He was there for a few months after the war, when there were no German bombing raids aimed at knocking out the CP Toolworks making armaments and munitions; no barrage balloons floating above the harbour protecting the all important fishing fleet, but the wee trawlers were still there and the herring gulls and girls with lightening fish-filleting fingers throwing guts to the mewing, snatching birds.

'Do you remember the air raids?' he asked.

'I remember my mother put my brother and I under an upside-down sofa when the sirens went. My brother had a red Pinnochio-like gas mask. One day after the all-clear a bomb went off and the blast threw my brother right across the room to land, astonishingly, in my mother's arms.'

Duncan's misadventures with the fishing hook that tore his hand apart exempted him from the army.

After his few months in the Broch, Fraserburgh, itchy feet of course took him again.

* * *

Then it was spring, feet got itchy again, and I made my way to Aberdeen. I landed in Old Aberdeen, and I found out there's Travellers was squattin in Old Aberdeen, in the squatter houses, derelict buildings. Traveller folk, wee Sandy and his wife. He had two wee lassies, Isabella and Nellie. I remember them well, and I stayed with him.

It wasna the lack of money: it was you could not buy a cigarette in Old Aberdeen. Everybody had cigarettes but they kept them for their customers. I was really pushed for cigarettes. I went doon one night, I said, 'I'll go and see if I can beg a fag from somebody or buy a fag, I'm going mad for a smoke.'

I walks down the street and just in front of the university I seen this young man standing. He had a big white polo-necked jersey on, I remember it well. He had plus-fours, long stockings and buckled shoes. He was standing, smoking.

I went up to him, I says, 'Excuse me sir, could you sell me a cigarette?'

He says, 'No, young man, I can't sell you a cigarette.' And he had the 20 packet in his hand! Box of Swan Vestas matches.

I said, 'Why can't you sell me a cigarette? I've never had a smoke. I've got money but I cannae get a cigarette to buy.'

'No,' he said, 'it's very hard to get cigarettes at the moment. The war, you know,' he said. Nae white collar, nothing, just a polo-neck jersey. He said, 'But I'll give you a cigarette.'

I says, 'Aye, mister, that's very nice of you, sir, very kind of you.' And he gien me a cigarette, a Capstan. Oh, a great old fag.

He said, 'Where are you from? You're not from around these parts are you?' He knew by my Highland accent.

I said, 'I'm from Argyllshire. I just came down from Fraserburgh, I was working up there in McConnachie's Soup Kitchen for a while.'

'And where are you working now?' he said to me.

I says, 'Nowhere. I'm squatting in the old squatter buildings with a cousin of my mother's and his wife.'

He said, 'Where did you say you come from?'

'From Inveraray,' I said, 'Lochgilphead, Furnace, that's my district.'

'Well,' he said, 'do you know Glen Aray?'

I said, 'I know Glen Aray as good as you know your own house, I used to cut peat there. I use to herd sheep there, clip sheep there. I used to build drystone dykes there for some of the farmers.'

'Well,' he said, 'if you know so much about it, who is the farmer of Glen Aray?'

I said, 'John Macintyre, of course.'

He looked at me and he smiled. 'I see you know what you're talking about,' he says. 'Young man I think you'd better come and meet somebody. There's somebody I want you to come and meet.'

I thought he was a shan gadgie, you know, kinda strange. I wasna sure about him.

He said, 'Oh don't worry,' he said, 'it's only I want you to meet my mother.'

'Ah, well, that's different, you want me to meet your mother,' I said. 'Why should you want me to meet your mother?'

He said, 'My mother is the full blood cousin to John Macintyre in Glen Aray. She's never seen him for a long time. I know you'd have a lot to talk about.'

He had an old Alvis car with wire spokes lying at the front of the house. With a big brass radiator at the front, and big starting handles stuck out the front, an Alvis! It was all covered in leather, old boot at the back.

He took me to the house and he took me in. The old woman was sitting by the fire, sitting knitting, grey hair, nice old woman.

He said, 'Mother, I've got a visitor for you. This is a young man from Argyllshire, your homeland. He knows your cousin, John Macintyre.'

I said, 'I worked for John Macintyre many times when I was younger.'

'Well,' she says, 'John is my cousin. I havnae seen him for some time.'

She got up. She laid her knitting down. She said, 'Would you like a cup of tea?'

'Ah,' I said, 'I'd love a cup of tea.'

I had tea with the old woman. I thanked her very much and we cracked about life in Argyll. She asked about my family and we got on really well.

'Come again,' she says, 'come again!'

The minister walked me out the front door.

'Well,' he said, 'You know I forgot to tell you,' he says, 'I'm a minister.'

I said, 'A minister?'

'Yes,' he said, 'I'm the minister for the parish of Seton.'

'Oh,' I said.

'I run a wood contracting business.'

I says, 'A wood contracting business? You're a minister!'

'Oh yes,' he said, 'but I need my business forbyes. I have a big quarry down here. I've got three men working for me at the moment. Are you able to handle an axe?'

I said, 'An axe! Handling an axe to me is like handling a cigarette, and I do cross cut.'

He said, 'Do you know anything about a circle saw?'

'Ah,' I said, 'I've worked with a circle saw many, many a time. I used to work with my father setting the circle saw.'

'How did your father set the circle saw?' he said.

I said, 'With a claw hammer. My father used to set the teeth of a big circle saw with a claw hammer – one to the right, one to the left, one to the right, one to the left, one to the right till he had filed it sharp.'

So he said, 'Would you work for me?'

I said, 'I work for anybody.'

Come doon tomorrow at eight o'clock.'

* * *

Duncan always spoke of Ian, the minister, with gratitude and affection. 'He was a wonderful person.' The nature of this minister was one of life's beautiful surprises, though he was yet to meet his favourite minister of all.

The Reverend Ian was as equally surprised by his new worker's resourcefulness. Duncan was reaping the harvest of the skills he had learned from his wise and provident father, handling and servicing a six foot circle saw, splitting knotted wood with wedge and 14 pound hammer. Here was a strong, charming and personable young man.

They became good friends and it was in a gleaming Alvis motor car chauffered by the Reverend Ian, minister of the parish of Seton, that the young Traveller lad was delivered to the army medical centre to be assessed for National Service.

He failed, or as Duncan put it, 'Passed grade four, unfit for service.' The hook that had torn his hand apart disqualified him.

'David, when I think about what happened to my brothers, the army wouldnae hae suited me and I wouldnae hae suited the army.'

That I had no difficulty in believing and so his time in Aberdeen was not interrupted by serving his Majesty King George the Sixth. Was I not in the army? he asked.

'I don't think it would have suited me either,' I said. Luckily, I was deferred while I was at university and by the time I had my degree, National Service was abolished.

We drank a whisky to our mutual escape.

* * *

Life on the whole was very pleasant in Aberdeen at that time. Working in the woods, travelling out every day in the old car with the minister, sometimes in a lorry with Arthur and Iain who worked there forebyes. Sometimes, we'd stay in the mill, at the sawmill, and work about the sawmill. Sometimes I would sharpen the saw, set the big saw, oil the engine, and do other little jobs about.

In Aberdeen, at that time, the only problem was cigarettes, and that was a problem. It was just after the war and things was still on ration. Anybody had cigarettes would keep them for their local customers. Even on the black market, cigarettes couldna even be gotten. But life was very pleasant because there were a lot of Travelling people, like myself, had squattered during the war and brought up their families. These Travelling boys knew I was a Traveller and I knew they were Travellers.

We'd go down the Castlegait on a Saturday night. There were dancing, singing, street playing and people playing the accordions, and there were girls and there were Traveller boys there. I mean, nobody never caused nae problems to anybody else. Everybody was out for just a nice time to theirself. We never visited in the pubs, and as for drugs, I never even heard the name of a drug. Didnae know what a drug was. Life was very pleasant, but there's always this longing.

I mean, people were happy, you were accepted, you were free to do as you please. I got my five pound every week from the minister. I just blew it with my mates. We used to buy a pig's foot, Foot 'n' Chips. A sixpence for a pig's foot. You know the funny thing was, you'd sit there on the side of the street with the pig's foot and you ate all these things – the're 21 bones in a pig's foot! You'd suck all these bones, throw them in the street. And I guarantee, if you were there when the scaffy man came along and he was sweeping up the street, you could hear the bones rattling under his brush! There were the fattest dogs in Aberdeen in the world. They cooked the pig's foot first and then they roasted it and you got a pig's foot with chips. Fantastic. Good for you, it was good food. Anyway, you just blew it as you got it.

The thing was I was accepted. There were no such a thing as discrimination between me and the local lads that was there, even though we were Travelling people. That was one thing about Aberdeenshire people, there was nae class distinction that we were different. We were accepted with them, and this was a kind of a new world to me, different by the way I was brought up back home in Argyll. I mean, even though you were pleasant to people and you worked with people, you could never become one of them. As if you were just living on the other side of the fence all the time. But in Aberdeen with the local community, with the minister and his mother, the local boys, the local Traveller people and the local people of Aberdeenshire, the shops, and the places and the chemist where you went for things you needed, you were treated like just another person.

The minister would come to me and say, 'Duncan, would you go up and keep Mother company tonight. I'm going out with Lily.' Lily Paterson was his girlfriend. I would go and old Mrs Begg would let me into the house, sit down and give me a cup of tea, and we'd sit and talk. She would ask about her cousin in Argyll and Donald Macintyre, what were you doing and when had you seen him last and all these things. We'd talk for hours! And this really made the minister happy because I was good company to his mother. Life was very pleasant indeed.

Then one evening, Ian said to me, 'Duncan would you like to come to the booth?'

Now, the word booth to me was foreign. I thought it was something to do with the church because Ian was a minister. I thought a booth was a kind of a pulpit where the minister stood and lectured to the people. I'd no clue what a booth really was.

But anyway, he says, 'Come anyway, have a look there.'

'What is it?'

He says, 'Wait till you get there and you'll see.'

So we jumped in the old Alvis and he drove up, and I saw him putting this bag in the back of the car. And I thought maybe it was the books, bibles or something. I'm looking forward to this booth, what the hell! We drove right away up to Seton and into the big circle of these prefabricated houses that's built during the war. In behind them was a big, long, fabricated building, and he pulled the car behind this.

'Right,' he says, 'we're here.'

He said, 'Duncan, a boxing booth.'

I said, 'What have you got a boxing booth for?'

He says, 'I'm the trainer.'

I says, 'What? You a trainer? Well, you're amazing.'

'Amazing? I'm the trainer,' he said.

He had a Nissen hut hired from the army and he taught 14 and 15-year-olds boxing. I seen fabricated houses before but this one was lighted up. It was a big long empty room. I says to myself, 'What will I do here?'

He says, 'Come in!' and he led me through another door. There was another room in there and there to my surprise was everything under the sun. Unknown to me it was a boxing booth. He had everything: there were dozens of pairs of gloves hanging on the wall, there were skipping ropes, there were weights, everything you could ask for inside this other room. I says to him, 'This is some kind of training place?'

He said, 'Duncan, this is a boxing booth. Have you ever done any boxing in your life?'

I said, 'I've done plenty fighting, I had to fight all my life – I had seven brothers and to be second youngest you had to fight for a way of life. When I went to school I had to fight – it's been a fight for me since the day I was born.' I said, 'I've never had gloves in my life.'

'Well,' he said, 'I'm going to give you a present.' He walks over and he picked a pair of gloves. 'There's for you.' Second hand gloves they were, but they werenae boxing gloves, they were training gloves. He says, 'Put them on. I'll be with you in a minute. Take off your boots'. And he threw a pair of sand shoes, white sand shoes. I took my boots off and put the sandals on. He went through a door, and he came back in, just dressed in his pants and a T-shirt and he was putting on a pair of gloves. Pulling the gloves on him.

I guarantee him being a minister, his body was nothing but muscle.

He says, 'Have you done any sparring?'

I said, 'Nah me, I never done that. I've done plenty of fighting.'

'Well,' he said, 'we're going to have a little spar till the boys arrive.'

I said, 'Boys arrive? What boys?'

'Oh,' he said, 'they'll be here in a wee minute.'

He got on and he shaped up, and I shaped up with the gloves. I had no idea about how to handle gloves. But I knew how to fight. I could fight like big guns. He hit me in the back of the neck and he spun round and he hit me. He must have hit me about a dozen times within seconds. I didna know where his punches was coming from. He was using me as a punch bag.

But anyway then he says, 'You're a strong man.'

I said, 'Aye.'

He said, 'You've got a good reach, but you'll have to learn how to handle your gloves.'

A wee while later in they come, about 14 laddies, aged from about 13 to about 15 and 16-year-olds. There's one wee boy, he had a club-foot, high boot.

I looked at his foot, you know. He was from Glasgow, a wee Glasgow laddie. They all went into the room and they started to come back out, and they all took seats around the hall. I'm watching this one with the club foot. He wasnae going to be very fast on his feet, but he went down and he put a pair of sandals on his feet. Alasdair was his name, Alasdair Cameron.

Ian says, 'You and you, out on the floor.' He just picked a couple.

Wee Alasdair, wee guy with the club foot and a big red heided laddie about 17. I said to myself, 'That wee boy's goin to be killed!' Was he what? You never seen the like of this in your life. With that club foot he hardly ever moved. He just went round in a circle and I guarantee that big red headed laddie would be taller than him, heavier than him, but he couldnae touch him in any way!

Iain watched them, and he stopped them, and he gien them a break, tellt them where they're going wrong. And then he got another two up.

Then he said to me, 'Would you like to have a spar with one of the boys?' Now me and him had a spar about ten minutes before the boys arrived, and I began to get the feel of this. I began to like this, the gloves, get the feel of these gloves. It was really good! Anyway, that went on three times a week for about a month.

One night he says to me, 'I'm going to drop you off at the booth tonight. I'm going off early, I want you to take care of the boys. I dinnae want nae trouble.'

I said, 'There'll be nae trouble, dinnae worry about it.'

'Just give them plenty of training, just sit back and just pick them. You know them all by name now.' This wee laddie Alasdair, he was my favourite, him with the club foot. Oh, he was exceptional!

Now there was a wee woman and I don't like to mention the name: shall we say she used to go with the sailors. She went to the docks, you know. Ivy they called her. She had a sniffle in her nose, she spoke through her nose. Of course, everybody spoke about Ivy, Wee Sniffy Ivy they called her. Sniffy Ivy. But one night we were sitting on after a break, all sitting round the stairs at the break, and somebody mentioned Sniffy Ivy.

It was the big red heided laddie, 'Oh,' he said, 'after that we'll go and maybe see Sniffy Ivy tonight.'

Well, this wee laddie with a club foot got up. He says, 'You, up, the floor!'

I said, 'What's going on about this? I'm supposed to...'

'No,' he said, 'it's all right, it's all right, Duncan, it's got nothing to do with you. It's between me and him.' He said, 'Oot, you! Out on the floor!' he said.

He says, 'Aye, I'm gonna enjoy this.'

He did enjoy it all right! I guarantee that wee laddie with the club foot near killed him, he near killed him. He says, 'I want to tell you now, Ivy's my mother. I don't know who my father is, but Ivy's my mother. They call her Sniffy Ivy, but she's my mother.' I guarantee, in that hall, I was there, for months and months and months after that. Not one of these lads ever mentioned her name again in the hall.

So, Ian got me to run this place. Him and I used to spar every night before the boys came down, and I began to get a great love for this. It was something very special with me, I never done this before. I couldna but wait, I could look forward to it, and Ian could see this and he let me run the booth for him from that time on till the day I left. And you know these lads were fantastic. There was a young lad there, the name of Jackie Gillon. He later fought in the Olympic Games, was a silver medallist in the Olympic Games. He became the amateur champion of Dundee, a great wee fighter. These boys were very good.

As I say, I really loved and enjoyed that time. It was a new way of life, a new world and something I'd never done before in my life, but I knew fine I couldn't go on like this. Deep in my mind there was something I really wanted to do, I needed to do, some kind of pull.

I took this longing. It was nearly a year since I saw my parents. I'd never wrote my parents a letter in my life, never got in touch with them. And, you know, you're always wondering what's going on with the little ones behind you. Even though life was pleasant there's always this longing for to get back to the old hometown, old home village and see the old folk and find out how things were. I had grown, put on some weight working swinging an axe in the woods. I was five foot ten, 13 stone, and I was only 17 at the time.

The next day was Saturday and I says to Ian, 'Ian, I'll have to go home and see my parents. I've got a longing to go back to Argyll.'

'Well, you better come and see my mother before you go!'

I came in and seen the old minister's mother. I told her I was going back to Argyll.

'Well,' she says, 'stop in and see John, my cousin John in Glen Aray.'

I says, 'Certainly, I'll go and see him.' I did too.

I told the minister I was leaving on Monday morning.

* * *

Duncan incarnated one of his favourite sayings. 'Don't let the truth stand in the way of a good story,' and knowing him as long and intimately as I did I was often stunned by the mantles he convincingly adapted. After we recorded the tale of his boxing exploits he returned on his next visit with a statue of a boxer which he gave me, asserting this to be one of his awards. Unfortunately, the inscription had been somehow scraped off. He had a great desire to please and add conviction and glamour. I heard him lay claim to being a Gaelic speaker, the author of songs he didn't write, and his version of the past told with absolute aplomb would baffle historians, though it convinced and delighted audiences from Israel to Canada.

Cheeny Feekin

AS I BEGAN TO travel more and more frequently with Duncan, to hear the story of his own travels, the running themes were: 'live for today, take no or little thought for the morrow. Hit the road and keep awake'. Without a penny, gasping only for a smoke, the only transport his feet, he was off, following the urge to move.

All the changes in my own life had also been prompted by the feeling that it was the time to move, from teaching, to the BBC, to wandering with Duncan: these shifts were how I had been travelling on in a very different world. But now our paths met.

We often discussed and compared our two journeys, joked about the impish fate that brought us to be rolling along in my old campervan to tell stories together in schools, libraries and at festivals from the tip of Galloway to the Western Isles. From such different worlds and educations we had each at different times followed the inner urge to move on not knowing whither.

'So, why did you leave the BBC, to be travelling with this old tinker man, David?' he asked.

In this mood it suited him to be not a Traveller but a 'tinker man'.

'I'll tell you the whole story one day,' I said, but in the meantime I told him that my department had been run by a wonderful man, who understood and trusted people and knew they needed freedom to make programmes, and it was taken over by a man who didn't understand people, didn't

Sunshine and Thunder; David and Duncan together

trust them and had never made a radio programme so he didn't understand how it worked. He bullied the women and deceived the men. I read Duncan a poem I'd written about it.

He asked her to
paint a picture
benign Medici.
But when he
told her
what colours to use,
the joy left her heart
her hand could not move.

The poem didn't impress Duncan. He doubtless agreed with the sentiments but consigned the art to 'classical shit'.

'Anyhow if I hadn't left I wouldn't be here as your chauffeur being suffocated to death by your cigarette smoke.'

In my old van that night we continued to record the story of Duncan's travels at the point where he enterprisingly garbed himself from an ex-army store, hitched a lift from a young horsey lady in her 'wee clooty top MG', who plied him with the paradise of Players cigarettes and dropped him in Montrose from whence he walked to Dundee.

* * *

I walked all the way from Montrose to Dundee. By the time I got to Dundee it was about nearly ten o'clock at night. I was hungry, I didn't have a smoke of any kind. I didn't have a penny to my name, but I had an old friend that lived in Dundee, a man cried Joe Hendry. Joe had squatted in an old squatter building and I knew where he stayed. He had just lost his wife. She died with childbirth, and he had two wee boys and a wee girl. He was a cheeny feeker. You know cheeny feekin? China mending.

He had this little bow and arrow made of leather and a wee drill, and he had this box of little lead pellets. He went about from door to door hawking, mending heirlooms, broken vases and antique plates. He was a specialist at it. Joe was glad to see me. He made me a cup of tea but he didna have any milk.

I said, 'Joe, I'm really sorry. I havenae a penny.'

'Never mind,' he says, 'we'll get the price of some messages tomorrow.'

He was doing really well for himself and he had a few orders to go back. He says to me, 'Will you come with me tomorrow?'

So the next day I says, 'Aye.'

He left his two wee boys and the wee lassie with his sister-in-law who lived in an old squat down in North Tay Street where we were staying. Me and him went off to cheeny feek. He would go to these big houses: he would get an old vase or an old plate, something that fell and broke by mistake. These old Willow Blue bowls, he was fantastic at them. He would sit down on the step of the door and he showed me how to work this wee drill, his homemade drill. It was just a bended stick like a bow and arrow and twang of leather across the front like a bow and arrow. He put a twist in it in the middle and he'd pull this back and forward and this wee drill would drill a hole into the clay. He'd push in one of these wee lead pellets like a lead plug, and you would never hardly see it. And after, he had a wee box, wee square box, white stuff like white powder – he used to wet the powder with his thumb and he would put the white powder over the top of where the lead plug was. You wouldna see where it was mended. He was really clever.

I said, 'Joe, that's near as the best job I've ever seen anybody ever do.'

He took me working for a couple of days. And it was a delightful time watching his mending. I'd never seen this done before: mending easily old Willow plates, vases and things that got broken.

He was really good to me, but cigarettes was my problem. I remember one night him and I sat up, nae cigarettes!

'Did you ever try this?' he said to me.

He rolled up in a cigarette paper a brown shoe lace. Now it shows you how hard people was for cigarettes. Talk about people on dope today. Him and I sat and smoked a brown shoelace rolled up in a piece of paper. It tasted like tobacco. Imagine sitting smoking a brown shoelace. He had money, but for the love of money you couldna get a cigarette in the whole of Dundee. I wish to God I had given up smoking at that time. I stayed three days with Joe and I left him.

I travelled on to Perth, all the way 22 miles to Perth. I mean I could walk in these days. An army battle dress and a pair of good strong army boots I had bought with the wee bit o' money the minister had given me. That night I slept in a haystack near Crieff. Hungry! No smoke, no nothing.

Anyway, I walked on, up to Crianlarich, up to Dalmally, down into Inveraray. Took me about two days. Down to Furnace to see my parents. They were pleased to see me but I didna have a penny to give them. Nothing. But they werena too bad off. I stayed with them for about a week.

Glasgow

BETWEEN CIGARETTES AND STRONG, sweet tea one morning in Dundas Street, Duncan was teaching me 'The Braes o' Gleniffer' which sang straight into my heart, a story of longing by a woman whose sweetheart is taken off to war. 'Join in, sing along,' he exhorted, his way of teaching by emulation and osmosis, a transfusion of his love for the song, his desire to pass it on, and to improve my singing.

I told him how I had been transfixed and inflamed when I'd first seen and heard Jeannie Robertson in a tent at Aikie Fair in Aberdeenshire singing 'Son David'. Shivers and the beginnings of an addiction and a huge desire to sing. 'Just keep singing,' he said.

In the love of ballad and folksong our planets swung into the same orbit. I recalled the Edinburgh folkscene in the '60s; he told me about Glasgow.

Later that afternoon, I had just played him a CD of Jock Tamson's Bairns with Rod Paterson's version of 'The Braes of Gleniffer' when, by chance, Norman Chalmers, a member of the group, paid a visit. This ignited an incendiary argument, Duncan unleashing a furious fussilade, eloquently dismissive of this ill-conceived 'beat-up' version with nothing to do with the sentiment or meaning of the song. To Duncan this was sacrilegious. No argument!

In the evening, in cooler mode, he told me, 'where it all began,' for him, another step into a new world. It was a world he could step into easily amongst fellow singing nomads of Scotland, wild lovers of music and song, people who like the great folklorist and collector, Norman Buchan,

> recognised that in Duncan was a mother lode of song-gold and ancient balladry.

* * *

My mother had told me my older sister Bella, with her husband George, a petty officer in the war, lived in Glasgow. So I says to my mother one day, 'I want to go to Glasgow.' I was never in Glasgow in my life. The old bus was eight shilling, from Inveraray to Glasgow, Buchanan Street Station. I saved eight shillings and I took the bus. I found my sister's house after a bit search and George was back from the navy, George Macfarlane. He'd come through all the war, but he was disabled some way. He wasnae wounded, but something happened to him, he'd seen so much. He liked a wee drink.

One night he says to me, 'You want a beer?'

I says, 'George, I dinnae take any beer. But I'll go with you.'

He said, 'The're a wee pub down the street here.' This is about 1948. I walked down with him, and he bought me a half pint of beer. He bought a pint for himself. I think that was about the first taste of beer I ever tasted in my life. I liked it. There was a lot of people. The place was full up. There were people singing, and George knew I could sing in these days.

He says, 'Give us a wee song.' Now he was known in the pub. I cannae remember the name of the pub but it was the place called Possilpark. It wasn't far to walk anyway, up one street, down another street to the pub. This is where it all began.

I said, 'I'll sing a song.' Everybody's sitting round, just nae difference in what it is in a pub today, but there were nae jukeboxes or nothing. One boy had a wee squeeze box and he was playing a tune. I seen a man and his wife sitting over at a table across the room. He had a grey bonnet on, thin faced chap. I would say he was in his 40s. They had a drink in front of them. I stood up, and I sang a song. It was the very same first song I ever sang to Linda, who was to be my second wife, when she came collecting later.

> The trees they are high, my love,
> The leaves they are green;
> The years are passing by, my love,
> That you and I have seen.

And I sang it really well. Then this man who was sitting at the table got up and he came across to me.

He says, 'Young man, that was a nice song you sang. Come over and meet the wife.'

She said, 'I liked your song. Where did you learn that song?'

I said, 'I learned it from my old granny. My granny was a folk singer.' I told them I came from Argyll.

He said, 'My name is Norman Buchan. What's yours?'

'Duncan Williamson.'

'Oh aye,' he says, 'you're a good singer, laddie. How long are you staying here?'

I said, 'I'm just here to see my sister. I'm with my brother-in-law.'

He had this machine with him sitting on the table. I know what it is now, but I didna ken what it was then. It was a reel-to-reel Uher tape recorder, one of the old big type, two big wheels. You know them well. I thought he was from the radio station or something.

He says, 'Do you know what that is?'

I says, 'I dinnae ken what it is. Is that a wireless?'

'No,' he says, 'it's not a wireless. You can record people singing.'

That thing was to become well known to me in the future. 'Well,' he said, 'I've got a few friends who are having a wee get together tomorrow night. If you come down here I'll pick you up.'

He bought me a half pint of beer. I sat down and cracked to his wife. When I walked over George was still sitting cracking to somebody else.

George said, 'Who was that you were talking to?'

I said, 'He said his name's Norman Buchan.'

George never heard of him. I never heard of him either. I was to know him better later! He used to call Bella his wife 'Ella'. He had a staish in his speech, called her E E Ella.

George said to me, 'Are you coming back?'

'Well,' I said, 'I dinnae ken my way back but I've to meet this guy tomorrow night.'

He says, 'You better watch what you're daeing. You know you're in the big city.'

I said, 'I can take care of myself.' I was 18 years old.

So the next night I came back with George between five and six. Norman and his wife were sitting at the table and a big tape recorder was sitting on the table in front of him. I came in.

I didna know if he was an MP at that time or no, but anyway we walked to another pub where he had a room at the back. Everyone had collars and ties on. They were all dressed. There weren't no person my age in the whole place. Nae lassies. There must have been about 50 people. There were people in their 30s, 40s and 50s. They were all sitting with their drinks. He put his tape recorder in the middle of the table.

I didnae know what this was. This was a folk revival club where people got together for a sing, nae stories, people got together and sang songs and he recorded them on his recorder. Norman Buchan, the great folklorist collector, I was to know later he'd come to be.

Anyway, I had collected all these beautiful songs from old Patrick MacDonnel where I was cutting the peats, some of his Irish songs.

He said, 'Well, give us a song!'

I said, 'I'll give you a song. What kind of song would you like?'

He said he would like an Irish song.

And I sang 'Glen Swollee' for the first time in public. Oh, the people just loved it, they loved it dearly!

He said, 'You're a great singer, man. You'll have to do something about this singing voice of yours.'

I said, 'I just sing, please myself. When I'm walking on the road I sing to myself all the time.'

'That's a good thing,' he says to me.

He could sing himself. Good beautiful voice. But not a musical voice, but good singing voice. Then the other people took a turn around, singing all round the room. I sang about three songs that night. It was a wonderful evening.

He introduced me to a lot of people, people that were to become well known to me in the distant future. People that I was to become great friends with in later years when I was much older.

The next day, I wanted to be on the move again, so George gave me a pound and he shook hands with me. I took the train – the first time I was ever on a train in my life. I didn't know how to get into the train; it was these old fashioned carriages. But if you gave me a thousand pounds, I didnae know how to get into that train. It was an old woman, and she said, 'What's up son?'

The doors was closing and it was an old steam train sitting choo-chooch-chook. She showed me. I took the train to Perth anyway. I think it was about seven or eight shillings on the train, left me a few shillings over and about.

I landed in Perth, I had a brother, Willie, just back from the war. He was working on a farm there, him and his wife. I stayed a couple of days, and then him and I went to Perth on the Saturday.

The Bold Man

WENT TO PERTH AND this was my Waterloo.

I met in with a Traveller family in Perth, a widow woman, her son and her daughter. Daughter was about 16. Her son was younger. They were Stewarts, related to the Stewarts o' Blairgowrie, Travelling singing Stewarts. I went home with that woman and her boy and the lassie. They lived in Auchterarder, outside o' Perth. I stayed with them for about a week. And eh, I went out with the young woman, the young lassie, to my regret. We done everything young people shouldn't have done. This is where I made the big mistake of my life. I stayed there for a week but I had a longing for Aberdeen.

So I bade them goodbye the next day and I landed in Aberdeen and this is about three months from the time I'd left. Everything was the same, the old squatter buildings were still there; there were still Travellers there, the minister was still there. He was glad to see me back. I started to work with him again, went to see his mother, sat in the house, the same old thing all over again, but unknown to me something was happening behind me. Something terrible was happening behind. I wasna to know about it for about a year.

I worked hard with the minister and at this time I had made up my mind I was going to save myself a few pennies. Far behind me I didn't know that the girl had given birth to a wee baby girl. It was some Travellers coming up from Perthshire who had come to Aberdeen, and they carried the news – that I was a daddy.

They said to me, 'The're a girl that had a baby to you back in Perthshire?'

I said, 'No!' And then I realised that it could have been true.

This began to worry me a lot, you know. I mean it was late summer. I was 18 past. I'd made up my mind I wasna going to be a squanderer and be the same I was before. I wasna going to leave Aberdeen penniless the next time. I tried to save a few pound back and forward, try to keep things together, build a wee bit of money for myself. I worked really hard. We travelled through Aberdeenshire, worked in the woods, sometimes we stayed in the mill. I think I took over the boxing booth. Ian hardly rarely turned up at the booth.

Till one night he said to me, 'I've arranged for a fight for you.'

I said, 'What?'

He said, 'I've arranged for a fight for you. You're the best here. So, I've had a request from some chap from the university. The Amateur Champion from the university.' I still had my gloves, the gloves he gave me. He says, 'He wants to have a fight, but not in the gym, in the hall.'

I said I wasn't too sure about this. I mean I was good with the gloves because he'd turned the whole thing over to me. I said, 'I don't know. A real fight?'

He says, 'Knock him to hell if you can, that's the idea.' That's the first time I ever heard him swearing. He said, 'Knock the hell out of him.' That's what Ian says to me, God rest his soul.

It was some kind of hall down in Aberdeen, where he had arranged for this fight, but it was amateur, it wasn't professional. I didn't know he was the welterweight champion of the university. He was older than me; he'd be about 22 or 23, and he'd asked Ian for one of his lads for a fight in the hall and Ian choose me. I would rather he had choosed the wee boy with the club foot, but no, he didn't. He choosed me. So it was arranged. I says, 'Well, if that's the way you want it.'

Oh, a lot of people turned up. Young lassies, old women, the local people. I never met the guy before, big, tall, dark-haired lad. They had the referee come in. There was nae ring: it was just pins on the floor, a rope and pins like. You could take them away.

They set up this ring and we go into the room, changed over, pants, T-shirt, gloves. Ian was my second, a minister, and here he's in plus-fours and long stockings and a white polo-neck jersey. This other guy, McGillivray was his name. Tom McGillivray.

Ian says to me, whispered in my ear, 'Ye better watch yourself, this guy can punch.'

Oh he punched right enough. Anyway, Ian wasnae the referee, another chap was the referee. We got into the ring and he came up.

'Now boys,' he says, 'I just want you not to be too rough.'

I was not accustomed to this. This was something new to me. I mean, I could punch like God knows what but I'd never done any fighting like this before in my life. It was always rough and tumble, you know what I mean. I was training the wee laddies in the training school. In he came and he had an old man at that corner and I was over here with Ian. The referee was in the corner on the other side.

He put his hand on my shoulder and he put his hand on McGillivray's shoulder, 'Now,' he says, 'I want you to be square, and touch gloves.'

We touched gloves, and the minute I touched gloves he hit me on the chin without even stepping back. I went down like a shot cock. He touched the glove and then he just hit me on the chin and down I went. I lay, I must have lain in a daze. I didn't even know where I was. Then all the people came out and they all gathered round. I sat up. I got up and my legs were shaked, felt really dizzy.

Ian came and says to me, 'That was a foul,' he said.

'If that's a foul, you didnae get what I got on the chin.'

He said, 'That was a foul. That wasnae right.'

So the referee came in, and they were talking among theirselves. I didn't know what they were talking about. These people knew what they were doing. I was just a stranger. I didn't know nothing about what they were doing.

But Ian says, 'We'll have to have a rematch.'

I said, 'What do you mean?'

He says, 'You have to fight again.'

I said, 'Not tonight.'

'No, not tonight,' he said, 'not tonight.'

So in the car going back I said, 'Ian, what was the problem? What went wrong?'

He says, 'Duncan, that was a foul. He should have stepped back, after you touched gloves with each other – then you come forward, but he didn't do that. Everybody's complaining. It was an unfair fight.' It wasn't the spar gloves that he gave me; it was tiny gloves, real wee tiny gloves. He says, 'You want a rematch. If you feel like going back for a rematch with him.'

I said, 'I dinna mind.'

I mind fine it was a Friday night and Ian took me down. A lot more people was there. Same thing happened again. I didnae ken the guy, he wasnae professional, but he was an amateur champion, welterweight amateur champion, and they just wanted a punchbag for him, to show, maybe he was going to turn professional or something, I don't know. God only help him!

So, the referee came up, we touched gloves. This time he stepped back, and I stepped back. Then he came forward and as Ian had taught me, I just hit him, a right cross, right straight across, right on the jaw blade and he went out, somersaulted, never gave a kick, and he lay there on the floor.

The referee went, 'One, two, three,' he said, 'he's out.'

One punch, I swear on my mother's grave, I wouldn't lie to you. One punch, that was all it took, one punch right square on the jaw blade. Out for the count.

On the way back in the Alvis, Ian said, 'D'ye know what you done? You knocked out the welterweight champion.'

I said, 'You put me in there with a champion fighter?'

He says, 'If I didnae know you were qualified to do it, I wouldn't put you there in the first place.' He said, 'You'll no be needing me in the gym very much after that. So I'll just let you take over.'

I stayed another month. I think it was about 13 months had passed by; I was worrying about the news I'd heard. I didn't have a lot of money, about 25 pound or something, but that was a lot of money in them days. About 25 quid I'd saved up, and then I tellt Ian I was leaving.

'Oh,' he says, 'you cannae!'

'I'll be sad to leave.' I mean I became a hero among the local Traveller laddies.

He said, 'If you're going this time, you won't be coming back.'

I said, 'I don't think so, Ian.'

'Well,' he said, 'I'll tell ye what we're going to do with you, I want you to take your gloves with you. Keep them for me.'

So the next morning, I went up and I said goodbye to his mother. I mind I kissed the old woman. I kissed her on the cheek and I shook hands with Ian. I put my gloves in the wee bag and I made my way back to Perthshire. I went to my brother up in Stanley. And he got on to me right away.

He says, 'You know, you dinna do that. A lassie had a wean to you.'

I says, 'Nah.'

He says, 'She did. You're a father of a wee year old wean. But you're too late. She's married.'

He said, 'Somebody else is looking after your wean now.'

This just tore the heart from me, you know. So I just squandered and spent the bits of money I had. I was really completely sick. I wanted to see the wean, but I didna want to see the mother of the wean. You know something, I never saw that baby till it was 16 years old. I was to marry another lassie, cousin of my own, and bring up seven of a family in the years to come, but I never saw that child until she was 16 years old, a little girl. Her mother had married someone else. He only died four years ago with cancer, and she was with him for 49 years.

Well, I was kind of mixed up after that when I found out. I wasna in love with her in any way but I wanted to be faithful and true. I wanted to see the baby, to look after the baby. I wanted to become a father to the wee lassie who was my first child. All my brothers were married and had children, except for my youngest brother. I wanted to see the baby, but things eluded me. She moved around. She was one of the Traveller women and married to a Traveller. He was a piper. They travelled a lot around Perthshire, never hardly in the same spot. You'll hear the end, what happens at the very end of the story.

* * *

The name of that Traveller girl was Martha Stewart. The little girl was Nancy, Duncan's first of ten children by three mothers, part of our story yet to unfold.

After nearly 50 years Martha phoned the bold man and he began to visit her again. I was curious to meet her. I visited her twice, once with Duncan (I did not record her then, Duncan's presence would have been something of an impediment). Later, I visited her and recorded her story of the meeting and mating with the handsome 'cowboy'.

Duncan was in high spirits when we drove to Dunblane to visit Martha. Here was a warm and couthy welcome, a comfortable woman. She greeted us, made strong black tea, sandwiches, scones. Cosy.

'He's never changed', she said, 'still the bold boy.'

Her affection for Duncan was clear, teasing, playful and his for her likewise. I left them cuddling, realised Duncan intended to stay the night and drove home alone marvelling to myself about the snuggling unabashed sexuality of their meeting.

When I later visited Martha on my own, she received me with great warmth and hospitality and I recorded her memory of walking out with the young Duncan.

* * *

'We were living at Auchterarder camped down the hill – they called it Chinafoot Burn on the old Dunning Road and I didn't really know Duncan then. We were gathering potatoes. Then we moved away but we all landed back at another camping place at Auchterarder on the Crieff-Madderty Road. Well, he was living up with his auntie and his cousins and that; and my mother, brother, sister and I were all working in the same field. Then they went away their way and we went our way. But before we went away, Duncan and I had a wee walk out, but nothing happened, because I was only about 15 then.

But when he came back the bold Duncan came round, and he used to come pretty, pretty regular. We used to walk six mile from Auchterarder to Madderty, him and I, over to see my granny. She smoked a pipe, we used to take tobacco over to her and that. Then, we would come back. We were just singing and whistling, carrying on, nothing, I can't say anything else. I loved him, but I don't think he loved me as much! Or he wouldn't have left me with the baby.

Oh, he was a cowboy, dressed in one of these hats, the full rig-out you know! From the head to the boots. Oh, he was a nice looking man. He would be about 19, well I was 17 when I got pregnant. I didn't tell my mum. I was sick in the mornings. I was one that would never eat any breakfast, even when working in the fields. When my mum noticed me getting sick every morning, she says, "I know the bold man done that." But she had no animosity, no way in the wide world. She liked Duncan very, very much, and he liked her. And by the time Nancy was born Duncan was already married.

I never saw him for eight years after I had my child. He must have heard about it because news like that travels fast, especially me not married. Eight years after that I saw his wife, Jeannie. I never was really talkative to her but one time when my daughter was about two year old, Duncan and his mother-in-law and his wife were living just outside Crieff, about six miles from where we were living. And I saw Jeannie and her cousin. She came to the camp. My mother and I were out sawing logs for our fire. My wee sister and my daughter Nancy, Duncan's daughter, were the two kids playing outside.

Jeannie came to me and says, "Martha, Duncan's saying that's not his daughter, Nancy."

"Well," I says, "between the two playing there, you go and pick the one that's more like Duncan." And she picked Nancy. So I just put my wee child in a pram I had and I walked all the way with her and her cousin right to where they were camped.

If Duncan had been there, I wasn't going to give him the child, but I was going to place her on his knee in front of the lot. But he cleared out, he wasn't there.

And his mother-in-law took my wee girl Nancy out of the pram and took her into the camp, in a tartan rug, and put the two children sitting side by side, Jeannie's and mine. And the mother-in-law said to her daughter Jeannie, "Look, they're like twins. You could hardly pick the one from the other."

Maybe his side of the story wasna as good as that.'

* * *

From time to time Martha phoned me looking for Duncan who was often staying with me. On one occasion when they had fallen out (they fell out and in frequently) she said, 'I'll tell you the real story about Duncan and me.' I didn't get the chance to record that version before she died but got Duncan's story and later, in November 2010, I visited the Traveller caravans near Dunbar where the extended Williamson family were following their Traveller life collecting whelks. I was welcomed with a cup of real tea by Duncan and Jeannie's first daughter Edith and Edith's husband, Willie. She told me what her mother said about Duncan, Martha and the baby, Nancy.

'My mum and dad were staying at Crieff. I was about four months old. We were at the tattie picking at Bains Drumness Farm. And Martha comes over to my mother and she says, "Take this, this is yours as well." The wee baby. And she puts it down in front of my mum. She says, "This is Duncan's." And he denied it. He denied it for years. He was there at the time. My mother never trusted him after that. Knowing my dad, my mother had her reasons for being jealous. He was a bit of a scallywag.'

And so we have three versions of the story, Martha's, Jeannie's and Duncan's.

* * *

I was a bit scattered. I didn't know what to do with myself. I didn't want to go back to Aberdeen. I was finished in Aberdeen. I said I'll go back to Argyll. I went back to my parents. And I stayed with my parents for one single year. I went back to work in Achnagoul with old Duncan Macvicar. My father was working in the quarry by this time, it was in the '50s. They started a new roadway by-passing Furnace, cutting Furnace off altogether. And my father got a job.

I remember he came back and he says to my mother, 'Betsy, I was offered a job driving a horse and cart. A shilling an hour. Eight shillings a day,' he says, 'good money.' Eight shillings a day! A shilling an hour he was getting in 1950. He says to me, 'Laddie, you want to have a job in the road. They're looking for a nipper.' You know, they call a 'nipper' for boiling the cans. You boiled their wee drums.

I says, to keep my father happy, 'I'll go along with you for a day.'

So, they stopped at ten o'clock and the nipper kindled a fire and boiled all the wee drums o' tea. Well, you built a big oven and you filled their wee drums o' tea and the men gathered. Just the wee billycans, them that was working, horsemen and carters and some of the workers. But I only stuck it for two or three days. I didnae like it. It wasna my thing.

I told the old man, I says to him, 'I feel like a move again.'

It was the last time with my Aunt Rachel, God rest her, the last time I seen her alive.

'I'll go doon,' I said, 'to Tarbert and see my Aunt Rachel.' She was still alive at that time. Aunt Nellie was still in the same old place. I stayed a couple of nights with her. They lived in a tent in a wee place outside of Tarbert.

I went on my way to Campbeltown. I had a bit of a carry on with some of the Travellers there. I had a fight at Campbeltown. I was arrested.

It was someone who was jealous, some man was jealous. Police arrested me. I was lucky, I got away with a warning. These people, they were the locals. I was an incomer. The sergeant kent all the Travelling folk, the Campbeltown Townsleys.

Well, there was a group of Travelling people sitting in the green in Campbeltown, what they always done. The men with their checkered bonnets on, their mufflers round their neck and the women with their shawls over their shoulders. This young particular woman, and her man, they were sitting drinking cans of beer. I mind fine, the lassie, the young woman knew who I was. Both of them were kind of distant relations to my mother, second cousins of mine. It was the lid of the can she took and she filled it full of beer.

She says to me, 'Duncan, would you like a drink?'

I said, 'Aye, I'd like a drink. Aye, I'll take a drink.' I drank from the lid of the can.

But her man, he had a wee sup on him. He had a wee drink. I could see that he was upset you know. He started talking about my people and he started talking about my father. I just couldnae take it anymore. He started talking about nicknames and what are you doing doon here, and 'What do you come down to this part of Campbeltown for? You hardfish should stay up in your ain part of the country.'

I said, 'It's a free world, you can go where you like.'

Every Traveller has nicknames. They used to call the Williamsons the 'hardfish' because my grandfather used to collect dried fish when he used to go hawking with his umbrella making. You see, the thing is... a hard fish is a dried fish. They used to catch a little cod. They used to hang them round outside the house to dry. He had a love for this dried fish. Some of the Perthshire travellers had met him on their visits to Argyll, and they saw old grandfather with his basket full of hard fish. They christened him 'hardfish' so their name passes down from generation to generation, passes on, a nickname but it's an insult, see.

And he started. So I hit him, and the woman screamed. The Travellers disappeared just in seconds. The guy was lying there and the police came.

Sergeant, 'You'd better come with me,' he says. Took me up to the police station.

The guy got up on his feet and he got away. His wife, his girlfriend or whatever she was to him, led him away that night. They packed their little cart and barrows, hand carts and away they went.

Sergeant took me over, put me in the cell for a while. I must have sat for two hours. The constable came and he gave me an enamel mug full of tea.

'Here's a cup of tea for you,' he said. 'What's the carry on about?'

I said, 'The're nae carry on!'

He said, 'You hit one of the Townsleys didn't you?'

I said, 'Aye, I hit him.' I said, 'So would you. I wasnae doing any harm, I just walked over. In fact, they're relations o' my mother's. My mother's second cousins.'

'Oh,' he said, 'we know them all. And what was the cause of the trouble?'

I said, 'He was being cheeky, he was being umperant, he was looking for a fight. I didn't want nothing to do with the man. But', I said, 'I couldn't take it any more, I just hit him.'

He says, 'You did him harm, didn't you? Do you no think you hit him a wee bit hard?

I said, 'I hit him.'

So the policeman, he went away and he came back, and the sergeant was with him. I remember him fine, the old sergeant had a patch on his knee. He was a sergeant of the police with a patch on his knee.

'You'd better come in here,' he says. 'Sit doon.'

I sat for a wee while. So he closed the cell door. Took me and sat for an hour. Oh he asked me all the questions. 'Where were you?'

I told him what I was doing. I just come fae Aberdeen. Told him about the boxing, told him I worked in Aberdeen.

'Well,' he said, 'I'll tell you what I'm going to do with you,' he says. 'I'm going to give you a wee tip,' he said. 'I'm going to let you go. He hasnae charged you. So there's not much we can do about it. Neither has his wife.'

The reason he didna charge was I had a father and a lot of brothers, and if they thought he had charged me and I got the jail, my father and my brothers would come looking for them. This was the kind of way with the Travelling folk. They believed it, though it would never have happened.

'So,' he said, 'he's pressing no charges. You're free to go, but I'm just warning you, if you come back to Campbeltown again keep away from these people.'

I left that day. I walked all the way back up to Aunt Rachel. I stayed that night with Aunt Rachel. Aunt Rachel had a wee job to do on a farm, a wee field of turnips, it was late (in the year) to thin the turnips. The're a wee farm doon near Kilberry. It was a good walk. She said, 'If you would like to come along and give me a wee hand to finish the neeps, I've got about ten or 12 drills left to finish.'

She'd been working two or three days before that. On her knees. You crawled on your knees and you singled out the plants. I was a good thinner of turnips. I'd done it hundreds of times before with my father when we were kids. So, me and her finished the wee puckle neeps. The farmer gave her nine pounds. She gave me two, two pounds.

So I says, 'Aunt Rachel, I'll have to move, I have to go.'

She says, 'Where you going, laddie? You cannae wander your age. You need to go and get a wife to yourself.'

I says, 'Nah, I'm no wantin nae wife, Aunt Rachel.' I tellt her about the lassie. I said, 'I've got a wean.'

'So I heard,' she says. 'Your sister was telling me,' she said, 'you've got a wee wean somewhere in Perthshire.'

I said, 'Aye.'

But she said, 'I hear the woman's married,' she says.

I said, 'Aye, she married someone else. I wasnae wantin her anyway, but I wanted the wean.'

'Oh the woman wouldnae give ye her wee wean,' she says. 'You're no able to look after a wean o' yir own!' She says, 'Ye have to get a wee wife to yourself.'

I says, 'No, Aunt Rachel, I'm no wantin nae wife to myself.'

So, she kissed me goodbye. And that was the last time I ever seen her.

I had a feeling I was needing something, but I didna know what it was. Then it dawned on me that, with being in the folk club in Glasgow, being in the boxing in Aberdeen, being at work with the minister, workin with my Aunt Rachel, fighting with the Travelling folk – where was my life leading me? What was I doing with myself? I couldna settle down with my parents. Where was I going?

One morning I left, I sees a lorry coming and I thumbed a lift over Crianlarich and Tyndrum. The driver, young fellow, dropped me off in Perth. Didna have any money, didna have a smoke. I was walking the street in Perth and lo and behold out of the blue who did I meet but my brother, Willie. God rest his soul.

'Where hae you been?' he says to me. 'You're no settled doon yet?'

I said, 'Not yet, no.' I said, 'Where are you going?'

He said, 'I'm going to the horse market.'

I said, 'You're going to the horse market? You're no wanting any horse.'

He says his old father-in-law had one leg, and he says, 'He sent me into the market to see the horses. He always keeps a pony, kept a horse and cart because he couldnae walk with one leg, went with a crutch.'

So I went to the horse market. This young lad came up. Curly hair. He had a strange eye. His eye was coloured, as if it was some kind of disease in it. He had short, curly hair. Willie, my brother, knew him.

He says to me, 'Come here a minute, I want you to meet somebody.'

This was to be the fate of my life.

He said, 'This is your cousin,' he says to me, 'John.'

I said, 'My cousin John, I never heard o' the lad.' So John shook hands with me.

This was the son of my mother's youngest brother who died with pneumonia when he was only 39. John was staying outside of Perth with his mother and two sisters. He kept horses, a horsieman.

He said, 'Would you like to come out and meet my mother?'

I said, 'I never met my Aunt Bella, never met her. I heard about her from my mother.'

He said, 'Come over with me.' He had a wee pony and a wee trap.

John yoked up his wee pony, nice wee pony, beautiful wee pony.

I jumped up and sat with him. He drove outside of Perth, way up by Scone up by the Blairgowrie Road, then up an old farm road. I seen two bow tents and a fire in the middle on the old road.

There's this woman, tall, dark woman, good looking woman. Woman maybe in her early 40s, you know. He says, 'This is your nephew, Naismort ['Mother' in Cant, the Traveller language].'

She says, 'You're Betsy's laddie?'

I said, 'Aye.' She shook hands with me.

Then I see these two lassies sitting. And this lassie about, what would she be, about 16. Beautiful young woman. Short curly hair. And I took an instant liking to her.

And that young woman was to become my wife. Jeannie.

I courted her. I stayed with my Aunt Bella for about three months in Fife. And I left again. I went away, because Jeannie had heard that there's another Traveller lassie that had a wean to me.

She says, 'You're goin back to find your wean. You canna have two wives at the same time.'

I said, 'I dinnae have a wife.'

Her mother wasna very keen about me carrying on with her daughter. I never had nae intercourse with her or nothing, but we were good friends. I liked her a lot but I didnae know if she liked me or no. Anyway I left her and I went back to Perth.

I went up to my brother Willie. I needed money. I had to get a job. I worked with him all winter long at the tatties on a farm called Shiellhill, Mr Petrie was the farmer. Then the spring came and I was getting wearied, wearied, wearied.

Then it came the berry time. Everybody came up to the berry picking, because the farmer had acres and acres of berries: he needed all the pickers he could get. He used to bring in buses, old fashioned buses from Perth and other places.

One day, who should appear but my Auntie Bella and her two boys and the two girls, and they pitched their tent in the field along with the berry pickers. Jeannie was there, God rest her.

So I went down to crack to Aunt Bella, had a nice talk to her. She seen I was still single. She found out that I was the father of this baby and the woman was married and there was no way that I was going to do anything about it. She kind of softened up a wee bit.

Me and Jeannie went for a walk and that night me and Jeannie eloped. We jumped the broomstick! We had a little stir, you know! We eloped – off we went. Where do you think we went to? Aberdeen! We went to Aberdeen. She had an auntie there. She knew all the roads because she travelled with her mother and we got on really really well.

At Her Majesty's Pleasure

JEANNIE AND I WENT to stay with an auntie of Jeannie's in Aberdeen, but Bella, her old mother, found out and caught up with us. See we'd been together for three months and Jeannie was gonna have a baby, so she told her mother.

'Well,' said her mother, 'the best thing you can do is come back and get married.' So we did. We got married in Glasgow. Jeannie was heavy expecting, a month to go before the baby was born, second oldest girl, Edith. Jeannie was a good while in hospital before and after. But I still didna have a horse and not having a horse was like a duck outta water, you wer'na accepted.

I went to a place called Darnley, outside of Glasgow. It had a big quarry. I went up to the office to the manager of the quarry and I asked him for a job.

He said, 'Have you ever worked in a quarry?'

I said, 'I was born beside a quarry, my father spent most of his life down a quarry. Sometimes I helped him quarrying. I know all about quarryin'.'

'You're a Traveller? Have you got a caravan?' he said.

'No, I've got a tent.'

'You can pitch your tent doon beside the quarry,' he said, 'this is our property.'

He took some kinda liking to me and says, 'You'll start tomorrow at eight o'clock.'

I wanted money for a horse and this was the only way I could get it. Next morning he took me to this shed made of steel. He had a bunch of keys, opened his shed and said, 'You see these boxes there? This is very dangerous stuff.'

I didn't know what it was.

'That's dynamite, and you see that?'

It was like your recorder cable.

'That's dynamite fuse. Now watch carefully,' he says.

He opened the box of dynamite, little long stick wrapped in brown paper, cut one through the middle and he said, 'I'll show you this once.' He folded back the paper, cut a bit of cable, about six inches long, took a cap, a wee kind of tube and closed it with his teeth.

'This is far from boxing and things like that,' I thought. A big boulder had dropped from a skip about twice the size of your bed. He took this wee cap, got a handful of earth, covered the cap and he took me back, say, 50 yards and all in a minute BOOM! And that big rock, twice the size of a bed, blew into a thousand pieces and he said to me, 'Now you see how dangerous that stuff really is young man?'

I said, 'Aye.'

That man took an instant liking to me and I was to learn later why.

Now I had a young wife, baby home from hospital in the tent with Jeannie, 'course she had her mother to help her. I was happy. I was working. I was settled and I was getting the price for a horse and food was cheap at that time.

There was the gaffer, himself, he never hardly spoke to me, this man; a Glasgow man, big guy, with a khaki shirt, sleeve rolled up, tattooed, a big man, eh? There was a wee shed and there was a big urn with hot water in it and all the workers come in and they fill their wee drums with tea, sat down and drank their tea. I walked up and I seen the drum empty, empty.

I said, 'Who boiled the drum?'

The gaffer said, 'I did, I boiled it.'

I said, 'You never left me enough water, did you, for my tea?'

He said, 'You dinna need fucking water, you're not doing nothing. Ye're workin' like a school boy following the manager around.'

I said, 'What's wrong wi' you, ye're supposed to be the gaffer, ye're supposed to boil that so that everybody gets some water for their tea.'

'What do you know about this?' he asked.

I said, 'I'm telling you plain, I take some water same as everybody else, I work here.'

Anyway, it came to a head. One word led to another. I said, 'Listen pal, I don't give a damn about nobody here and I don't give a damn about you.' And then an old man chipped in.

'That's enough boys, we don't want any trouble.'

I said, 'He's looking for trouble, and he will get it if he wants it.'

The old man says, 'Do you live in a tent down there?'

I said, 'Aye, I live in a tent but don't let it deceive yer.'

Then, I saw the manager come in. 'What's going on here?' He asked, 'What's the problem Duncan?'

I said, 'Nae water for my tea.'

He said to the gaffer, 'Did you no fill the urn?'

The gaffer said, 'I thought there was enough for everybody.'

'Well,' said the manager, 'the young chap hasnae got no water for his tea.' He said, 'Come wi' me.' And he walked me over to his house. Big enamel tea pot sitting there.

'Take a cup. Are you quite comfortable in the tent down there?' he said to me.

I said, 'Aye, I'm fine in the tent.'

'Aah, we only have a wee while,' he said, looking at his watch, 'so have yer tea. Have yer tea and a fag.'

That gaffer never spoke to me again, all the time I was there. But the manager took me in one day. That man taught me everything you want to know. I could blow a fly from a rock. And he said to me one day before I left.

'I had a boy once, but I never had the pleasure to bring him up. My wife took him off when he was only a year old. Went off to Africa. I would have loved to have him here working with me, and you being here with me for the last two months has been what it felt like to have a son, that I could teach all the things that I've learnt. Are you sure you wouldnae stay on? I could give you a better place to stay.'

I said, 'No, I couldnae stay.'

He said, 'Why?'

'Have to move on.' I said, 'we are Travelling folks, we have to move on.'

'Well,' he said, 'I'll tell you something. It's been a real pleasure having you here.'

So, keeping myself and buying things for Jeannie, God rest her, and the wean, I managed to save 26 pounds and we left Glasgow and went all the way to Fife, a wee place called the Star o' Markinch. There was an old pig-man there and he kept ponies. For 23 pounds I bought a little float and a wee pony and a set of harness. 23 pounds! It carried my wife and my stuff around the countryside. Now I was a man of my own. I had a wife and a wee baby and I'd never seen my parents for over 18 months. I was gonna take off in the world and be a Traveller and travel the countryside. Show off my wife to my brothers, show off my wife and baby to my parents and do things that other Travellers would do.

I was qualified. I could blow a fly off a rock. I could work on farms. I could handle a horse. I was happy. I had a wife, a wee baby running round my feet. I was capable of joining the Traveller community, being a young Traveller man but there was something missing. For the love of me I couldnae find out what it was. I wanted to go back and see my parents but now my wife was pregnant again. I couldnae trail my wife away over the hills, away from hospital over to Argyllshire because there was no doctors on these roads away back into Argyll. I would have to postpone the trip till next summer. I was needing to find a job, get myself a place to stay, a field to put my horse.

Above Leven I see this farm in the distance. It was surrounded by barley fields and wheat fields. There was an old road called Kennoway Old Road. And I camped on this road and I said to Jeannie – God rest her – I said, 'I'm going away up to see the old farmer, see if I can get a job on the harvest.'

She says, 'Dinnae stay too long away.'

There was a collie dog at the door, barked at me but it never come near me. I patted it. I went up to the door. A wee old fat man like Santa Claus came out. 'Eh laddie,' he says, 'what is it ye're after?'

I knew the accent – Ayrshire.

'Er, I'm looking fer a job at the harvest.'

'Er, you worked the harvest before?'

I said, 'I worked the harvest all my life.'

'Och aye,' he said 'when could you start?'

I says, 'I'll start the morning.'

He says, 'Very good.'

'Jeannie,' I says, 'I got a job.'

'You got a job?' she says. 'That's fine. So I've got to sit here,' she says, 'all day while you go.'

'Well,' I says, 'maybe your mother will come and move in.'

Honest to God, the words were just shooting out my mouth, when

I heard the horse's feet on the road, and sure enough it was her mother and her two brothers and wee sister. And I was glad.

But that old farmer was to become a great friend of mine. I was with that man Sandy Kerr – Alexander Kerr for 16 years.

* * *

Duncan often spoke of that time. Chancing on Sandy Kerr for the harvest in 1950 put a congenial routine into his life with Jean and the family. 'It was fun.' He and Jeannie's brother, John, were wonderfully well fed. 'Beautiful chunk o' mutton and tatties, two bowls of soup, eh? Teapot and two mugs of beautiful tea. God bless you.' They were well fed, well paid. 'A pound a day. Money for old rope.' They were accepted and happy.

Even when, as an ominous note of things to come, a friendly policeman visited their roadside camp, 'Boys I'm afraid you'll have to move. You're only allowed 24 hours, you know,' Sandy rescued them, giving them camping space in a 'nice wee sheltery place in a field.'

To their surprise and delight harvest came to tattie time, sociable and robust with squads of women of all ages from Methil, a fine core with bawdy blatant tales. 'The most pleasantest folk you ever saw in your life.' The tatties gathered, they were ready to decamp, but no, 'Yer no gonna awa?' They were needed for dressing, riddling, 'chug, chug, chug, the old machine shook the tatties.' Then, packing and loading the potatoes in countless hundredweight bags. 'You could lift one under your arm.' And they were not above a wee bit of trading, the odd bag of tatties, for fags. 'Packets o' Woodbines.'

The endless seasonal rhythm of the farm, next: 'Oh you'll bide tae shaw the neeps.' So Duncan and John shawed and carted the rows of turnips and filled the shed, cattle feed for Sandy's hundred dairy cows. But the spring fever was on them and they were dying to be on the move when canny old Sandy says, 'Eh? He, he, you wouldnae go off without giving us a hand with the plantin'?'

He was 'the nicest old soul you ever met.'

Every winter for 16 years they returned, Duncan ending up as head dairyman.

When the two months summer school break came along old Sandy would say: 'Yer off fer yer wee wander.' Off they would set to visit Duncan's parents, granny and grandpa, now in Argyll. In the early days it was horse and cart.

To the children, as Duncan's eldest daughter Edith told me, these were marvellous journeys, tourists taking photographs of this colourful family on the road, Duncan loading the horse and the kids sitting on the cart. A household on wheels, everything for cooking, sleeping and shelter, another world.

* * *

We packed up, cleaned up the field, you'd never have kent there was a soul there apart for the marks o' the tents. Yoked the ponies, packed the tents and off we went. Now, in these days with the horses you couldnae travel very far. You know what I mean? Bonnie wee bairns and my wife curly hair sitting on the cart. Little cart tidied up with a green cover, all these possessions we had with blankets, with cooking utensils, with clathes fer the weans, everything we needed on the cart. And I would walk the horse. We had regular camping places. We would maybe go sometimes 15 miles, sometimes it was 20 miles in between campsites. From Kennoway say to Strathmiglo, camp there; next night we'd camp outside Perth. Next time outside Crieff, then Loch Earn then Crianlarich, on to Dalmally into Inveraray. I wanted to go back and see my parents. They had never seen my wife. Never seen the children. Parents had left Furnace.

The old Duke of Argyll had died. What do you think he did, the young Duke? Right up near the castle in Inveraray there was a woodman's hut. Beautiful hut, wooden hut. Two-roomed hut, stove, and the young Duke said, 'Mr Williamson, I want you and Betsy to move up to the hut in Inveraray. It will be more comfortable for you because we're going to cut the forest.'

When I got to Inveraray, first person I see was my mother in the street. Introduced her to my wife. That was her brother's wee lassie, you know. Mother was happy.

'We've got another place,' she said. 'I'm working in the Duke's kitchen in the castle. Your father's working in the woods.'

I moved down to the shore at Inveraray. The kids were completely crazy about the shore. I showed them whelks, I showed them mussels, I showed them how to cook whelks. It was happy times, but then a change was to happen in my life.

One night, Jeannie and me took a walk up to see granny, my mother, in the wee hut. And there in the drive was a wee grey Morris 1000. Who was in the car? None of my family had a car. There's a young woman sitting in the hut when we goes in. Granny, my mother, was making tea. My brother George was there, he'd come from Dunbarton. He'd come with this woman. This woman was Helen Fullerton. The folklorist who later became a great friend of Hamish Henderson.

She was a great friend of Hamish Henderson in The School of Scottish Studies. She was a great friend of Norman Buchan, of Peter Hall, of all the folk singers. She collected many tapes, recorded many folk singers. She was over recording granny on the mouth music. Granny was a great singer at the mouth music. Helen had picked up my brother George in Dunbarton. George and her was great friends. I think my brother George and she were more than friends. Anyway, we sat there and my mother asked me to sing a song and Helen asked me could she record it.

I said, 'Sure.'

I sang two or three songs for her. She recorded them. She says, 'That's beautiful, I have to get you through to Glasgow.' My wife Jeannie was looking daggers at me as if to say, 'That'll be right.'

Anyway, I made my way back to Perthshire. I worked on a farm and in comes the Morris 1000. It was big Helen Fullerton again. She was with my brother George. She was wondering if I wanted to go along to sing.

'No, I cannae go along. I cannae leave my wife.'

'I want you to come to Glasgow and sing in Glasgow for me,' she says, 'and you'll get paid well for it.'

Now, trying to convince Jeannie for me to go away with a woman was impossible. I tried to persuade her that I was gonna do no harm. I never got with Helen to Glasgow that time.

So we moved over to Fife and I got back to work at Sandy Kerr's at the farm again. This time we got a wee cottage. Old Sandy says, 'Eh, eh, you'll no need to go back to the field this year. There's an empty hoose up there, if you want that.' I was over the moon. We moved into the cottage and put my horse in the field and started to work again. It was a wonderful time but things weren't going to be as good as they were. Things were to change.

There was something deep inside me that I needed. I didn't know what it was; I was to discover later. I was wanting to get away. Couldna wait for the spring fever to come. What was it I wanted? I was making a few shillings, I got a bigger horse, I had two children and another on the way, I could go home, see the kids, sit with the children at night, tell these wonderful stories to the kids, sing songs, have fun with the two, with Edith and Jimmy, my two oldest children who were beginning to grow up and it was nice. And we were close, Jeannie, my wife, and me. Life with her was great. But I knew I wanted something else and you know, when the spring comes in you got this kind of spring fever. It happens to all Travelling folk, even today. There's something within that pulls you onto the road. There's no Traveller can settle down and have this nine o'clock till five o'clock job. Even if you got a comfortable house and a good home. You can't be content with that kind of thing if you are born and bred as a Traveller. There's some kind of pull within the body and it has to get out. So then my problem started.

You see, my wife, God rest her, was very, very jealous. She was nice when we were together by ourself, not that I encouraged, gave her any cause, any reason to be jealous, no, I gave her no reason to be jealous. I think she thought I would find somebody else because it did happen even among Travellers you know, leaving their wives and taking off wi' another woman. It did happen. They are human beings. And she thought maybe I would leave her and go off with someone else. I think not until the day she died, God rest her soul, at the age of 39, did she ever forgive me for my first baby. Even though it had nothing to do with her, she knew I had intercourse with a woman before I met her and she never had a man in her life till I met her. She was only 16. And the other wee girl I made love to before I went to Aberdeen, she was only 16 too, of course and I was 18. It was okay when we were alone by ourselves, Jeannie and me. She couldnae read, she couldnae write and I use to read stories. She loved to hear stories. She loved story books. Romances you know, and I use to sit and read a story to her. It was alright as long as we would be by ourselves on our own wi' the two kids. But sometimes

I needed a bit of male company, so I went took my wee son with me, five year old, to go and have a crack to other men around the campfires and that, and she one time followed me with a torch, went from tent to tent looking for me.

'Is Duncan there? Is Duncan there?' And then when I had come back she wouldnae speak to me all night. 'Where were you?'

I said, 'I was away talking to some of the boys.'

'Oh, I went round looking for you with the torch and couldnae find you. Where have you been?'

I loved her, I respected her and I did everything that a husband should do for her. Never argued with her, never lifted my hand to her, never beat her; she never had a black eye in her life or a fight, or an argument. But she never trusted me. I trusted her. I knew she wouldnae even look at another person. She could do what she liked but if I went away walking, I had to face a court of law when I got back.

'Where were you? Who were you talking to? Why were you so long?'

And this permeated into your mind, you know, till it came to the crunch. Now, the kids were getting a bit older and I walked up on my way to granny's, my mother's. I left Jeannie and the three kids playing on the beach. When I got there, to my mother's, Helen Fullerton was there. She was from Glasgow University. George was with her. Wherever you find George you found Helen and Helen says to me:

'You must come to Glasgow, you've got to come and sing in Glasgow.'

Now here was me caught between the Devil and the deep blue sea. I definitely wanted to go and sing in Glasgow. I knew fine it would mean to stay the night. I knew fine that my wife would be safe alright at home 'cause an old man and his wife had moved into the shore. The police would never bother her. She could camp on the shore for as long as she liked. She would be safe enough. So I said to Helen, 'I'll come to Glasgow.'

And she said, 'I'll pick you up and I'll drive you over to Glasgow. I cannae take you home, you'll have to stay the night.'

So I go back home and Jeannie was there and we were sitting on the shore and the old couple was sitting at the fire as well. I says to Jeannie, 'I'm going to Glasgow tomorrow.'

She says, 'What?'

I said, 'I'm going to Glasgow to sing in the concert.'

'How are you gonna get to Glasgow?'

I said, 'Helen Fullerton.'

She knew Helen, she'd spoke to her before. Then she went completely berserk, crazy. She took all her clothes and put them on the fire. Burnt them up, every single clothes that she wore, put them on the fire and burnt them.

She said, 'Yer no going.'

I said, 'I'm going to Glasgow. There's no way about it, I'm going to Glasgow, that's what I want to do.'

One thing led to another and she never spoke to me all that night. I had this great feeling in my heart, in some ways it was kind of enlightening. As if I had a new lease of life in me, no matter what Jeannie said, no matter what she cried, no matter what.

The kids said, 'Where are you going, Daddy? When are you coming back, Daddy?'

I said, 'I'm only going away for one night, I'm going to sing in Glasgow.'

And the kids, my two wee boys and girls. Jimmy, a great singer today, said, 'Aye, alright Daddy, just stay away for one night.'

There was plenty company there for Jeannie. My brother moved in; he was camped at the shore. She was no lonely, she had plenty of food, my horse was in a good place. There was firewood around, the kids were playing, a clean wee stream ran by where she could get clean water. I knew she was alright. Here was me given the chance of my life to go to Glasgow to sing in a concert. I didnae know many people, I wasnae caring. The more people that would be there, the better for me. This was something I wanted.

I tidied and cleaned myself up. Jeannie wouldnae talk to me. I walked up to granny's (I always called my mother granny), to the hut and granny says, 'Where are you going?'

I says, 'I'm going to Glasgow, Granny, to sing.'

'Good, you'll sing alright, you know you're a good singer. Give me a wee song before you go. You sit down.' She always had a bottle of sherry in her hut. I felt really good, great joy in my heart. I wasnae forgetting the kids, I wasnae forgetting the wife but this was something new. The new world to me. I think this was the beginning, this was the beginning for me.

Helen turned up about three o'clock next day in her wee Morris 1000. A young woman maybe in her 30s and we drove to Glasgow up to her little flat in Hyndland Road. She made me a cup of tea. Helen was a folklorist, long before Linda Headlee that was to be my wife, long before Jeannie Robertson or Betsy Whyte or The School of Scottish Studies, which was started in 1953. Hamish started the school then, I think. Hamish was a great friend of Helen, so was Geordie MacIntyre, so was Dr John Purser, so was Norman Buchan. These were the folklorists coming up for the '60s and she was studying Archaeology at the University of Glasgow. She even took about 50 of my tapes and gave them to Ewan MacColl when she moved down to England. I've heard Ewan singing some of my songs. Songs I wrote myself, singing them on the radio, but that's another story.

We went to the hall and I was introduced to people. People were walking around with wee glasses of white wine and things like that, didnae bother me. Norman Buchan was there with his wife. I was so excited to be there. It came my turn to sing. Helen introduced me. The first song I sang was 'The Cruel Grave' and it was the first time I was to sing it in public. There was silence, you could hear a pin drop. I sang it really well, everybody loved it, the applause was great. I sang another song, I think I sang three songs.

After I'd finished, all the people gathered around me. This was the thing I wanted. I felt that here was what I wanted to do with my life. I wanted to sing folk songs. I never wanted to go on radio or making records or anything like that, I just wanted to be at folk clubs and sing folk songs like it was back with granny, back with my Aunt Rachel, God rest her. Singing folk songs. I felt I was paying them respect to keep the whole thing alive because I was singing some of their songs. From the first time I sang 'Lady Margaret' in public that night, Dr John Purser, he didn't have his doctorate then, came up and said to me, 'Where in the world did you learn that song?'

I said, 'From my grandmother.'

He said, 'That's another version of 'Tam Lin',' he said, 'look you don't know what you've got.'

That was the words he said.

'It's just another song to me,' I said.

And I was to meet him again later on in time.

Anyway, it was a lovely evening. We went back to Helen's flat. She made me a little bed on the floor with a couple of blankets, and the next morning we had breakfast and she said to me, 'I'll run you back to

Inveraray. I've got to see your mother to record some mouth music.' Helen gave me an envelope and I stuck it in my pocket.

She said, 'Peter Hall wants you to go to Aberdeen.'

I said, 'There's no way I'm going to get to Aberdeen.'

She said, 'I could take you there.'

I said, 'Helen, it's impossible. You don't know the problem I'm going to face when I go back with Jeannie.'

Jeannie didnae have much time for her. She was jealous. She was jealous of everybody, not that she wasn't a good looking woman herself. She was a beautiful young woman. So Helen dropped me off and I walked down. Jeannie was sitting there. She never spoke to me. The kids gathered round me, the wee one was about two. I pulled the envelope out of my pocket and opened it. There was 11 pounds in it. Two five pound notes and a single pound and in these days that was a lot of money. I mean, I was going to work on the beach for days, for five shillings a stone. I had to collect whelks, put them in a bag, take them all the way to Campbeltown on my horse and sell them for five shillings a stone. There were no cars in these days and here was me getting 11 pounds.

I said to Jeannie, 'Look, I got 11 pounds last night.'

She said, 'Maybe that's not all you got.'

I said, 'What do you mean?'

She said, 'You were away with that woman all night, weren't you?'

I said, 'Of course I was, I was singing.'

Wee Jimmy and Edith said, 'Was it good Daddy? Did you enjoy yourself?'

The kids were delighted.

'There's ten pounds for you,' I said to Jeannie and she clutched it as if it was dirt.

'You take that for you and the kids, and I'll take this pound for fags,' I said.

She never said anything. There seemed to be a split somehow. Even in bed together she would turn her back to me. It was now a case of, we couldnae get through to each other in some way. There was mistrust. I thought if this is what it's going to be, then what's the point. Something happened to our lives at that time. Even though I stayed with her until she died, things were never going to be the same again.

I said, 'We'll move on tomorrow.'

So, we went back to Campbeltown, camped somewhere amongst other Travellers, it was nice for the kids. But summer passes quickly and so it was time to get back over the hills and dales, back to Fife. I knew when I got back to Sandy Kerr's and Letham Farm, I had work. The horse was in the field and I could start right away but I knew fine I would give Helen my address. I told Helen where to find me and it's not so far from Fife to Aberdeen.

I told Helen, 'I'll come to Aberdeen.'

She said, 'I'll take you. Wherever you are I'll find you.'

Maybe she had a wee notion for me. I don't know, but we never had nothing together, in that way. Never even kissed her on the cheek.

For Jeannie and me, God rest her, it was a good summer in Argyll. So we came to Inveraray, said goodbye to granny We had a few pennies from the whelks in the summer and enough money to buy food and the horses shoes were fine. My horse came first. I couldnae go to bed, couldnae eat or sleep if my horse hadnae food. No way! Horse was always the first thing. You unyoked your horse, took its harness off, hung it up to dry because the horse would have been sweating, you rubbed your horse down, took care of your horse, before you even kindled your fire or made your kids a cup of tea even though your kids were hungry.

We packed up and we went on our way back to Fife up to Leven. Yoked the horse, told old Sandy we were back. 'Okay laddie,' he said, 'you came back, you can get back to your hoose.'

So, life went back to normal when out of the blue one day I came back at dinnertime and there was the Morris 1000 lying outside of the house. Helen Fullerton. I think for Jeannie to see Helen Fullerton, it was like seeing the Devil himself. I liked her and I liked her company, I liked what she stood for. She never went without her recorder.

I said to Helen once, 'Helen dear, you're a very nice person and it's nice to be in your company.'

She said, 'I don't think it's me that's company for you, Duncan, I think it's my tape recorder.'

And of course, many times she played me back the tape and some of the songs I'd sang. It was nice to hear your own voice on tape for the first time.

This was about the end of October. She said, 'There's a big concert coming up in Aberdeen. There'll be great people there. The Corries are going. You've been invited. Peter Hall wants you to sing. I'll take you but you'll have to take the train back.'

Then, it started. Helen didn't stay long. Here was Jeannie back in her moods again.

'So, you're away back to Aberdeen again, what's the farmer going to say?'

I said, 'I'll ask him for the day off or I'll work late.' This feeling within me had blossomed again. I'd come through the first step with Jeannie and her jealousy and her hate and her scolding and the backlash and all the things she had said, but something stood out in front of all that, the idea that I wanted to sing to people, to sing granny's songs. The songs people have never heard. These old songs from Aunt Rachel, from my mother. I was keeping them alive and I think this appealed to people because I was giving them something.

I had hundreds of stories. Stories of all description I had collected through time but they were all locked away in my head. I never gave a story a thought. Oh, I told stories to the kids at night-time, they were brought up on stories, Edith and Jimmy. Their heads were packed with stories, every night. All types of stories, I would say, 'Come and sit down and I will tell you a story. This is a story from my daddy and when he told them I was wee like you and someday I want like you to tell it for me.' I would tell the kids all these beautiful stories. They loved the stories.

But I wanted to get out there, to be with people, to sing. This kind of gave me enlightment about what to do. It was coming up for the '60s and folk music was taking a grip and here was me with all these beautiful songs, a knowledge of songs and stories that some people had never had. That's all I wanted to do. I'd never heard nor never been to The School of Scottish Studies, even though they told me about it.

Now I had four children, Edith, Jimmy, Willie and Betty the baby. Jeannie, God rest her, was the mother of four children and would someday be the mother of seven. If only she had a little faith in me, and understood that if I had wanted another woman I would never have stayed with her all these years. If she had just given me a little trust, a little faith. She never could. I always believed it was stemming back from the first mistake I made. I wasnae looking for sex, I wasnae looking for women, I was looking for something else.

I just wanted to have a bit of time, maybe once or twice a week sing in a pub or club, go and teach songs, do a recording for people, that's all I was asking from her. But I couldn't get that, never got it willingly. But I had to do it anyway, and so I did. She accepted it but she never learnt to live with it until the day she died.

Helen was going to come on a Sunday.

I said, 'Helen, I can't stay the night.'

She said, 'The concert finishes about ten, we'll put you on board a train to Cupar.'

From Cupar to Letham, where I lived, was about six miles. I knew if the worst came to the worst I could walk it. Six miles to me then was nothing. But Jeannie dreaded this day coming up, this Sunday. Jeannie was so beautiful, I wouldnae have left her in a million years. I would never have gave her up for anybody, but try to tell her this was out of the question. Maybe she knew somehow in her own mind, but she didnae know then she had a bad heart. If I had known then, what I know now, that Jeannie was going to die when she was only 39 and I was only 41, and that I would have the whole world in front of me and my children would be partly grown up, I could go wherever I please. But I didn't know and I thought me and her were going to grow together as a couple and me not doing the things that I wanted to do.

Anyway, this Sunday morning, Helen turned up in her wee car. Jeannie never said 'cheerio' to me. We got to Aberdeen, I went to the concert, MC was there, the Corries were there, leather waistcoats, Ronnie Brown and Roy. I sang three songs that night and then I went to the bar. In comes this woman, big white scarf round her neck, good looking woman.

She said, 'Are you Duncan Williamson?'

I said, 'Aye.'

She said, 'I'm a great friend of Hamish Henderson.'

There was nobody ever said a bad word about Hamish Henderson. Hamish Henderson was a legend among the Travellers even though, like me, they'd never met him at that time. He'd come to their tents. He sat with his big car battery and his bicycle. He'd let them hear themselves on the tape recorder and people couldnae believe it could happen, to hear their own voice telling stories. It was amazing. Hamish brought a new world to the Travelling people. Around the berry fields of Blair, he brought a new world for them. He gave them something to look forward to. They were always looking forward to having a cup of tea or coffee with Hamish. Maybe a wee drink. He is a legend among the Travelling folk.

Anyway, this woman come up to me, she says, 'You've a lovely voice laddie. I'm Jeannie Robertson.'

I said, 'I've heard of you. Are you going to give us a song tonight?'

She said, 'I'd love to, but I've a sare throat and I'm no booked for this anyway.'

So I finished about ten o'clock. I'm getting a bit worried, you see, I've got to get back to Fife and Jeannie Robertson came up to me and said, 'That's a braw song, would you like up to our hoose and I'll gie ye a ballad or twa, a lang sang, a wee perty?'

I said, 'Jeannie, if you couldnae sing tonight what's the point of going down to your hoose?'

She says, 'My throat's no as bad as it was, I think I could sing a few songs to you.'

I said, 'I'm really sorry, I can't come down to your house tonight.'

'That's a pity,' she said, 'I wanted to hear you sing, to hear mair about you and hear mair of your songs.'

I said, 'So would I.'

Anyway, that was the first and last that I ever met Jeannie Robertson. Peter Hall gave me an envelope with 15 pounds. Helen dropped me off and I got a train to Cupar and I walked home.

It must have been one o'clock in the morning by the time I walked from Cupar Station to Letham, nearly six or seven miles. But I felt happy, this great weight was gone from my life, somehow. I was beginning to be recognised and people were liking my songs and I wanted to do more of it. But this didn't make my life with Jeannie any happier. She still had the idea that I was looking for other women. I felt that I was paying respect to my old ancestors and singing the songs of the old singers Harry Lauder, Will Fyffe, Harry Gordon, Joe Mercer, Jimmy McBeath and some day people will be singing Hamish Henderson's songs when he's gone. I hope some people will sing my songs when I'm gone. I had found what I wanted to do, I loved it and I need to keep on with it as long as I survive.

Anyway, the winter passed quickly enough working with old Sandy. Usually, we'd go away down to Argyllshire but this time we crossed over the ferry, from Queensferry over to Edinburgh – no motorways in these days, just the old back road. We carried on down to Dumfries, the Borders, Galloway and Peebles.

The willows were growing wild and I could make baskets. We could make a living from baskets when we were on the road. We would see the willows on the roadside, stop the horse, cut a big bunch of willows, put them on the cart. When we came to the campsite, I'd put up the tent, I'd make a fire and Jeannie would make meals for the kids. We'd sit down and I taught the kids to help me peel the willows. I made a little thing called a 'slide' like a clothes peg, and you'd take the skin off because in the spring the willows are full of sap and the skin comes off easily. The kids would peal the willows and I'd sit down and make a couple of baskets. Maybe a message basket, shopping basket, and Jeannie would hawk them at the doors for five shillings a basket, which was cheap. At the end of spring that year we camped at Coalton of Balgonie. Travellers have been camping there since the 18th century. It was an old right of way.

But tragedy was to haunt me on this journey. The night shift miners would come cycling down on their bicycles with a little lamp on their head. My horse had too much scope. It had eaten one side of the road, and it crossed to the other side to eat along the bank, leaving the rope across the road. A miner came cycling down, ran into the rope and he somersaulted from his bicycle. We heard him cursing and swearing. So, I tied the horse short so he couldnae dae the same thing again. Well, in our camp there was a man, Albert McMillan, a non-Traveller who had married a Traveller lassie. He knew these miners, was a cronie drinking in the pubs with them and that miner told him, 'Bloody tinkers down the road: horse knocked me off my bike.' So this Albert McMillan came back from the pub shouting, 'Out youse. You put your bloody horse across the road, knocked a miner off the road.' He challenged us to a fight.

I says, 'Away you go to your bed, you're annoying folks, nobody's wanting any trouble with you.'

He says, 'Could you put me to my bed?'

I says, 'Look, I'll give you two minutes, two minutes to get to your bed.'

He says, 'You put me to my bed. You think you're a big man, don't you?'

I says, 'I'll put you to your bed.' Smack! Right there on the jawbone. He fell.

People came out, his wife came out. She saw him lying there in the road unconscious, sent for the police, ambulance. He was put in the ambulance and they sent him to Kirkcaldy, but they couldnae do anything in Kirkcaldy so they took him to Edinburgh. His jaw was broken in three places. He had to be wired up. Police came. Sergeant said, 'We're not going to arrest you but don't leave the district.'

I said, 'I cannae stay.'

'Don't leave the district, we want to see if this man dies or lives. If you're going to move, keep in touch, report to the next police station.'

So nobody ever bothered me as long as I reported. We left Coalton of Balgonie. I'd forgotten all about it.

I moved down to a little roadway near Kingskettle in Fife. A little Morris van came, two policemen.

'Duncan Williamson?'

'Yes.'

'Right, in the back!'

I was arrested, they took me to Cupar, put me in the cell. I lay all night in the cell, I left my wife and kids behind me, nobody took care of her, no company, nothing. I didn't know how she was going to get on.

I says, 'What's the charge?'

He says, 'You're charged with assault and breach of the peace.'

They took me to the Sheriff's Court in Cupar the next morning and the Procurator Fiscal stood up, Sheriff Moore.

He said, 'Why has this case taken so long to come to Court? It's been three months ago.'

'My Lord, the accused absconded and he cleared out of the district and we couldn't find him. It was a drunken brawl, My Lord.'

The Sheriff with his wig was sitting at the table. He said, 'Have you anything to say for yourself?'

'Well, My Lord,' I said, 'it was not a drunken brawl. He came drunk commanding to fight and upsetting and disturbing the whole family. He was under the influence of drink. He forced himself upon me, My Lord, I kept in touch with the police. If they wanted me they could have found me.' They hummed and hawed and the Procurator Fiscal said, 'We don't have that statement in Court. I have no option but to send you to prison for 30 days.'

I said, 'My Lord, can I have time to pay?'

He said, 'No time to pay.'

I turned round, I could have got myself Contempt of Court, and said to that Sheriff, 'I am innocent of the crime you accuse me of. I think I'll be the last person you ever send to prison.'

I was took off to Perth and I was put in prison. That night Sheriff Moore dropped with a heart attack and died. At five o'clock that night, anyone will tell you.

Anyway I spent the first night, and the next day went for a walk out in the exercise yard. There was another Traveller man there, Jimmy Johnson, who I knew well. He was in for beating his wife or something. Anyway that's another story. He was good company. Now you couldnae get a smoke. No smoking of any kind. Jimmy had a wee box. He had a burnt rag, a razor blade and a wee flint. He held the flint into the burnt rag and you scratched the razor blade and the sparks set the cloth alight. You got a wee light and you could puff off it. You got this stuff called Digger, black, like ground up black tobacco.

He says, 'Take my box with you.'

I said, 'I've no cigarette papers.'

He says, 'Maybe you could borrow a paper off somebody.'

I says, 'Thanks Jimmy, I'll take your box.'

Old Bayne, a wee screw, he was built like a woman, slim and tender like a woman, locked me in the cell and I had this little box. Now, I'd never had a smoke for four or five days. I was going mental. I looked over and there was the Bible. Bingo! The inside page was blank. Nothing on it. I tore the page off. I made myself a cigarette paper. Quick! Window open, I'm sitting and in comes wee Bayne. Civil as the day is long. Treated you good. He saw the bit of paper, he saw the Bible lying beside me, he saw the bit I'd tore out and he says, 'You took a bit out of the Bible?'

I says, 'Aye, I couldnae get a bit of paper.'

'That's it!' he said. He picks up the Bible and says, 'Leave that down there.'

I left the fag and the wee box on the floor. I was brought before the governor. There he was sitting, old man in his suit, gold rimmed specs. Twenty packet of Gold Flake in front of his ashtray. The screw closed the door.

'Have a seat,' he says. 'You know why you've been brought before me?'

I says, 'I havenae done any harm.'

He says, 'You've been making a cigarette, haven't you?'

I says, 'Well, I was trying to.' I was looking at the fags on his desk. Twenty Gold Flakes, matches and his ashtray. Half smoked bits that he'd just taken a wee smoke from.

He said, 'You know, young man, you've torn up the Bible.'

I says, 'Look governor, I'm a Traveller. You'd call me a tinker. I'm getting 30 days here for nothing.'

'It's nothing to do with me,' he says. 'I don't know what goes on outside the prison. That's for the law to deal with.'

I said, 'I've had five days here since I had a smoke.'

He said, 'You'll be getting five Woodbine at the end of the week and then you can smoke to your heart's content. Now about this Bible affair.'

I said, 'I'm a Traveller and a tinker, religion means nothing to me. I believe Jesus was a man, just like me and you, and he died for his sins and people didnae understand him, at that time. He had no magical powers, he couldnae turn water into wine.'

'Look,' he says, 'I don't want to hear your ideas about religion. What you think is nothing to do with me. All you're here for is destroying prison property.'

I said, 'Prison property! It was only a page of the Bible.'

'Ummmm, yes,' he said, 'today, it's only a page of the Bible. Tomorrow, it could be something else.' He said, 'I have to refuse your five days remission.' And there was the Gold Flakes, 20 packet, sitting on the table and me never having a smoke. I was led back to my cell.

Sitting on the floor was a pail full of water, bar of soap, scrubbing brush and sponge. Written in chalk on the floor was *please scrub concrete floor*. I got down and scrubbed. Down on my knees, clean as I could, never even got my little roll-up. You could have eaten a meal off the floor. Anyway, we did get our five Woodbine and I said to the screw, 'Can you give me a light?'

Wee Bayne took a lighter out of his pocket, old fashioned lighter, he gave me that, he gave me five Woodbine. He says, 'That's your quota, make them last now.' And I sat there with that five Woodbine, and the one light I had, and I smoked one fag after the other. When the cigarette was burned down I lighted another one and another one, and I smoked that five cigarettes one after the other, and I never enjoyed anything like it in all my life.

So along came Sunday and wee Bayne says, 'You want to go to chapel?'

'Yes, I want to go to chapel.'

I went to chapel with the Catholics and I went to church with the Protestants to get out of the cell, but the happiest day of my life was *click*. Cell door. You're not going to believe this. There's a man standing in his shirtsleeves, a book under his arm, white jacket on him and a screw with him.

'Williamson!' They never called you by your first name.

He says, 'This is Dr such and such. Would you like to give some blood?'

'Aye,' I said, 'definitely.'

He said, 'You'll get a cup of tea and a cigarette.'

I said, 'You can have all my blood for a couple of cigarettes.'

The doctor smiled and he said, 'That's the spirit, young man, that's the spirit.'

We went down the stairs into the wee room. A young woman sitting at the table.

'Pull up the sleeve.' Needle, and she filled a glass full of blood.

I said, 'Have you got enough? Do you want some more?'

'No, no, that's fine.' The lassie went to a wee box and pulled out an enamel badge. Enamel, beautiful – *Blood Donor* – it said on it. She pinned it on my shirt. Everyone who is a blood donor gets one of these.

I said, 'Thank you very much. I appreciate that.'

She said, 'Cigarette and a cup of tea?'

I said, 'This is fun.' Big cup of tea, good strong tea (prison tea was just like water), and a biscuit, a digestive biscuit. I thought this was great. So I had my cup of tea and I had my fag, and then the warden says, 'Back up the stairs again.' Standing at the cell door was old Mr Crawford. He was from the next cell to me. An old tall man, glasses on, roman nose like an old Indian Chief, grey hair, Englishman, spoke good English.

I said, 'Hello, Mr Crawford, how are you?'

He said, 'Fine, fine. Can I have a word with you?'

I says, 'Aye.' The warden is standing there in my cell.

He says, 'Jimmy here was telling me you're a bit of a singer!'

I said, 'Aye, I sing at folk clubs. I've been in Aberdeen and Glasgow and I would like to be a real singer. I want to sing more.'

He said, 'I'm a singing teacher.'

I said, 'What?'

He said, 'Well, I teach it. I would like to hear you sing sometime.'

I said, 'You wouldnae be allowed to sing in here.'

'Well, maybe not,' he said, 'but we could talk about it.'

'I would love to,' I said.

'I'll see what the screw has to say.' He was a gentleman, Mr Crawford.

Anyway, I managed to smoke Jimmy's wee roll-up with the black Digger tobacco. It was strong! Made with holy smoke, made with the Bible page. I really enjoyed that too. At exercise time Jimmy Johnston and me use to talk in *cant* language because the people wouldnae know what we were talking about. He was very fluent in this language. He told me that old Crawford was a sword master. Taught sword fencing. He said, in fact, he had taught Errol Flynn to sword fence. That he was in here for embezzlement. Jimmy knew all about him, he had asked around. But he says, 'He's a gentleman.'

I said, 'He telt me he's a singing teacher.'

He said, 'If you want to know what singing is about, you go and talk to him. He can teach you all you want to know.'

So I got in touch with old Crawford in the exercise yard and told him I was interested. I said, 'I cannae read or write music.' I can now, but I couldnae then.

He said, 'Don't worry, maybe we could have an appointment. I think it could be arranged. You come to my cell or I'll come to yours. I'll talk to the screw about it.'

Anyway, he must have talked to the screw because Bayne says to me, 'Mr Crawford wants to see you in his cell.'

I went through and Mr Crawford's sitting on the stane bed and he says to me, 'We've got permission to talk about your ideas for singing.'

I said, 'That's very nice, very friendly.'

He was a pleasant gentleman, he said, 'Sing me a wee song, you're allowed to. I got permission.'

I sang one of my granny's old songs. 'Oh the trees they are high my love, the leaves they are green' and he sat and he listened to every word. He said, 'You've a beautiful voice.'

I said, 'I know nothing about notes, Mr Crawford.'

He said, 'You carry your notes well. There's one thing I want you to learn and that is, breath control. Every time you sing a line you should draw your breath without it being heard. To be a singer you need breath control. The drawing of the breath should never be heard.'

So, we sang a few lines here and a few lines there. That was the first half hour. I had nearly five hours with him and he would be in his late 60s. An old gentleman. When I went to exercise I used to join up with him. We walked round the ring you know.

Then one morning, 'Right, Williamson!' Back before the governor again. 'Have a seat.'

He opened the packet and gave me a Gold Flake. Gave me a light. 'Have a cigarette with me,' he said. 'Did you know you're getting out this morning?'

I said, 'Yes, I'm glad to hear that.'

'You really behaved yourself didn't you?'

'Well, I had no option,' I said.

'Well,' he said, 'this is not the place for you. They say you've been having a nice time with old Crawford.' He was the one who'd given permission for Crawford to talk to me, to come into my cell and teach me about music and breath control and singing.

He said, 'It was good for him to be with you.'

I said, 'Well, it was good for me, too.'

Here am I ready to be released, sitting before the governor after receiving a cigarette off him. To tell the truth, he was very pleasant. Different man from the time we'd met when he took my five days off me.

'Young man,' he said, 'this place is not what I'd like for you.'

'No, I understand that, governor,' I said.

'I don't want to see you back here again.'

'I don't think I will be.'

'Here's a little purse for you,' he said, 'four shillings, a little pass. This is for your bus fare back to Cupar.'

I said, 'Thank you very much.'

He said, 'They'll be coming for you in a minute. The screw will take you out the front door. It's been very pleasant for old Mr Crawford, it was good for him.'

I said, 'I enjoyed his company.' I said, 'Jimmy, I mean, Mr Stewart, told me that Mr Crawford taught Errol Flynn to sword fence.'

He said, 'Yes, man, he's a swordsman grand master. Errol Flynn came for many lessons as a young man to his sword fencing.'

The screw arrives standing with a bunch of keys. The governor said, 'This is your time, Mr Williamson, goodbye and behave yourself.'

The screw led me out to the next door to the great door. He let me out and I walked away and I felt relief but I had also learned something. I sat in a chapel with these people, these prisoners, I sat in a church. I'd been with another Travelling man, I'd been with Mr Crawford, the old sword fencer and teacher who'd once been a rich man. I saw a prisoner governor through two different ways. I saw two people in old Crawford, two people in Jimmy Johnston, I saw him as the piper, I saw him threatening his wife. I saw Crawford was two people, a businessman behind a desk, someone who embezzled somebody's money. I saw two people in the governor, one who sat, who took my five days off me for making a roll-up from a page from the Bible, and the other one sitting there giving me cigarettes after I'd spent my time. And from these three people, who actually in my mind were six people, I learned some beautiful things. Instead of taking my bus, I walked home on my way to Cupar. An old farmer stopped with a pick-up and I thought he might give me a lift.

He said, 'Where have you been young man?'

I said, 'I was in jail.'

'You were,' he said, 'that's not a nice place to be at this time of the year.'

I says, 'Farmer, it's not a nice place to be at any time of the year, but,' I says, 'it's like anything else. In jail you learn many things, probably things you'd never learn if you'd never been in jail.'

The old farmer picked me up in his old pick-up just outside of Newburgh. I'd never seen my wife or my family for over a month. No one sent me a letter, I never got a card, no one came for a visit, but I'd done my 30 days in jail. It was behind me. Good memories of the old governor and old Crawford. I walked up the road and lo and behold there was my brother, my mother-in-law and his young wife who I hadnae seen for a whole year. My wife and the kids, the children were glad to see me.

Jeannie said, 'Hello.'

I didn't say why didn't you come and see me. Nothing. My brother didn't have any young children but he had taken good care of my horse. The horse was alright. The kids were fine. Good to be home again. The next day I said to my brother, 'I'm going back to Letham.'

So we goes to old Mr Kerr and I explained that this was my younger brother.

'Oh,' he said, 'Aye, we can do with another hand.'

Jimmy came to work with me and one day old Sandy said, 'Eh, would you like to move out of the tent, Jimmy? Move into the bothy, it's empty. Your brother's got a house, so why don't you move into the bothy?'

So, Jimmy moved into the bothy with his mother-in-law and his wife. We were right close to the farm. Potatoes, milk, everything was exceptional, wonderful. Then one day, it must have been about eight or nine months later, out of the blue once more around comes the Morris 1000. My brother George and Helen, Dodie we called my brother. Helen says, 'I want you to come and sing in Perth.' They were beginning to do what they're doing here now, you know, branching out, Folk Clubs. They had one in Perth.

I said, 'Okay, I'll come.'

Jeannie was humming and hawing, I was only about a week or ten days out of jail, so we went to the Skye Hotel. The jail was just up the road, I was remembering old Crawford and his breath control and I guarantee, I'm not bragging, I really did sing well that night. The song I sang was 'Jock o' Breadislee'. It was exceptional, went down like a dream. I sang Country and Western songs because I was very fond of that. We had an old gramophone and I'd learned a few of old Jimmy Rogers records and you know, when we'd no steel needles, what we used for these old records? Hedgehog quills. Anyhow, Dodie was there, he didnae sing anything, he was too interested in Helen at that time.

They took me back, dropped me off and I walked back. The two kids were sitting, the oldest one reading a book, wee one was in bed, Jeannie was in her bed. I went into the bedroom, kids were in one room, we were in another. Two kids slept with us. We had four kids at that time. Jeannie wasnae very happy about my going and singing as usual.

Time went by and we moved to Crieff and Jeannie was took into hospital in Kirkcaldy because of her heart. One day this chap, Stewart, come to me and he says, 'Would you be interested in singing at the Baillie Nicol Jarvis up by Callander, they're having a Scots night? Do you sing any Scots songs?'

I said, 'Aye, hundreds of Scots songs.'

'So, I was wondering if you'd come along.'

I said, 'Aye, I'll come long, but I'll have to visit my wife, Jeannie, God rest her, she's in hospital.'

'It starts about seven or eight,' he said, 'we need to leave about five.'

I went to see Jeannie and sat and had a crack with her. I never told her about the Baillie Nicol Jarvis, I didn't want to upset her. I said, 'Well, I'll need to go now.'

She said, 'Oh well, come back when you can.'

But that night I went to the Baillie Nicol Jarvis Hotel, but the thing was when I got there everybody was dressed in tartan. Women in long tartan frocks, white blouses, men in kilts, a real Scottish night. A choir of four or five women singing the same song together. They didn't think very well of me at all, but I'm sitting there waiting my turn. 'What the hell am I doing here,' I said to myself. 'This is no my kind of thing. They're having their Scottish night, women with their scraggy necked voices, when it comes to my turn I'm going to cheer this place up a wee bit.' And there's four or five old women sitting, ken, with their tartan dresses and the man came over to me, white collar and tie.

He says, 'Mr Williamson, would you like to come and give us a song?' This is true! 'Could you give us something Scottish with a wee bit of a lilt?'

I goes up and said, 'Thank you, ladies and gentlemen, it's a pleasure for me to be here. I'm going to sing a song for you.'

When I started singing these two old women with their tartan skirts on, their feet started tapping.

Oh I'm 94 this morning and I'm 94 the day,
I'm no as young as I used to be, I'm getting old and grey,
I'm fond of fun and I'm awfy pleased to see ye,
I'm getting married on Thursday though I'm 94 the day.
The people doon the village, they will get a big surprise,
They neednae think it is a joke with the minister telling lies.
I will get a laugh at them as sure as I'm alive,
There'll be another christening yet, before I'm 95.

And the whole place went completely crazy. More! More! I gave them the best Scots night they ever had in their life. Old Harry Lauder, Will Fyffe. I'd hundreds of them. I learned the tunes because me and the kids used to play them on the gramophone at night-time. It was the greatest evening you ever saw. The guy came over gave me 15 pounds.

Now in hospital, we thought Jeannie was going to be alright because they said they were going to operate on her. She was supposed to get a plastic valve in her heart but she never got it. They discovered that she was pregnant. The doctor said this should never have happened. And Jeannie would never have an abortion or anything like that.

She says, 'I'm going to keep my baby no matter what.'

So she kept the baby but they kept her in hospital for eight months. Then I got words from the hospital that Jeannie was coming home for a while. Oh, it was a delight! I got the tent in good order, kept it clean and this time Edith was getting a bit older, maybe 13 or 14 years old. She was a great help at that time. We got her mummy home from hospital so we could take care of her. She'd given birth to little Sandra and little Sandra was about ten or 11 days old when she came back. Of course, she still had the heart problem. But anyway, we were sitting one night in the tent after tea and a car pulled up on the road. It was not the wee Morris 1000 this time. This was a young couple in the car and they came walking up.

They said, 'Hello Mr Williamson.'

I said, 'No, no, Duncan. Come in.'

'What a good tent you've got.' he said.

This was Pete Shepherd and Lena his wife. Pete and me were to become great friends from that time on.

'We'd like you to come along and sing in the Folk Club in St Andrews.'

I said, 'That would be nice, but you'll have to pick me up.'

'We'll come and pick you up.'

So Jeannie made some tea. Lena came and took me down to St Andrews Folk Club and Pete introduced me to all the crowd. I didnae get any money but it was a good night. Pete came up on many nights and recorded many of my songs. I sang many songs at St Andrews but never got a penny. The funny thing was because I didnae stay all night long, and Jeannie had taken some kind of liking to Lena, and maybe it was while she was still in hospital, I don't know, it was as if she knew there was something far wrong because she completely changed. It was our last baby. Life was really well, I was happy now, I was getting known as a singer and I wanted to spend more time with Jeannie.

I told Jeannie, 'Look sweetheart, if somebody comes and asks me to go and sing for them for the night, I won't stay a night away. I promise. I'll go and sing for them but I won't stay the night.' This seemed to make her happy. She felt better after that. Things went alright for a year and by the time Sandra was about a year, beginning to toddle around, life was okay with us. We travelled Fife but I didn't want to go far out of Fife because I had an idea in my mind. You see, Jeannie was on tablets and she needed to see a doctor now and again, and there was no way I was going to trail her away up to Argyll, away to Ayrshire, or off to see my parents, because I thought maybe she could take a relapse miles from hospital with no doctor to see her. I was really worried about her. Her condition affected her breathing and walking. She couldnae walk very well, she couldnae dae much. If it had been today, they could have given her a bypass but maybe she was too weak to stand an operation anyhow: she could barely walk. The doctor told me afterwards she should never have had that last child. Before that she didn't really have such a problem. She could hawk tatties. It just seem to come on all of a sudden.

* * *

> This was 1969 and as Duncan told me, 'It wasnae a very good year for me.' His father died of a heart attack, Jeannie's health was deteriorating and his first baby by Jeannie, Edith, followed her father's footsteps, jumped the broomstick and he wasn't best pleased.

* * *

> 'Father was very strict with us, we weren't allowed to pubs and dances. We weren't allowed boyfriends. I only had one boyfriend when I was 19, Willie. When I ran away wi' Willie, father was gonna kill him. He searched for three days and he was gonna kill him. We ran to Glasgow and I sent a letter to my father. He cooled down and accepted it then. He was furious because I'd just left. Left my clothes, my money, my car and never told him. Me and my dad was so close. But he was close to all of us.'

* * *

Things was difficult, my oldest daughter Edith was married, 19 years old. Father died with a heart attack and in the month of May my wife was took once again to the hospital. We took her for a check up at the hospital, once a month, but she wasnae getting any better. My sister-in-law Edith and my brother Jimmy had taken the two little girls, Sandra, a year old and Isabel, three, off her hands to make it easier for her and they had moved back to Argyll after father died. So, Jeannie was in hospital and I was left with the three boys but things was to get worse.

I remember the last day I went to visit Jeannie. This was the last time before she died. I drove over to see her, she was really ill. She was on a heart machine.

I said, 'Now my dear,' just to cheer her up a bit after all these years we were together, I said to her, 'I have to go away home. I'd better get away home and look for a woman for myself. It's been a while since me and you made love.' This is the last words I said.

If she could have smiled, she would have smiled but she never did. She turned round and she said to me, 'If they are foolish enough to give it to you, you're a fool if you don't take it.' This was the last word she ever said, I swear on my mother's grave those were the last words she ever said to me. She died that night. I was camped outside Cupar in this field and when I got home I was very sad. About one o'clock in the morning in comes the police in a van. Pulls up and I came out to see what was the problem.

He says, 'Mr Williamson?'

I said, 'Yes!'

He said, 'You've got to phone Kirkcaldy Royal Infirmary.'

There's a little phone box along the road, I phone the hospital. Probably a nurse or somebody. They said, 'Mr Williamson, we have very bad news for you, your wife passed away at 12 o'clock.'

I stood in the phone box for a long time and now I'd to go back to the three boys and tell them their mammy had died. They were still living in the tent in the field. I came back and told the boys and of course they were very upset. We never spoke much that night.

The next morning, I had to go into Kirkcaldy. The doctor took me into the room and he said, 'Mr Williamson, I'm very sorry your wife has passed away. Her heart was very weak, you know. I want your permission to perform an autopsy on her, to have a look at her heart.'

I said, 'No doctor, that's one thing I can't do, I can't give you permission.'

He said, 'It won't help your wife, but it may help someone else in the future.'

'Well,' I said, 'look doctor to be quite honest with you, you've probably performed many autopsies doon through the years on other people apart from my wife, and it didnae help my wife very much, did it?'

'Well,' he said, 'that will be that then.'

I had to go down to Kirkcaldy to register her death.

Travellers have got an underground grapevine. You don't need to phone people, the words spread far and wide. She would be buried in Strathmiglo with her mother who died two years before. She was buried at two o'clock and people came from all around. In these days Travellers had cars. The horses were fading out. Cars coming round the whole village. People from Perthshire, Aberdeenshire, as far away as Campbeltown. Cousins, friends, relations, strangers. Helen Fullerton came from Glasgow. All the people who knew her and it was a great funeral. We never had a ceremony in the church, just everybody stood at the graveyard waiting for the hearse to come. Four men carried the coffin, not us, we never touched it. The undertaker and the minister and people stood and talked for a while and everyone went their own way. I had to go back home to my three boys. The two wee girls were in Argyll with Jimmy and Edith and they brought them up as their own.

The next week I made a big decision in my mind. My wife was gone, I had the three boys and my two little girls were gone with Edith and my brother Jimmy. I went in and sold my horse, sold my cart, sold my harness, went into Cupar and went to the School of Motoring. I could drive tractors, I'd driven before but I was not a specialist in driving. I passed my driving test and I bought a van.

The four of us went away to Argyll down near Campbeltown. Jimmy at that time would be about 16, Willie, 14, John would be 12 when their mummy died. Everything that belonged to my wife was put in a fire and burned. The tent was burned. All her clothes, all her possessions was burned, we kept nothing belonging to her, not a single thing, as was the custom. Only a few photographs. It was a new beginning.

My oldest son, Jimmy, stayed with me until he was 25. The youngest one got married and when I met Linda many years later, I told Jimmy that me and Linda were going to get hitched up. She was going to leave her husband and get a divorce. He says, 'Daddy, you'll no have anything for me anymore. I'll go and find a wife for myself.' And so he did. And my life was to travel into new worlds.

* * *

The new worlds were to see Duncan, the tinker born in a tent in Argyll in 1928, who died at the age of 79 in 2007, acclaimed as the best-known and best-loved storyteller in the English-speaking world.

That journey, encompassing his dramatic second marriage to a young American student, international travels and fame, triumphs and sorrows, is the story told in the forthcoming second volume of *A Traveller in Two Worlds*.

Another book published by **LUATH** PRESS

Out of Mouth of the Morning: Tales of the Celt

David Campbell

ISBN 978 1906307 93 6 PBK £8.99

How did the warlords of the Celtic Kingdoms combine ferocity with compassion?

How did the druids lose their sacred power?

What is the dark origin of the fairy folk?

The Celtic lands of Scotland and Ireland carry a rich heritage of legend and lore: myth comes to life in tales of feisty saints, elite warriors, powerful fairies and ordinary folk.

Distilled by a master storyteller, *Out of the Mouth of the Morning* eloquently unfolds these tales for our times. They are a reminder of our primal relationship with the land and the connections between all things. The author skilfully traces the carrying stream of Celtic consciousness from its origins in ancient landscapes and tongues, to the men, women and stories of today. Deftly weaving the ancient with the modern, he illustrates the essential nature of the folklore of the Celts in today's Scotland.

This book is an invitation to savour the essence of ancient peoples linked into a communal spirit by legends, and to retell the tales of the Celt.

This Celtic collection is drawn from various age-old sources, lovingly and lyrically retold by a master storyteller.

SCOTLAND ON SUNDAY

Details of this and other books published by Luath Press can be found at:
www.luath.co.uk

Luath Press Limited

committed to publishing well written books worth reading

LUATH PRESS takes its name from Robert Burns, whose little collie Luath (*Gael.*, swift or nimble) tripped up Jean Armour at a wedding and gave him the chance to speak to the woman who was to be his wife and the abiding love of his life. Burns called one of 'The Twa Dogs' Luath after Cuchullin's hunting dog in Ossian's *Fingal*. Luath Press was established in 1981 in the heart of Burns country, and is now based a few steps up the road from Burns' first lodgings on Edinburgh's Royal Mile.

Luath offers you distinctive writing with a hint of unexpected pleasures.

Most bookshops in the UK, the US, Canada, Australia, New Zealand and parts of Europe either carry our books in stock or can order them for you. To order direct from us, please send a £sterling cheque, postal order, international money order or your credit card details (number, address of cardholder and expiry date) to us at the address below. Please add post and packing as follows: UK – £1.00 per delivery address; overseas surface mail – £2.50 per delivery address; overseas airmail – £3.50 for the first book to each delivery address, plus £1.00 for each additional book by airmail to the same address. If your order is a gift, we will happily enclose your card or message at no extra charge.

ILLUSTRATION: IAN KELLAS

Luath Press Limited
543/2 Castlehill
The Royal Mile
Edinburgh EH1 2ND
Scotland
Telephone: 0131 225 4326 (24 hours)
Fax: 0131 225 4324
email: sales@luath.co.uk
Website: www.luath.co.uk